Drugs and Crime

Drugs and Crime

Philip Bean

WILLAN
PUBLISHING

Published by

Willan Publishing
Culmcott House
Mill Street, Uffculme
Cullompton, Devon
EX15 3AT, UK
Tel: +44(0)1884 840337
Fax: +44(0)1884 840251
e-mail: info@willanpublishing.co.uk
website: www.willanpublishing.co.uk

Published simultaneously in the USA and Canada by

Willan Publishing
c/o ISBS, 5824 N.E. Hassalo St,
Portland, Oregon 97213-3644, USA
Tel: +001(0)503 287 3093
Fax: +001(0)503 280 8832
e-mail: info@isbs.com
website: www.isbs.com

First published 2002

ISBN 1-903240-36-0 Paperback
ISBN 1-903240-37-9 Hardback

British Library Cataloguing-in-Publication Data

A catalogue record for this book is available from the British Library

Printed and bound by T.J. International, Padstow, Cornwall

Contents

List of figures

List of tables

For
Charlotte, Stacie, Celina and Jade

Preface

When I wrote about drug taking and crime in the late 1960s, I thought any link (such as there was) between drug taking and crime would be complex and full of pitfalls for the unwary. I little realised then how true this was nor how many and deep were the pitfalls. Nor was I able to see that drugs and crime would come to dominate government thinking. In the 1960s, questions related to this issue were rarely about crime but about over-prescribing; about the role of the medical profession; and about how best to explain drug taking within the context of the social attitudes of the 1960s.

In the last 25 years or so things have changed. Drug users were once rare; now they are commonplace. Once they were likely to be pitied; now they are likely to be scorned. Previously there was no supply system except through over-prescribing doctors; now cocaine comes from the Andes, heroin from Afghanistan, Turkey or South East Asia, and amphetamines, ecstasy and similar drugs are manufactured in Britain or on the continent. In the last five years or so the government has reacted to the drug problem – but whether with the appropriate vision or the right direction are matters for debate. Some of the policies seem to be right but others that have led to the Drug Treatment and Testing Order are surely not. Government-funded research is scanty, often promoting short-term atheoretical epidemiological studies, seemingly uninterested in large-scale longitudinal studies that would provide detailed information about the natural history of the phenomenon. Nor do non-governmental agencies fare better for they, too, rarely promote high-quality research.

What have also been missing are texts that provide an overview of the drugs–crime debate. In this book I have tried to make amends in that respect and offer this text as a way of assessing what is broadly known about drugs crime and related matters, such as policing, drug testing and treatment. I have also made suggestions about how best to proceed. Inevitably the topics selected represent a personal view and I make no claim they comprise a compendium of the subject matter. None the less it is hoped sufficient areas have been covered to sustain the claim that this book includes most of what we mean when we talk of drugs and crime, particularly with regard to how this issue affects Britain.

I want to thank all those people (too numerous to mention) who have assisted in the preparation of this book, especially those colleagues in the Midlands Centre for Criminology and the Department of Social Sciences, University of Loughborough, who provided help and encouragement throughout. Nigel South also read the draft and made many valuable comments. I want to take this opportunity to acknowledge the help given by him and others, including my friends and immediate family. That this book is dedicated to some of my grandchildren is a further indication of their importance.

I am grateful to John Corkery at the Home Office and the Home Office itself for permission to publish a number of the figures and the tables in Chapters 1 and 3.

Philip Bean
January 2001

Publisher's acknowledgements

Tables 1.5, 1.6, 3.1, 3.2 and 3.3 are reproduced by kind permission of John Corkery, and Figures 3.1, 3.2 and 3.3 by kind permission of the Home Office Drugs and Alcohol Research Unit.

Chapter 1

Drugs and crime: an overview

A great deal has been said about the links between drugs and crime and, in Britain, increasing amounts of resources are given to drug-crime prevention programmes. For example, the Criminal Justice and Court Services Act 2001 involves estimated costs for the national implementation of the new drug-testing proposals at approximately £45.5 million (House of Commons, 2000: 24). This is a small part of an ever-increasing spiral of expenditure aimed at reducing drug use – rightly described as the scourge of our age – and the corresponding social and economic problems it brings.

For our purposes, 'drugs' are defined as those substances controlled by the Misuse of Drugs Act 1971 (henceforth the 1971 Act), of which there are a number. (The terms 'drug misuse,' 'substance misuse' or 'drug abuse' will be used interchangeably.) Cannabis, amphetamines, heroin, cocaine, LSD and ecstasy are, for these purposes, the most important as they tend to be the most widely used illegally. Debates about what constitutes a drug, about the moral connotations attached to the term and about how or under what circumstances certain substances are selected for control are important but not considered here. These are topics in their own right warranting more consideration than space permits. Our task here is different: it is to examine some of the major criminological implications of the drugs–crime nexus, to determine how drugs and crime are linked, and to determine the responses that should be made to those links.

It is not just the 1971 Act that is under scrutiny: in the 1990s, major pieces of legislation were introduced dealing with drug offences and drug trafficking. The Criminal Justice Act 1993 and the Drug Trafficking

Act 1994 deal with drug offenders and trafficking, and the Criminal Justice and Public Order Act 1994, the Crime and Disorder Act 1998 and the Criminal Justice and Court Services Act 2001 deal with similar matters. These will be considered where necessary. The drugs–crime debate also extends beyond the legislation to include, *inter alia*, policing (whether on matters of interdiction – i.e. before drugs enter Britain – or local procedures, including the use of informers) and the sentencing of drug offenders involving treatment programmes, whether as part of a sentence of the court or not. It can and, indeed, should include the impact of drug use on local communities – not least because of the deleterious effect drugs have upon them.

To complicate things further, many of the substances controlled by the 1971 Act can be prescribed by selected physicians to substances misusers, the latter being defined as 'producing a maladaptive pattern of use manifested by recurrent and significant adverse consequences related to the repeated use of substances with clinically significant impairment or distress' (Ghodse, 1995: 162). This should alert us to some of the complexities. If substances can be prescribed, the question must be: for what reason? Are they to assist the offender or to reduce crime? And what after all is a 'maladaptive pattern'? Or, how are we to talk of dangerous drugs when some prohibited substances are not dangerous, whilst others not included *are*? Moreover, what are the boundaries of the debate? Hopefully some of these questions will be answered here, but some remain elusive and difficult to unravel. We can begin, however, with a workable definition of what we mean by 'drugs'. For our purposes, and to avoid a lengthy and acrimonious debate, a pragmatic, circular definition has been used: 'drugs' are what are usually included in the debate about drugs.

Extent of drug use

Who, and how many, are the users? Drug misuse is largely an illegal activity, making it difficult to measure prevalence or incidence. Traditionally, national estimates have been based on a set of indicators that have included convictions for possession or supply, drug seizures by police and HM Customs & Excise, and notification to the Addicts Index where notification was required under the Misuse of Drug (Notification of and Supply to Addicts) Regulations 1973. Taken together, they provided some evidence of trends of use throughout Britain. These standard indicators are still used although to what effect remains unclear. The Addicts Index has been replaced by what is now called a 'starting agency episode'; this is where users are recorded when they first attend a selected agency or reattend after a break of 6 months or more. Unfortunately data from these starting agency episodes are not comparable with that of the older Addicts Index and, of course, seizures or possession offences in themselves are uncertain indicators, reflecting the activities of the police rather than measuring the extent of use. At best they provide a crude estimate but an estimate none the less and, incidentally, more than we would otherwise have.

Other means of assessing prevalence and incidence have been through self-report studies. The British Crime Survey (BCS) is by far the most comprehensive, providing some of the best data on the extent of substance misuse. The BCS is a large-scale household survey representative of the general public in England and Wales where, although the main focus is on the victims of crime, drug taking has been included. The key points from the 1998 survey are as follows (Ramsay *et al.* 1999):

1. Young people aged 16–29 reported the highest level of drug misuse in the 1998 BCS. Some 49% indicated they had taken a prohibited drug at some time within the last month or year. For the 16–29 age group, this figure was 25% in the last year and 16% in the last month.
2. The gap between male and female rates appears to be widening. Female rates remained steady at 19% for 1998 but for males it increased from 1994 to 1998 by 5% – from 23 to 28%.
3. Whilst higher rates of substance abuse can be found in deprived areas and amongst the unemployed, those people living in areas with a preponderance of affluent professionals have rates double the average. Being married and responsible for children produce lower rates.
4. There was a significant increase in the use of cannabis and cocaine in the 16–29 age group, mostly among young men.

The 1994 BCS came up with 'best estimates' of the number of people aged 16–59 in England and Wales who could have tried four specific substances (Ramsay and Percy, 1996) (see Table 1.1). The data given in Table 1.2, however, are not directly comparable to those in Table 1.1 – the age range differs and the drugs recorded are also different. These 'best estimates' for 16–24-year-olds using drugs in the last year and month in England and Wales in 1998 show about 65,000 were using an opiate in the last month and a similar figure were using cocaine (Ramsay and Partridge, 1999). The picture in Scotland during 1996 was similar to that of England and Wales except that females in Scotland were less likely to continue using drugs on a regular basis after initial experimentation (Corkery, 1999: 14).

Table 1.1   The number of people aged 16–59 in England and Wales who could have tried four specific substances (according to the BCS 1994)

	Ever	Last month
Cannabis	6,307,000	1,486,000
Amphetamines	2,486,000	303,000
LSD	1,324,000	152,000
Ecstasy	728,000	121,000

Source: Ramsay and Percy, 1996.

Table 1.2   The number of people aged 16–24 in England and Wales who could have used drugs (1998)

	Last year	Last month
Any drug	1,865,000	1,220,000
Cannabis	1,735,000	1,095,000
Cocaine	195,000	65,000
Opiates	195,000	65,000

Source: Ramsay and Partridge, 1999.

The age and gender of those starting drug use, according to the definition of starting agency episodes for the 6 months ending 30 September 1999 for Great Britain, are given in Table 1.3. John Corkery (*ibid.*) notes that these figures replace those derived from the Home Office Addicts Index but that they are not a complete replacement. First, notification to the Addicts Index was compulsory (even if often flouted) but, even so, was likely to be better than that currently collected using the starting agency episode. These new data are collected by anonymous reports and there may be duplication in reporting. Also from 1987 onwards, the index recorded 'renotifications' but this is not used in the data for Table 1.3, which gives episodes not persons (*ibid.*: 9). Table 1.3, therefore, shows little more than a set of general trends but trends that none the less confirm what has been shown before – that is it is males users who outnumber females (in this case by just under 3 to 1), that the peak age for starting drug use is 20–24 and that this is so for both males and females. After the age of 24, the decline is steady and dramatic, at least after the age of 35.

Table 1.3 Age and gender of users starting agency episodes in the 6 months ending 30 September 1998

Age group	Male	Female	All persons
<15	175	74	249
15–19	3,353	1,517	4,870
20–24	6,845	2,570	9,415
25–29	6,788	2,190	8,978
30–34	4,656	1,412	6,068
35–39	2,228	732	2,960
40–44	975	306	1,281
45–49	453	161	614
50–54	173	92	265
55–59	54	29	83
60–64	28	21	49
>64	22	21	43
All ages	25,750	9,125	34,875

Source: Department of Health Tables (C2), 1999.

Table 1.4 gives data for users' starting agency episodes for England, Wales and Scotland for the 6-month period from 30 September 1993 to 30 September 1998. The picture that emerges is that there has been a steady but relentless increase in drug misuse, with occasional decreases, which were themselves almost always offset by an immediate increase in the following 6 months. Table 1.4 also shows that the figures for Wales remain steady (in fact there was hardly any increase over the 5-year period). Those for Scotland and England show a different pattern. In Scotland they have more than doubled, made worse when seen as a proportion of the population of the UK generally. Those for England are only marginally better, but there was massive 19.6% increase over the last 6 months shown – as too for Wales, with an 18.9% increase.

It is not easy to link these figures to other indicators such as drug seizures, except to say that, in spite of the obvious shortcomings, all the data point in the same upward direction. That means we should accept the likelihood there is a measure of validity about them and we ought not to try to talk ourselves out of a problem because we see the data as inadequate. There are few good longitudinal studies in Britain to provide better data, and this is a serious failing (Aldridge *et al.*, 1999 being one of the exceptions).

Data on seizures of controlled drugs for 1967–97 are given in Table 1.5 (the data on offenders are given in Chapter 3). The totals for each drug in

Table 1.4 Users' starting agency episodes by period and country

Six months ending	England	Wales	Scotland	Great Britain
30-9-93	16,810	1,204	2,207	20,221
31-3-94	17,864	1,261	2,457	21,582
30-9-94	19,331	1,159	3,217	23,707
31-3-95	20,733	1,320	3,387	25,440
30-9-95	22,848	1,211	3,876	27,935
31-3-96	23,313	1,288	4,255	28,856
30-9-96	24,879	1,220	4,193	30,292
31-3-97	25,925	1,141	4,618	31,684
30-9-97	21,996	1,107	4,159	27,262
31-3-98	23,916	1,068	4,781	29,765
30-9-98	28,599	1,270	5,006	34,875
% change between last 2 periods	+19.6	+18.9	+4.7	+17.2

Source: Department of Health Tables (C1), 1999.

the respective years will not add to the subtotal, nor will the subtotals add to the main total as some seizures will be recorded more than once, and the categories are not discrete. Some seizures include both possession and trafficking. However, from Table 1.5 it is clear that seizures have increased for almost all drugs in the last 20 years or so (even though no data were available for 1967).

From Table 1.5 it can be seen that seizures rose in 1997 to over 139,000. This is an increase of over 6% on the previous year. Table 1.5 also shows cannabis was involved in 77% of seizures for 1997. There was a massive increase in seizures involving heroin and cocaine in 1997 over 1987. Seizures of cannabis also rose in that decade. Table 1.6 shows that the quantity of most Class A drugs seized rose alongside the numbers of seizures – and that heroin and cocaine use rose to an all-time high. (Incidentally, the amount of LSD and ecstasy-type drug use fell by 34% and 67% respectively over the previous years – Corkery, 1999.)

It is not known, of course, to what extent these seizure figures represent patterns of use but, as they correspond with other data such as the starting agency episodes, it is reasonable to suppose they do. If this is in fact the case, Tables 1.5 and 1.6 confirm that same rise in the use of illicit drugs and show, too, that certain age groups dominate.

Table 1.5   Number of seizures of controlled drugs, UK, 1967–97

	1967	1977	1987	1997
Cannabis	NA	12,316	26,175	106,735
Amphetamines	NA	1,347	2,852	18,575
Heroin	NA	270	2,058	12,474
Cocaine	NA	204	717	3,687
LSD	NA	202	302	851
Ecstasy type	NA	NA	NA	5,087
Total	NA	13,006	30,690	139,174

Note
NA = not available.
Source: Corkery, 1999.

Table 1.6   Quantity of seizures of controlled drugs, UK, 1967–97 (in Kg unless otherwise stated)

	1967	1977	1987	1997
Cannabis plants	196	4,352	16,936	149,996
Amphetamines	NA	36	152	3,296
Heroin	0.260	27	236	2,255
Cocaine	0.253	14	407	2,350
LSD (doses)	7,720	148,800	62,000	164,000
Ecstasy-type (doses)	NA	NA	NA	1,925,000

Note
NA = not available.
Source: Corkery, 1999.

Links with crime

Crime is one of the (if not major) attendant problems of drug abuse. Clearly, from the data above crime is extensive, if only because it is an offence unlawfully to possess these substances. However, it is the so-called secondary criminality that is important, especially where drug use is linked to property crime. The *prima facie* evidence for the links are clear: drug users require large amounts of money to support their habits and, as they are able rarely to meet these costs from legitimate sources, they need to commit crime. An out-of-control male drug user is likely to commit 80–100 serious property offences per year or, if a female, may resort to prostitution to pay for the drugs (Chaiken and Chaiken, 1990). At this level the evidence, anecdotal and otherwise, is compelling – all suggesting that drugs and crime are inextricably bound together, perhaps even causally connected. A closer look will show the matter is not that simple but, before considering the more complex side of things, we will look first at what appears more straightforward.

A number of ethnographic and longitudinal studies of drug-using criminals (many in the USA) show that high levels of drug use are associated with high levels of crime, and that low levels of drug use are associated with low levels of crime (*ibid.*: 235). This is particularly true for heroin users but less so for the persistent use of other drugs – except perhaps for cocaine (*ibid.*). Moreover, there is strong evidence that predatory offenders who persistently and frequently use large amounts of multiple types of drugs – what we call polyaddicts or polyusers – commit crimes at significantly higher rates over longer periods than do less drug-involved offenders. Predatory offenders commit fewer crimes during periods in which they use no heroin (*ibid.*).

Similar research evidence has been found in some British studies. For example, studies of heroin users in Merseyside show how burglary rates increase when heroin use increases (Parker and Newcombe, 1987). The Shadow Home Secretary in 1996 produced evidence that he subsequently used to introduce the Drug Treatment and Testing Order (DTTO), showing that the growth in the rate of crime was accompanied by a similar growth in the rate of substance abuse (Labour Party, 1996). Offenders themselves often say they committed their crime to feed their habit, even going so far as to imply that, were they not drug users, they would not be offenders. This type of evidence (supported by the research findings above) tends to support the drugs–crime link.

But how clear is that link? How much credence should we give to research that shows that crime rates increased when drug use increased, when there was no control group of non-drug users to make comparisons? (Lack of a control group is a common failing in British research, linked incidentally to another failing – the small sample size. Studies involving interviews with 20 or 30 drug users are commonplace.) Assume for the moment that the link is clear, how then has it been explained?

Numerous explanations have been offered – some psychological, some sociological and some economic. Consider two psychological explanations, one that suggests the criminality is as much a product of the drugs as the need for the drugs and the other that suggests the drugs change the drug user's personality. In the first the supposition is that users are said to be 'enslaved' by the drug and, in the second, 'out of character' when they behave in ways unlike any ways they have done before.

In the first model the drug user is said to be unable to offset the impact of the drug so that, being 'enslaved', he or she commits offences with little or no control over his or her actions or with no consideration for any one else, let alone the victim. 'Enslavement' means behaving in ways that may be criminal in order to satisfy the craving – this is a mild version of the economic necessity model. The second, the 'out of character' model, can overlap with the 'enslavement' model but it need not. Being 'out of character' means behaving in a different way than hitherto; it might involve abusing close family members, or not showing concern about personal appearance or hygiene. It may also involve committing offences to satisfy the habit and, in extreme circumstances, these offences may be over and above that needed to pay for the drugs (i.e. the user may become violent or damage property in a way alien to his or her erstwhile character). In both models similar psychological mechanisms are at work, except that the 'enslaved' user is more powerfully driven by the demand for the drug, whilst the 'out of character' user behaves in ways that may be highly unusual, and this may or may not include crime.

These psychological models help make a wider point – that being 'enslaved' or acting 'out of character' are not precise terms and could as easily explain non-criminal behaviour as criminal behaviour. They do not provide information on the extent of 'enslavement' or being 'out of character'; they offer merely a series of assumptions that, however useful, permit only wide generalisations to be made. Some drug users are 'enslaved' and some do behave 'out of character' – but that does not give a satisfactory explanation of their criminality.

Or consider the stronger version of the economic necessity model (that drug users commit crime to fund their habit) – a position strongly implied by the Parker and Newcombe (1987) study noted above and also by that of the Labour Party. The problem here is that it is difficult to disaggregate the crimes committed *qua* offending and the crimes committed because of drug taking. Offenders might say they burgled because they were drug takers but they were burglars in any case. What is required, and almost impossible to achieve, is a means by which those offences committed as a result of drug taking could be separated from those that would have been committed anyway. Drug users might believe, or want *us* to believe, their claims to be seen as being some how *forced* into criminality to fund their habits, hoping this might somehow invoke a less condemnatory reaction. (They suggest the fault lies elsewhere – for example with the government for not making drugs legal or with the dealer for raising the prices.) This is a risky strategy that could easily backfire with an unsympathetic judge or magistrate and could lead to a longer spell in prison⨉None the less, some offenders might see this as a useful ploy. The problem for them is to convince all around them they were committing offences only because of their habit and not because they were burglars (or whatever).

All these examples (interesting though they may be) fall a long way short of establishing that drug abuse causes crime. To establish a cause or to say an event has a cause is to say there are universal laws that, along with statements about initial conditions prevailing at particular times, will, when taken together, allow a prediction to be made. That prediction will be of an event called an effect. So, under certain conditions water will freeze and, given that those conditions exist, we can predict the effect of temperature upon water. Here we have a typical causal relationship and those conditions are regarded as sufficient to explain the event. It is also a causal explanation (Benn and Peters, 1975: 199).

No one doubts that, for many drug takers, there is a link with crime, but how much and to what extent crime is a sufficient condition to produce drug taking are difficult to determine. Can we say being 'enslaved' leads to crime in the sense that 'enslavement' causes crime? Clearly not. Many drug users could be said to be 'enslaved', at least in some respects, but the term 'cause' is appropriate only if the drug user could exercise little or no control over the behaviour and is caught in an unwinding pattern as a prisoner of the drug. Or similarly for the 'out of character' drug user, how many crimes are committed as a direct result of this condition and, even if that could be established, will they always be of the same order, the same amount and the same type irrespective of the drug user's previous experiences? In other words, how is there a causal (sufficient) connection between the drug and the criminality in these two models? And the answer is that it is difficult, in fact almost impossible, to determine.

Social scientists have rarely been able to determine cause in the manner in which natural scientists have. This is not therefore a criticism of research workers in the drugs field. The trouble is, however, they use terms that imply causal connections; they talk of 'links' with crime or create the impression of somehow being trapped in certain social or psychological circumstances so the drug user can do no other – either to become a drug user or, when that is the case, to become an offender. What they should be doing is offering something less deterministic; that is, to use the term 'cause' in its weakest sense where there is no sufficient condition but there may be a necessary one. This is much more acceptable for rarely in social science do we have the type of knowledge that allows us to state those essential conditions; more likely, the type of generalisations made are those that state the sort of things that will tend to happen under certain conditions. Here the term 'cause' is couched in much wider terms than when sufficient conditions prevail so that to say drugs cause crime is to say nothing more than there is a tendency or a trend to associate drug use with criminal behaviour.

Often the best social scientists can do is to avoid the term in its strictest sense (sufficient condition) and consider it in its weaker form (necessary condition). Sometimes this means going no further than stating drugs and crime are two morbidities that tend to occur together, which for these purposes means a statistical connection, usually presented in the form of a correlation. For example, one might say (as in Trevor Bennett's 1998 research) that offenders seen at the police station often tested positive for drugs. Or as with Chaiken and Chaiken (1990: 231) that drug addicts who have entered treatment commit fewer crimes during the period of treatment than when they were addicted. In both examples we are talking of a statistical relationship (a correlation), although in the latter we might suggest it is rather more pronounced than in the former.

All this suggests the strongest causal connection (sufficient condition) remains elusive and that the weakest is more appropriate. Other evidence supports this contention. First, not all drug users are offenders and not all offenders are drug users. There may be an overlap but they are not identical populations. Studies in Britain and America show that about 50% of drug users were criminal before they started taking drugs (Bean and Wilkinson, 1988) but, of course, that means 50% were not, and many drug takers remain crime free for all their drug-taking careers. These data are more consistent with the common-sense notion that minor predatory crime is a precursor to serious predatory crime, suggesting the presence of two morbidities rather than a strong causal connection between the two (Chaiken and Chaiken, 1990: 216). If there is a link between the two morbidities, the most likely inference to draw is that both are expressions of the same deviant lifestyle.

That large numbers of drug users are not criminal, do not commit property offences and have no convictions except perhaps for illegal possession means the use of illicit drugs does not appear to cause (sufficient) participation in predatory crime. Similarly, that some drug users *are* criminal does not lead to the conclusion they are criminal because of their drug use. Some offenders might commit more crimes as a result of their drug use – and this would be a reasonable conclusion to draw – but how many and which offences are causally (sufficiently) linked cannot be known. (See particularly Hammersley *et al.*, 1989 for a useful discussion on this.) Similarly, some otherwise non-offenders might be drawn into committing offences, and some offenders drawn to non-offending. In both cases the behaviour may be 'out of character' but, again, how many and which offences are committed or not committed as a result of this are difficult to determine. It is reasonable to infer there are links with drug taking and crime (necessary) but even then what they are, how they affect crime rates and how offending might be reduced are more difficult to establish. There was no sudden increase in the crime rate in Britain when drug cases became more common; the rates of recorded crime had been rising relentlessly since 1960. Sudden changes in the rates of specific crime might alert us to structural changes in society of which an increase in substance abuse would be one. But in 1960 there were none of these. What one can say is that crime increased as drug abuse increased, but it is difficult to go much further than that.

Moreover, there is evidence to suggest that some types of drugs are less strongly associated with crime than others, implying this might have more to do with the background and personal circumstances of the user than anything else. For example, ecstasy (MDMA) use is not usually associated with crime, and it is reasonable to suggest this is because of the socio-demographic features of the population taking it (i.e. ecstasy users are more likely to be occasional drug users, employed, of higher social class and single or restricted multiple drug users – i.e. taking similar types of drugs but not the heavy end of the drugs scene). They will not likely have a criminal history or a subsequent criminal career. This in contrast to the heroin user, who is usually working class, unemployed (probably unemployable having never had a job), homeless and a polyaddict (taking heavy amounts of all drugs, including cocaine). Drugs and crime are strongly associated with this group (especially if a street user) but, again, the socio-demographic background of this group of users puts them at a higher risk of criminality in the first place.

However, this should not stop us promoting policies for this high-risk group. For example, Chaiken and Chaiken (1990: 235) say that criminal justice programmes that focus resources on preventing persistent drug use other than heroin or cocaine use are not likely to reduce the numbers of persistent predatory offenders. We need, therefore, to promote policies that concentrate on those users. Various avenues could be explored. Hammersley et al. (1989) say that rather than tackling the 'drugs problem' in the name of crime prevention, it may be worth while to tackle crime in the name of drug abuse. They see this as likely to have much the same effect.

To summarise, all this suggests we should be wary of trying to establish causal (sufficient) links of the type that state that those who take drugs are compelled in some way to commit crime. At best the term 'cause' can be used as a necessary condition, offering a weak form of explanation that does not imply much more than a statistical association.

Moreover, extracting causal explanations, of whatever sort, from the available data is a risky business given we know so little about the types of behaviour we are examining, whether before or after drug taking. That is why the suggestion by Hammersley *et al.* is so interesting.

Chapter 2

Theoretical assumptions

Michael Tonry (in Tonry and Wilson, 1990: 2) says of American drug research that 'the literature is scant, much of it fugitive, the research community fragmented, and too much of the research is poor in quality and weak in design'. He goes on to say that in a number of central questions very little systematic knowledge is available from methodologically rigorous research (*ibid*.). If so of America, how much more so in Britain?

The British literature on drugs and crime tends to be dominated by epidemiological considerations aimed at establishing the extent of drug use in a particular cohort or at showing that drug taking and crime go together, whether before or after the user is arrested. There is little by way of trying to establish links with established sociological theory or other theoretical propositions. Only a very small number of theories have been offered. I remember in 1965 being particularly taken by one that linked drug taking to the aristocrats of eighteenth-century France. Then the nobility were financially independent as well as eschewing ties and responsibilities to the less fortunate. During such times, experimentation developed in the form of sado-masochism. Parallels were made with the drug users in Britain in the 1960s; they were economically independent and had limited social obligations. Hence their interest in self-experimentation, but this time with drugs not sex. I do not know how much credence I would give nowadays to such a theory – it fails to account for the interest in drugs rather than another form of experimentation – but it was interesting none the less. There were after all few attempts to explain the sudden increase in drug use and then, as now, few theories to account for the continued use of drugs.

Where theories exist (and the drugs literature has not always been connected to the social science literature), there tend to be two main sets of theories, determined entirely by the academic disciplines: psychology, in which can be included psychiatry, and sociology or the economic. Often, however, there has been little attention to theory, but researchers have worked within a set of paradigms that have provided a way of looking at things and that has given a useful overview. Speaking very generally, it is possible to see these paradigms as coinciding with specific stages in the development of the growth of drug use. Each tended to last for about a decade. We begin with the 1960s, for this was the period when drug taking first became recognised as a problem, although it had begun slightly earlier in about 1957 when certain London clubs were known to have a number of cannabis users who openly proselytised its use (see Bean, 1974). This first period was from about 1960 to 1975; the second was from 1975 to about 1985. The third, from 1985 to 2000, is much more complicated.

In the first period the psychiatric paradigm dominated. Explanations of substance abuse (which were mainly about heroin addicts) were sought in terms of the drug takers' individual pathologies. Looking back on this period we should not be surprised that the psychiatric paradigm was dominant, for this was the most likely response to any new or unusual phenomenon. Other countries seem to have followed the same pattern. In this period (around the late 1960s) sociological explanations were rare and other types of explanations (e.g. economic) were unheard of. Amongst psychiatrists there was no shortage of psychoanalytical explanations linking drug use to nascent experiences, such as narcissism (through the process of injecting) or to other ontogenetic factors – this was, after all, the height of that type of psychiatric influence.

By the mid-1970s drug taking (or rather heroin addiction) began to arouse less attention, although the number of users continued to increase. There was concern about alcohol and glue sniffing but the addict remained the major preoccupation. Research interest began to emphasise the growth of the working-class addict and the social deprivation seen to be a breeding ground for addiction. Drug taking had ceased to be solely a psychiatric problem and the emphasis – as far as there was one – centred round the sociological features of the drug taker's background. The drug taker was seen as a product of the deprivation of inner-city poverty – drug taking was transferred from psychopathology to a form of social pathology. There was much debate, however, about the role of cannabis and amphetamines as gateway drugs and of the physician as a supplier of drugs, especially heroin. It is in this period that the treatment centres were born and when physicians, except those who were licensed, were prevented from prescribing heroin as a maintenance drug.

By the 1990s the emphasis had begin to shift again. The sociological model was retained but there was renewed interest in the psychological. What had happened was that theoretical interest had broadened and a wider range of models began to emerge – especially as British drug research expanded. Interest in drug markets developed alongside a socioeconomic model that considered drugs and drug taking in terms of commodities bought and sold like other commodities governed by the laws of supply and demand. Solutions were along the same lines, as either supply- or demand-reduction programmes.

The guiding theoretical principle here was that the prices of drugs were the central issue (Wagstaff and Maynard, 1988). Price affects consumption in terms of the quantity consumed, who uses the drugs and how the drugs are used (Reuter and Kleiman, 1986; Caulkins and Reuter, 1996). Price can also affect entry into treatment (i.e. the user enters treatment when he or she can no longer afford the drugs; likewise the incentive to remain in treatment will weaken if prices decline). The numbers using the drugs are also affected by price: a reduction in the price of heroin in Britain recently led to a sharp increase in heroin use. Lower drug prices, as with all commodities, lead to an increase in use. This type of market model was used to help explain levels of violence: drugs have an enormous valuable per unit weight and if large quantities are sold, the incentives to protect those markets will be huge. Or as Caulkins and Reuter (1996: 1262) say, the same could also be said for the corruption of authorities: high prices provide the incentive for corruption, and the incentives for organised crime are also affected by price and quantity.

There are, of course, wide variations in the type of socioeconomic model used; there is a Marxist, a socio-demographic and a laissez-faire market model. The one that has begun to dominate is that fostered by American research, specifically that from the Rand Corporation, which is closest to the laissez-faire type capitalist market model (*ibid.*). Take the example of policing. This type of market model shows the cost of policing drug markets is as important as the number of offenders prosecuted; that police corruption occurs most often where drugs are involved and where informers give information to take out the opposition or for monetary rewards in spite of the risks from other dealers. It has also been used to examine government policy that is in itself dominated by the costs of drug-linked crime, of money laundering and of prison sentences, and by the economics of the illicit supply system, including the cost of interdiction.

This economic model does not meet all requirements – no single model can – but it permitted the material to be ordered in a different way to include a wider range of information than hitherto. It was based on the premise that drugs are produced and sold for profits, that their use is determined by price and that the rates of crime are also related to price. It does not account for the specific features of the users nor their determination to continue taking drugs, but it can show that changes in supply or price affect which drugs are taken and for what period.

Inevitably, many theories of drug abuse have grown up, some closely related to the periods noted above (i.e. psychiatric during the first period, sociological during the next and so on), but some less so. Here, I want to give a brief overview of some of the more interesting and pervasive theories whilst recognising that the aim is not to examine the theories as such but to examine drug taking in the context of criminal justice.

In the psychological field, or under the psychiatric paradigm, Anglin and Hser (1990, quoted in Hough, 1996: 8) identified three models that had their own particular approach to prevention or treatment. They are as follows:

1. The *moral* model, which considers dependence to be the result of moral weakness and punishment or moral education the solution.
2. The *disease* model, which sees physiological or psycho-biological dependence as the problem and where medical treatment is emphasised alongside managed withdrawal.
3. The *behavioural* model, which views addiction as a pattern of learned habits to be modified by cognitive or behavioural techniques, such as psychotherapy, group therapy or the like.

These models are not discrete; for example, the moral model appears in the behavioural as well as in the disease model, and vice versa. Treatment programmes within the criminal justice system draw heavily on all these models, but the behavioural model is more commonly used. Unlike sociological models, the psychological models have been adapted directly to the demands of treatment.

The moral model (which perhaps had its greatest impact in the early part of the twentieth century) emphasises the importance of moral education and of moral fibre as a solution. It is still practised by many religious and charitable organisations and, although few programmes have been evaluated, there is little evidence to suggest their success rates are lower than those of their professional colleagues. The oft-heard demand 'to pull oneself together' is a powerful moral exhortation that is not confined to the moral model but overlaps with others and is used in their treatment programmes. A number of such programmes, if not exclusively devoted to the moral model, none the less encourage the development of character formation or aim to build up character to resist drugs (DARE or 'Just Say No' are two examples). Hamid Ghodse (1995: 171), a major British authority on treatment, says 'not all interventions are suitable for every patient, nor are they mutually exclusive'. He goes on to say 'there is no approach that is right or best. If there were then problem drug abuse dependence would be rapidly overcome and petty controversies between the advocates of different treatment modalities would disappear' (*ibid.*). Examples abound of ex-users becoming 'born-again Christians' or of religious movements claiming successful treatment programmes, as well of members of religious organisations providing help at the personal level. However, just because the moral model is less fashionable than hitherto, we ought not deride it.

The disease model, the centrepiece of which is AA/NA (Alcoholics Anonymous/Narcotics Anonymous), dominates American treatment programmes but is less popular in the UK. There are about 300 NA group meetings each week in the UK, with about 100 in London. The NA programmes gained scientific credibility after it was shown that results were similar to those treated by conventional programmes (Royal College of Psychiatrists, 2000). As the term implies, addiction is seen as a lifelong disease from which all drug users will, at best, be for ever recovering. AA (which has grown into NA and which was founded in 1953) requires abstinence from all drugs and a spiritual surrendering to a higher power if treatment is to be successful. Treatment is derived from the Minnesota model, or the '12 steps model', which incidentally has within it more than a passing moral flavour. The 12 steps are as follows:

1. We admitted that we were powerless over our addiction, that our lives had become unmanageable.
2. We came to believe that a power greater than ourselves could restore us to sanity.
3. We made a decision to turn our lives over to the care of God, as we understood him.
4. We made a searching and fearless moral inventory of ourselves.
5. We admitted to God, ourselves and to other human beings the exact nature of our wrongs.
6. We were entirely ready to have God remove all these defects of character.
7. We humbly asked him to remove our shortcomings.
8. We made a list of all persons we had harmed and became willing to make amends to all of them.

9. We made direct amends to all such people wherever possible, except where to do so would injure them and others.
10. We continued to take personal inventory, and when we were wrong promptly admitted to it.
11. We sought through prayer and meditation to improve our conscious contact with God, as we understood Him, praying only for knowledge of His will for us, and the power to carry it out.
12. Having had a spiritual awakening as a result of these steps, we tried to carry this message to addicts and to practise these principles in all our affairs.

The basic premise is that it is impossible to overcome the drug problem without the help of the group, which offers friendship and the sharing of common experiences. The Royal College of Psychiatrists (*ibid.*) say that for those who can accept the 12-step programme (and it notes the principles are interpreted with varying degrees of flexibility), the programme provides a comprehensive treatment package with an excellent network of support. Yet for all its apparent certainty the model involves that interesting but curious mixture of contradictions; the patient has a disease but can overcome this by moral and spiritual effort.

Finally comes the behavioural model. This is the most commonly accepted model of substance abuse, whether as an explanation of the phenomenon or whether used in its treatment. In some ways it is a catch-all model including almost anything that can be included, whether it be rational choice (Ditton and Hammersley, 1994) or 'enslaved' or whatever. Treatment involves various forms of therapies, which follow usually after an initial detoxification programme. Those therapies are all directed at understanding the user's personality and identifying the flaws that led to drug use. This is followed by an eradication of those defects, where the expectation is this will lead to new and less defective responses.

In sociology, Mike Hough (1996: 8) identifies three models that have begun to dominate. These are as follows:

1. The *coping* model or self-medication model, which tries to explain why drug misuse goes hand in hand with social deprivation. Drug taking is seen as a palliative to the poor quality of life.
2. The *structure* model, which emphasises that those who are denied legitimate opportunity to achieve society's goals do so by achieving them through illegitimate routes.
3. The *status* model develops opportunity theory, identifying status and identity as associated with economic exclusion. It identifies the

19

positive social pay-offs from drug use in subcultures that respect anti-authoritarian machismo, risk taking and entrepreneurialism.

What is interesting about these three models is how little they are connected to the main theories of the sociology of deviance. They seem to have developed outside mainstream deviance sociology almost as if earlier theories had never existed. For example, control theory is not mentioned, nor is labelling or differential association. Nor is anomie, which for many years (at least up to the late 1960s) was the dominant theory of deviance (Merton, 1957). In anomie theory, drug taking was a deviant adaptation to anomie, itself created as a mismatch between culture goals and legitimate means. That adaptation was described by Merton as retreatism where the substance misuser (then mainly an alcoholic) no longer accepted or strived for the culture goals of success, nor accepted the legitimate means to achieve them. Anomie theory depicts the user as an escapist – a passive respondent to the world around him or her. It gave way to subcultural theory which, in turn, gave way to labelling theory where the user was either labelled as a drug user (the important factor being the manner in which the label was applied), or responded to and took on board the effect of the label. Surprisingly, none of these is mentioned in the theories listed above.

Why should this be so? Largely it seems because those mainstream sociological theories fail to consider the social reality of the current user. Drug use is heavily concentrated in the deprived areas of cities and, although not exclusively so, often enough to be more than coincidental. That community is invariably a poor neighbourhood (Advisory Council on the Misuse of Drugs, 1998). In her description of Bladon in northeast England, Janet Foster (2000) describes it as containing 'drug abuse and crime combined with a debilitating range of other social problems, high levels of truancy, poor health and pervasive unemployment (about 50%) where exclusion and deprivation are very much in evidence'. She prefers to link social exclusion and social deprivation to drug taking, a view that echoes other British studies but does not appear to resonate with those earlier sociological theories of deviance. Her solution: a more inclusive society, but in this she is pessimistic. She fears that many of Bladon's residents did not dare to hope for a better tomorrow and, for those accustomed to living on the margins, it is for them a long and impossible path back (*ibid.*: 327). Coping in this environment requires strength of character and, for those who fail, drug taking is the palliative they need in order to survive.

Of course locating drug use in the poorest parts of the city comes dangerously close to harking back to the pathology models of yesteryear.

Nonetheless, the empirical evidence is there to support it, for the highest concentrations of drug abuse are in run-down derelict inner-city areas. Blotting out the awfulness and hopelessness is an understandable reaction. However, even this is only part of the problem for if drug use is a palliative, what of that undertaken by the successful middle classes? Clearly it is not a palliative to them nor to the never-ending stream of celebrities who daily appear at expensive treatment centres. Their lives are as different as could be. How can we explain their drug use? Do we have to have different explanations based on class or status? If so we are back to that age-old problem in criminology – how to account for middle-class delinquency. And there are no satisfactory theories for this, whether now or otherwise.

The second model (the structure model) is, however, based on an earlier theory derived from the Cloward and Ohlin thesis. It modifies or rather removes one of the main features of Cloward and Ohlin's argument: that of the emergence of the retreatist subculture. Cloward and Ohlin (1960) posit the user as facing two opportunity structures, the legitimate and illegitimate. In their terms, the drug user fails at both: he or she is a double failure having failed as a non-offender and as an offender. Drug abuse is the retreat from both opportunity structures. However, the modern structure model does not see the drug user as a double failure but one who is still striving to achieve success goals, albeit by illegitimate means. He or she has not retreated; he or she may not be a successful entrepreneur in the legitimate sense but is still trying to make it illegitimately. Indeed, the very nature of modern drug markets is that buying and selling, along with 'hustling' in all its forms, is a *sine qua non* of contemporary existence. Again, there is evidence to support this model but how far this is different from the third model discussed below is almost one of emphasis or degree rather than content.

The third model (the status model) is closely associated with the structure model in that both emphasise the use of entrepreneurial skills. The third model, however, emphasises and adds the positive pay-offs associated with dealing. This model draws heavily on some carefully focused ethnographic descriptions of drug users that do not show the drug user as 'a man or woman on his or her back'. Rather they see the drug user as an active participant in the life of the community, who (if not a 'mover and shaker') at least is someone who acquires status from drug dealing. The defining research on this came from Preble and Casey (1969: 14):

> Their behaviour is anything but an escape from life. They are actively engaged in meaningful activities and relationships seven

days a week. The brief moments of euphoria after each administration of a small amount of heroin constitute a small fraction of
their daily lives. The rest of the time they are aggressively pursuing
a career that is exciting, challenging, adventurous, and rewarding.
They are always on the move and must be alert, flexible, and
resourceful. The surest way to identify heroin users in a slum
neighbourhood is to observe the way people walk. The heroin user
walks with a fast, purposeful stride, as if late for an important
appointment – indeed he is. He is hustling, trying to sell stolen
goods, avoiding the police looking for a heroin dealer. He is in short
taking care of business.

The key phrase is 'taking care of business'. The heroin user, according to
Preble and Casey, is busy and purposeful and an important figure to those
who live in the drug areas of our cities.

These theories cover only a small part of the drug taker's world – and
that of the drug user in the inner city. They say nothing about the impact
of drug taking on the local community, of the recreational drug user or of
the non-criminal user. Creating distance from mainstream sociological
theory may turn out to be an error. Perhaps control theory, alongside
other theories of the sociology of deviance, may turn out to have much to
contribute. Centring the debate around ethnography may eventually be
seen to be too narrow, but that is the currently fashionable direction for
research.

A framework for examining drugs and crime

None of the models listed above is sufficiently adequate or able to
provide a framework for analysing the drugs–crime link. Moreover, little
would seem to be gained from pursuing further the drugs–crime link in
the form presented above – especially where the aim is to establish causal
links. Given the orientation of this book, which is to link substance
misuse to the criminal justice system, what is needed is a framework for
marking the boundaries of the debate and for understanding the social
context in which drugs are taken. Consider alcohol: only a small number
of people using alcohol commit crime. What, then, explains those who do,
and what distinguishes them from those who do not? The answer is
multifaceted but in part seems to be found in the social situations in
which alcohol is taken and in the users' behaviour when not under the
influence of alcohol. Violence is most likely to occur when the alcohol has
been taken in social situations where violence is approved and en-

couraged (certain types of pubs or clubs), and by those who are violent when not under the influence. It is not the alcohol *per se* that is the problem but factors external to the alcohol.

One of the most useful frameworks is provided by Paul Goldstein (1985), which itself is not free from notions of causality yet, none the less, allows an assessment to be made of varying crimes and provides guidance for future research. Goldstein concentrates on the drugs–violence nexus but the framework can be extended to include non-violent crimes. There are three parts to the framework or, in Goldstein's terms, there are three possible ways in which drugs and crime are related: the psychopharmacological, the economically compulsive and the systemic. These are ideal types and, whilst recognising they may overlap, Goldstein believes this does not detract from their heuristic value. These ideal types are largely derived from role theory, although not acknowledged by Goldstein as such, and presumably are not exhaustive – others could be added as and when required.

Psychopharmacological crime

Goldstein (1985) says that the psychopharmacological model suggests some individuals, as a result of short or long-term ingestion of specific substances, may become excitable and irrational and may exhibit violent behaviour. He regards the most relevant substances as alcohol, stimulants, barbiturates and PCP – although he recognises that others (such as cocaine and heroin) could be added, the latter of relevance during the period of withdrawal. Goldstein says it is impossible to assess the extent of psychological violence because most cases go unreported or, if reported, then no record is made of the physical or psychological state of the offender. He believes victims 'can be just about anybody' as this type of violence 'occurs in the home, on the streets, in the workplace, in bars and so on' (1995: 257).

Although Goldstein restricts the model to the study of violence, it can readily include other offences. For example, the psychopharmacological impact of a substance can presumably lead to offences such as vandalism or to other property offences. Or it could lead to a mental disorder (the problem of dual diagnosis is a real one – see Bean, 1998), which in turn could lead to other deviant activities, including crime.

Interestingly, Goldstein (1995: 256) also sees drug use as 'having a reverse psychopharmacological effect by being able to ameliorate violent tendencies' – that is, act as a crime-reduction agent. Heroin and other tranquillisers dampen down violent impulses or make it difficult to commit property offences whilst under the influence of the drugs. Heroin typically produces a soporific effect – 'going on the nod' is how the users describe it – it removes aggressive impulses and takes away initiatives. Goldstein does not give examples or cite evidence of the impact of drugs on the crime rates or of how often the so-called reverse psycho-pharmacological effect operates, but its impact is likely to be small. It is also likely to be offset by the violence commonly associated with the withdrawal stage of addiction, where the urgency to obtain supplies can easily lead to further crime (e.g. property offences or violence, domestic and otherwise). (Goldstein (*ibid.*) gives examples of prostitutes in the withdrawal stage robbing potential clients of their money to purchase sufficient heroin to 'get straight'.)

Goldstein also talks of victim-precipitated psychopharmacological crime. That is, drug use may alter a person's behaviour in such a manner as to bring about victimisation. For example, the alcohol-intoxicated man or woman may have his or her wallet or purse stolen by being an easy target for street property offenders, the drugged pedestrian may become victim to the dangerous driver or the drugged/drunken householder may leave his or her property unattended, thereby encouraging or assisting the burglar. These and numerous other examples illustrate the general point that drugs or alcohol can promote high rates of victimisation.

Parenthetically, the psychopharmacological model also suggests that perpetrators or victims have a reduced control over their actions and, on that basis, cannot be held fully responsible. However, in England (as in most common law countries) the law holds that a person who voluntarily ingests drugs or alcohol cannot use this in his or her defence to a crime (such as automatism or diminished responsibility) (Ashworth, 1995; Verdun-Jones, 1997). For example, the Court of Appeal has held that alcoholism can be recognised as an abnormality of mind arising from disease or injury to the brain, but only in very specific circumstances. In a reported case relating to homicide (*Tandy*, 1988) the Court of Appeal held that, for a defence of diminished responsibility to succeed, it must be established that the first drink on the day of the killing was involuntary. Ashworth (1995: 279) says this is an extremely demanding test manifesting deep judicial suspicion of any defences based on alcohol and drugs. That 'deep suspicion' emanates in part from a fear that few offenders would be successfully prosecuted if drugs or alcohol could be used as a defence. Refusing it can be more a matter of policy than of law.

Economic compulsive crime

The economic compulsive model illustrates the populist view about the links between drugs and crime. Here, drug users engage in economically motivated crime in order to support costly drug use (Goldstein, 1995: 257). Goldstein (*ibid.*) says heroin and cocaine are the most relevant drugs, being the most expensive, and produce the greatest demand on the user. He says (*ibid.*) violence may occur during the perpetration of other crimes as a result of 'the offender's own nervousness, weaponry, the intercession by bystanders and so on'.

In the light of the earlier discussion it would be difficult to disaggregate those committed by offenders *qua* offenders and those committed to purchase drugs. Nonetheless, popular perceptions of the links between drugs and crime (as supported by research) endorse Goldstein's thesis. Evidence from the British Crime Survey (BCS) shows that most people see drugs as the main cause of crime. Poor parental discipline came second. The Home Office requested the Office for National Statistics to include questions on perceptions of illegal drug misuse and drug-related crime in their February 1997 *Omnibus Survey* (Charles, 1998). Random samples of 1,585 people aged 16 years or over were interviewed in England. They were asked how much of a problem they felt illegal drug use and drug-related crime to be, whether locally or nationally. Drug-related crime included stealing to buy drugs, offering drugs for sale and committing crimes under the influence of drugs. In the sample, 23% saw drugs as the main cause of crime – slightly higher for those living in the north of England (25%) than in the south (21%).

The Home Office *Research Findings Pamphlet* (Charles, 1998) shows that a third of those questioned said they or a number of their household had been the victim of a property crime in the previous two years. Of those who had been victimised, 15% believed they were the victims of a drug-related crime but 26% were not sure. It is not clear how victims came to this conclusion as few could have had direct contact with an offender or could have known of his or her drug habits, but this was the general perception of the causes of crime. Moreover, about a third of respondents felt stealing for drugs was a 'very big' or 'fairly high' problem in their local area (*ibid.*: 3). Again, how could they know this? Perceptions of the causes of property crime remained steady: 29% in 1997 compared with 28% in 1996.

These perceptions find support in research. For example, what we know of property offences generally, and burglary in particular, is that the offenders rarely move out of their own neighbourhood so that areas with high drug abuse will mean the drug users committing offences against those living in their immediate locality – and that includes other drug users. In our Nottingham study, we found that drug users were active burglars – but were just as often victims of burglary (Bean and Wilkinson, 1988). They stole from others and were stolen from. Similarly, Trevor

Bennett (1998) found that nearly half of the arrestees who reported taking drugs within the last year said their drug use was connected to their offending. Among the various factors emphasised was the need for money to buy drugs, where an estimated 32% of all income was spent on purchasing heroin or crack cocaine (*ibid.*). Coid *et al.* (2000) also note that most subjects in their study (85%) reported they committed offences to buy drugs, the most common offences being shoplifting, fraud, deception and drug dealing. Following treatment, theft decreased by 52%, and those who spent longest in treatment showed the greatest reduction in daily expenditure on illicit drugs. Joy Mott (1987), for the Home Office, estimated the proportions of various types of acquisitive crime attributed to heroin users in England and Wales in 1987 to be between 6 and 24% of all burglaries, between 6 and 23% of all thefts from the person, and between 0.6 and 8% of all shoplifting. These calculations were based on a tentative set of assumptions (for example, about the number of heroin users at the time, the frequency of offending, the extent of their habit, etc.). Small changes to these parameters would affect substantially the final figures – if the extent of the drugs used is greater or lesser than estimated, the rate of burglaries will change accordingly. Mott kept the confidence intervals wide, and rightly so (Mott, 1987; ACMD, 1994).

Goldstein (in Goldstein *et al.*, 1991) produces much lower figures. He sees economic crime as consisting of only about 2% of the drug-related crimes. In his study of 414 homicides in New York, 8% were classified as psychopharmacological and only 2% as economic (*ibid.*). However, he used criteria that were more stringent than most. For example, he did not include a robbery of drugs from a dealer in which the user and dealer were killed. He saw this as systemic crime (i.e. crimes within drug markets). This low rate of economic crime is extraordinary, although Reiss and Roth (1993: 200) report there were differences between the assessments by the police and the researchers in this study, the police regarding more crime as economic.

Almost certainly, offenders help promote the view that they commit offences to buy drugs, and their explanation (or excuse, depending on how one sees it) has been largely accepted. Differences, however, are not just of passing interest: if criminal justice policy is based on the assumption that economic factors are the major driving force, and they are not, then resources will be directed inappropriately.

Systemic crime

As we have just noted, Goldstein regards systemic crime as the most common. Reiss and Roth (1993: 202), however, say systemic crime can take three distinct paths:

1. *Organisational* crime, which involves territorial disputes over drug distribution rights, the enforcement of organisation rules, informers and battles with the police.
2. *Transaction-related* crime, which involves theft of drugs or monies from the buyer or seller, debt collection and the resolution of disputes over the quality of drugs.
3. *Third-party related* crime, which involves bystanders to drug and disputes in related markets such as prostitution, protection or firearms.

Studies of organisational crime are rare, especially outside the USA. Organisational crime involves crime in drug markets where its high level of profits, the lack of skills required to enter as an entrepreneur and the ease of transportation of a commodity with an enormously valuable per unit weight are likely to be attractive for crime at whatever level. Protection of those markets requires high levels of corruption, whether of senior politicians, business people or low-level bank tellers. It also requires organisational skills to hold on to that part of the market in which they operate. The tensions within that market, whether concerning informers or other dealers, are always likely to make the market unstable.

Transaction crime refers to crime involving the interpersonal relationships between dealer and dealer, or dealer and user. Debts need to be collected, ownership and property rights need to be established, and countless other activities need to be carried out as befits any business contractual arrangements. Dealers collect debts in a number of ways: one is to use violence and another is by burglary to take whatever is available as a means of collecting debts (Bean and Wilkinson, 1988). An easy recourse to violence is a *sine qua non* of all dealings, for discipline has to be asserted and debts collected – the system runs on some sort of credit that needs to be overhauled at regular intervals.

Third-party-related crime is less common. There are also very few studies of this type of crime, but prostitution, protection rackets, etc., are common to all drug markets without necessarily being part of them. How and under what circumstances they mesh into the system is far from understood, but it is thought they operate at the perimeter and may well be more important in the scheme of things than is believed.

A note on violence

Goldstein (1995: 255) was particularly concerned with violent offenders where, he says, research has consistently found strong connections between drugs and violence. For these purposes violence can be defined

27

as behaviour by persons against others that intentionally threatens attempts or actually inflicts physical harm (Reiss and Roth, 1993: 35). It does not include self-inflicted harm as in suicide, unintentional harm or harassment or psychological humiliation in which trauma may occur. In Britain as elsewhere, the introduction of drugs such as crack cocaine in the late 1980s and early 1990s made people realise that drug markets could be violent places where death was increasingly commonplace and violence a standard feature of drug dealing (Bean, 2001a).

Violent people involved in drug misuse are not a subset of violent offenders nor a specific subset of offenders generally. The evidence suggests a measure of convergence has accrued – that is, substance misusers and other criminals have become one and the same. Drug-selling organisations frequently recruit those with previous histories of violence or those who are comfortable with violence, and ask them to fulfil roles within the organisation (Johnson *et al.*, 1990: 35). These roles can include intimidating ordinary citizens who may refuse to co-operate or otherwise with their demands (*ibid*: 35–36).

As with other forms of crime, there has been much research linking the ingestion of drugs with violence, especially alcohol. Jeffrey Fagan (1990) concludes there is no empirical evidence for attributing a strong causal relationship between intoxication and aggression regardless of the type of substances and, in any case, conditional factors make causal connections difficult to demonstrate. For example, interpersonal violence occurs more frequently in some bars than others, and violence in some sports stadiums occurs more often in some than others. In Britain, violence is more likely at football matches rather than cricket or rugby matches, yet more alcohol is consumed at the latter than the former.

As a general rule, violence is greater when drug dealing takes place at street level, and is even greater where the seller has less control over access to the purchaser. For example, Reiss and Roth (1993) confirm that call-girl operations are less violent than open-air street walking. 'Similarly in drug markets, runner-beeper delivery systems may entail less violence than open air markets, while heavily fortified crack houses experience still less risk' (*ibid*.: 18). In our Nottingham study, we thought that levels of street violence decreased in amount and changed in form and quality once control of the profits was taken over by an outside organisation, thereby making the financial system more organised. Then, as with high-level dealing, violence becomes more focused and instrumental and is used to enforce discipline and collect debts (Bean and Wilkinson, 1988). It is not likely to be random or haphazard. At the very highest level of dealing, violence is entirely instrumental and focused, aimed at taking out the opposition or removing internal disagreements. It occurs according to a prearranged set of signals that almost always involve co-offending i.e. with two or more offenders against one victim and based on a scale of punishments determined in advance.

Male violence in domestic situations is often ritualised. That is, alcohol is consumed in settings that give approval to male violence, where violent incidents occur as part of a considered demonstration of masculine authority. In contrast, female violence in domestic settings does not have the association with alcohol as found with male violence. Nor is female violence associated with other drugs as is common with male violence. In our Nottingham study (Bean and Wilkinson, 1988), we found that female drug dealers were prepared to use violence and did so as often as their male counterparts, either to enforce discipline or collect, but they tended not to do it themselves; male partners had to do it for them. Incidentally, they changed partners regularly when existing partners failed to deliver as required. Similarly, Inciardi *et al.* (1993), in their study of women heroin and cocaine users in Miami, found that like their male counterparts female users offended in similar ways – except that over half (54%) of their offences were for prostitution – and the heavier the drug use, the more likely was the use of violence.

Fagan (1990: 261) shows that male violence associated with substance misuse was no different from other forms of criminality in the sense it has the same antecedents (i.e. family pathology and early childhood victimisation experiences). Early childhood aggressiveness and alcoholism as an adult were found to interact and predict the highest levels of interpersonal violence. Violent men under the influence of a substance including alcohol were violent men when not under the influence of those substances.

Sadly, one of the most important changes in the British drug scene has been the increasing use of firearms on the streets where low-level crack dealers display firearms openly in areas where firearms were hitherto unknown. No one knows how many homicides in Britain are drugs related but the police believe they are increasing annually. McBride and Swartz (1991: 160) in America note that in addition to the willingness to use lethal weapons, there has been a significant increase in the lethality of the weapons used: machine-guns and semi-automatic weapons had significantly increased in use and scope in the 1980s during the increase in crack cocaine use. The large profits and the way in which coca growing and distribution in Central and South America have become increasingly intertwined with political revolutionary groups (*ibid.*: 161) may help explain the growing levels of violence associated with drugs. So too must be the recruitment of violent individuals to drug trafficking and the approval given to violence in those situations.

An overview

Few would dispute there are links between drug taking and crime, irrespective of the mere fact that possessions of selected substances are themselves crimes. The problem is to determine the precise nature of that link. As noted above, establishing causal connections (sufficient conditions) is additionally difficult, and the best that can be done is to make a weak causal link (necessary condition) and begin from there. The main problem is that many drug users would have been offenders anyway so that determining those offenders whose offences relate to drugs and those that do not is almost impossible.

Numerous theories of drug use have provided useful and interesting areas of research but, for our purposes, a wider framework is required so that rather than looking for causal links or concentrating on one theoretical approach, the framework developed by Goldstein has been modified to include all crimes (Goldstein, 1995). This framework involves the psychological (where drugs alter behaviour, including reducing inhibitions or increasing aggression), the sociological (which emphasises the social situations where crimes are committed in the effort to secure funds or to purchase drugs for self-use) and the economic (where crimes are committed to secure, maintain and extend drug markets). The emphasis on violence offences is important: there is a strong suspicion that violence in British streets has increased considerably with the arrival of crack cocaine in the late 1980s and that Goldstein is correct to point to this as an important dimension to the drugs–crime debate.

The Goldstein framework provides the basis of a great deal of what is to follow, particularly that related to systemic crime. The supply networks, particularly those within Britain, attempts to police them and the corresponding drug markets, whether local or otherwise, require considerable attention. What is often forgotten in the drugs–crime debate is the impact of drug use on the community and on the buyers and sellers – the dealers and users. Goldstein's model of systemic crime draws attention to this. Bruce Johnson *et al.* (1990) make the point that while a few upper-level suppliers make 'crazy money' from cocaine and heroin sales, the vast majority of inner-city youths who enter this world rarely improve their economic positions. Instead, the regular use of heroin, cocaine and crack frequently brings impoverishment (*ibid.*: 43). The oft-heard lament from ex-dealers was 'dealing doesn't last' (Bean and

Wilkinson, 1988); they made their pile of 'crazy money' but lost it as quickly as they made it, whether from drug use, burglary by other dealers, the need to pay to avoid threats and intimidation or simply by being 'busted' by the police.

There is also the impact on the community – an under-researched area. Anecdotally it seems the impact could be devastating, especially among some ethnic minority groups where community structures are fragile. When a 15-year-old dealer taunts others with his new-found wealth, what does this do to a community where unemployment is high and job prospects limited? How do parents tell children that hard work and effort will lead to rewards 10 or 20 years hence when the rewards appear to be available now, with few entrepreneurial skills required and even less education? Or how to cope with some of the more ill-considered comments from drug researchers who claim that drug use in Britain is 'normal'? Statistically speaking, this may be correct, but how do parents tell their children not to take drugs when their response is that it is normal to do so? We do not have to live with high rates of drug abuse: there are things we can do, one of which is to lay the appropriate foundations and then secure the political will to meet the task.

Chapter 3

Sentencing drug offenders

In this chapter I want to look at the way in which courts deal with drug offenders, or rather with those charged with drug offences under the 1971 Act. I want to include those offenders whose Index offence is other than for drugs but who are users. Unfortunately, the data on these are sparse. For the drug offenders there are two major types of offences: first is possession (that is, illegally possessing one of the prohibited drugs) and, secondly, is supply (that is, giving or selling one of those prohibited drugs). Of course, the 1971 Act is more extensive than this but these are the main types of offences.

Producing the data

The data collection and analysis processes relating to drug offenders who appear before the courts in England and Wales are – according to John Corkery from the Home Office – 'currently very complicated, old fashioned and time consuming'. As far as being old-fashioned, that means the figures always relate to a period some 12–18 months earlier, although discussions are taking place between the Home Office and data suppliers throughout the UK on the provision of more timely data. Inevitably, there will always be something of a delay, if only because of the time it takes for offenders to come before the courts and for any subsequent appeal that might be heard but, even so, a greater sense of urgency would be welcomed (*ibid.*). At present (2000), the courts supply their own data.

That the data is 'very complicated' is clear from the method by which it is recorded. At present, the data on drug seizure are compiled from a

Crimsec 38 form, which is used throughout England and Wales. It is apparently very simple to complete and can contain basic information (i.e. police force, date of seizure, drug involved, the type and quantity, and whether the drugs were sent for forensic analysis) (*ibid.*). Only 3 of the 43 police forces in England and Wales, plus the British Transport Police, submit data electronically on floppy disks. Steps are under way to encourage other forces to do so (*ibid.*).

By contrast, the form used in Scotland and Northern Ireland is quite complicated. There, the Crimsec 19 is a two-sheet partly carbonated form. The top sheet is completed when a drug seizure is made and sent to the Home Office once the substance has been forensically tested. In addition to the information outlined as being required by the Crimsec 38, other fields have to be completed (e.g. place of seizure and by whom). Details of the suspects are entered on to the form and these are copied through to the second sheet. This part of the form is supposed to be completed when the results of any police or court decision are known; it is then sent to the Home Office (*ibid.*).

The in-built delay concerning the time cases take to come before the courts is further complicated in the case of Scotland because the courts there tend to 'roll up' offences. This means that when an offender appears before the court, all offences of whatever nature are dealt with together. This makes it difficult for the police to decide on what action was taken for drug offences and, hence, what to enter on the Crimsec 19. These difficulties appear to have led to a significant shortfall in the number of forms being received by the Home Office, especially in the 1994–96 period. The second part of the Crimsec 19 form gives details of the date of the offence, the date of the disposal (e.g. court appearance), the offence(s), the action taken (court sentence, amount of fine, etc.) and the drugs involved, as well as the offender's name, age, gender and so on, the court and police force area (*ibid.*).

To complicate matters even further, since 1995, instead of supplying data on magnetic media in a format compatible with the Crimsec 19, HM Customs & Excise have provided data on their seizures and what happened to the individuals involved in unlawful import and export offences (almost exclusively the former) on floppy disk and computer printout. However, there is a fundamental difference between their data and those provided by the police and the courts in that the drugs seized by HM Customs & Excise are not attributable to individual suspects or offenders (*ibid.*). One wonders, of course, why these variations persist and why it takes so long to introduce a coherent system, but there it is. The data presented below are therefore the best available but should be seen as having limitations.

One of the most important limitations is that these data are on drug offenders – that is, those who are convicted of offences against the principal Act in Britain (the 1971 Act). They do not include that large unknown number of drug users convicted for an offence other than under the 1971 Act. Sometimes in the discussion that follows (for example, on the use of imprisonment) all offenders with a drug problem are included; at other times, such as in the discussion on sentencing, they are not. It would be unrealistic to exclude those whose Index offence was not a drugs offence but, sadly, the data on these are scantier than on the drug offenders.

Before looking at the sentences available, a brief overview of the legislation is required. The 1971 Act divides the drugs it controls into three main categories that determine the maximum penalties for possession, supply and other offences.

Class A

This is the highest class and includes heroin, methadone, cocaine, LSD, cannabinols and ecstasy. The maximum penalty for possession by the Crown Court is 7 years' imprisonment and/or an unlimited fine, and in the Magistrates Court it is 6 months' imprisonment and/or a £2,500 fine. For supply (i.e. trafficking and dealing) the offence in the Crown Court carries a maximum life sentence and an unlimited fine.

Class B

The drugs included here are amphetamines and cannabis. In the Crown Court, possession carries a maximum 5 years' imprisonment and/or an unlimited fine, and in the Magistrates Court 3 months' imprisonment and/or a £2,500 fine. For supply in a Crown Court, the maximum is 14 years' imprisonment and/or an unlimited fine, and in the Magistrates Court it is 6 months' imprisonment and/or a £2,500 fine.

Class C

The drugs included here are the benzodiazepines and some synthetic opiates. The maximum Crown Court penalty for possession is 2 years' imprisonment and/or an unlimited fine, and in the Magistrates Courts 3 months' imprisonment an/or a £1,000 fine. Supply carries a maximum of 5 years' imprisonment in the Crown Court and an unlimited fine.

In addition, the Customs and Excise Management Act 1979 prohibits the import and export of controlled drugs except for approved purposes (i.e.

medicinal or research). The Drug Trafficking Act 1994 creates further offences in respect of money laundering and gives courts powers to order the confiscation of assets obtained through drug trafficking.

Drug offenders

The number of drug offenders appearing before the courts in the UK from 1967 to 1997 is given in Table 3.1. Figures 3.1–3.3 show the actions taken against drug offenders over that period (that is, how the offenders were dealt with by the courts for the principal drug offences). The term 'offender' will be used in this and subsequent chapters although, legally, an offender must have been convicted of an offence but the term has been used here when the person may have been found not guilty or may not yet be convicted.

Table 3.1 is in two parts. First it gives data on the total number of offenders (i.e. not offences) and on the sentences passed for those offenders. Incidentally, the subgroups in Table 3.1 will not tally with the subtotal, as more than one offender can be in the subgroups. So, for example, the totals for 'unlawful possession' and 'trafficking' will not coincide with the total number of offenders listed. Similarly, the total for those sentenced will not tally with the numbers of offenders as those sentenced on one occasion only. The second part lists the drugs.

The key points from this table are as follows. First, it shows the relentless rise in the number of possession offenders – although these have not gone up as fast as trafficking offenders in the 10 years from 1987 to 1997. Secondly, the number of drug offenders increased by 19% to almost 113,000 in 1997, with almost 90% for possession cases, mainly of cannabis. Thirdly, there was a massive increase in the number of heroin offenders to 8,759, and a fourfold increase in cannabis offenders to over 86,000 for 1997 over 1987. Finally, in 1997 just under half of offenders were cautioned, 22% were fined and 9% were sentenced to immediate custody in each case a similar proportion to 1995 and 1996. The number of persons given immediate custodial sentences rose by 19% between 1996 and 1997, but this did not affect the proportion sent to immediate custody.

Figure 3.1 gives the same data on the trends in sentencing practices against drug offenders from 1987 to 1997. It shows that the use of the fine has decreased whereas cautions have increased considerably, and that the numbers of offenders sentenced to immediate custody remain low and have now fallen to under 10%. Figure 3.2 sets out the same data as Figure 3.1 but includes a wider range of sentences. It shows that the proportion

Table 3.1 Drug offenders, UK, 1967–1997

	1967	1977	1987	1997
Total offenders	4,498	12,907	26,278	113,154
Of which:				
Unlawful possession	2,604 under DDA and 1,992 under other legislation	10,987	22,017	108,808
Trafficking[1]	NA	1,923	5,077	17,604
Of which:				
Immediate custody	832	1,450	3,939	10,422
Fine	1,355	8,015	10,789	24,421
Caution	–	203	6,217	56,756
Compounding[2]	–	–	522	547
Fiscal fine (Scotland only)	–	–	–	500
Of which:				
Cannabis	2,393	10,607	21,733	86,086
Amphetamines	NA	1,788	2,299	13,354
Heroin	274	393	2,151	8,759
Cocaine	86	309	518	3,369
LSD	97	279	300	725
Ecstasy type	NA	NA	NA	4,164

Notes
NA = not available.
1. Unlawful production of drugs (exc. cannabis), unlawful supply, possession with intent to supply unlawfully, unlawful import and export. Production of cannabis included from 1995.
2. Financial penalty imposed by HM Customs & Excise in lieu of prosecution. Typically used for unlawful importation of small amounts of drugs for personal use.
Source: Corkery, 1999.

found 'not guilty' remained fairly stable and confirms that the use of 'immediate custody' is falling, but only gradually.

Figure 3.3 gives similar data to that in Table 3.1 but presents them in graphic form. It shows the dramatic increase in the use of the caution, a fall in the use of the fine and a fall in the use of immediate custody – and, incidentally, where immediate custody was awarded it was almost

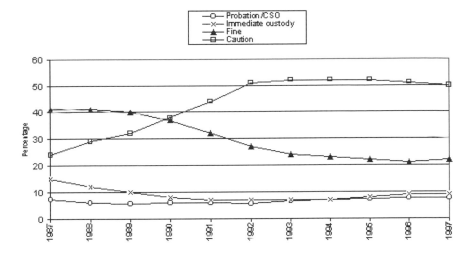

Figure 3.1 Trends in action taken against drug offenders, UK, 1987–97
Source: *Home Office Seizures and Offenders Bulletin*

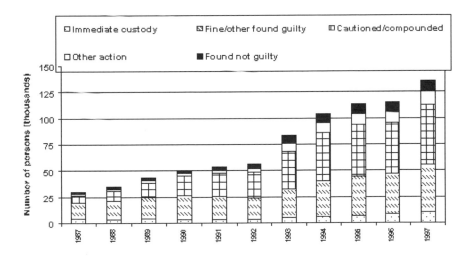

Figure 3.2 Persons dealt with and action taken, UK, 1987–97
Source: *Home Office Seizures and Offenders Bulletin*

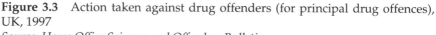

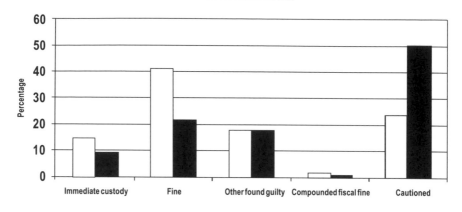

Figure 3.3 Action taken against drug offenders (for principal drug offences), UK, 1997
Source: Home Office Seizures and Offenders Bulletin.

always for trafficking offences rather than possession. As shown earlier, the proportionate decrease masks an aggregate increase where the percentage going to immediate custody has risen but not as fast as the rise in convictions generally.

We cannot of course assume that the rise in convictions as shown in the table and figures given here points to an increase in drug use but, as the figures are dramatic and the other indicators on seizures, etc. (as shown in Chapters 1 and 6) are similar, it is reasonable to conclude the increase is real. Anecdotal evidence is available in abundance and points in the same direction – that is, drug use has risen in all categories and for all drugs, especially over the last decade. That being so what, then, are some of the health problems common to drug users, especially those concerning HIV/AIDS, and what are the death rates associated with that drug use?

HIV/AIDS and the mortality of drug users

For reasons that are obvious, drug users have special health problems in addition to any psychological or social problems they may exhibit (some of these additional problems surround mental health matters, i.e. the problems of dual diagnosis). Drug offenders, or rather drug users generally, have high rates for mental disorder but, as is shown below, they also have high rates for HIV/AIDS and a high death rate.

Consider first HIV/AIDS. Again, the data are taken from the report by John Corkery (1999). Table 3.2 gives the HIV and AIDS statistics. These were obtained from the UK's Public Health Laboratory Service AIDS Centre (PHLS) and the Scottish Centre for Infection and Environmental Health (SCIEH) on AIDS and HIV. These two organisations publish a quarterly bulletin, the latest issue of which (as used here) giving details for the quarter ending June 2000 and published in July 2000.

First AIDS. The data show that about 6% (1,071/17,072) of AIDS cases are accounted for by heterosexual injecting drug users and a further 2% (303 cases) by homosexual injecting drug users. For HIV, then, 10% (3,608/42,125) of HIV cases were contracted by heterosexual injecting drug users and a further 2% (629 cases) by homosexual injecting drug users. Table 3.2 gives details of such cases by gender and region. Clearly, the extent of HIV/AIDS is worrying and it is understandable that the Advisory Council for the Misuse of Drugs (ACMD) made it clear that AIDS was a more important problem than drug abuse. Table 3.3 translates the data from Table 3.2 into age group and gender, showing that, not surprisingly, the 15–34 age group is the greatest age at risk.

Table 3.2   HIV and AIDS cases by region of report – injecting drug use

| | AIDS | | HIV | |
	Male	Female	Male	Female
England				
Northern and Yorkshire	19	8	64	30
Trent	28	11	102	36
Eastern	32	9	96	31
London	286	121	950	481
South East	61	20	194	70
South West	19	11	79	35
West Midlands	9	6	56	21
North West	41	16	113	48
Total	495	202	1,654	752
Wales	7	4	22	7
Northern Ireland	1	2	4	3
Scotland	257	103	803	355
UK	770	311	2,483	
CI/IOM	0	0	4	3

Source: Corkery, 1999.

Table 3.3 AIDS and HIV cases by age group at diagnosis and by gender - injecting drug users

	AIDS		HIV	
	Male	Female	Male	Female
15–19	1	1	128	89
20–24	30	21	506	322
25–29	165	78	690	322
30–34	267	120	604	227
35–39	172	54	317	100
40–44	87	30	134	29
45 and over	38	7	66	16
Total	760	311	2,445	1,105
Not known	0	0	42	16

Source: Corkery, 1999.

Wales and Northern Ireland have low rates of HIV and AIDS, with Scotland having a figure almost as high as London – with the exception of female HIV. There are also wide variations in the regions, with the West Midlands being the lowest. In terms of Table 3.3, which gives the data in terms of ages, the peak ages are 25–29 with 1,255 cases, closely followed by 30–34 with 1,218. Thereafter the fall is quite rapid. In almost every respect, and not surprisingly, the data in the above tables follow the trends for drug use generally.

Looking next at death rates, again the data presented by John Corkery (1999) are the best available. Table 3.4 shows that, in 1995, there were 1,805 drug-related deaths in the UK. Of these, about 602 were attributed to drug dependence or non-dependent misuse of drugs (other than alcohol or tobacco but including volatile substances). A further 470 deaths resulted from accidental poisoning and 259 by poisoning from controlled drugs where it was uncertain whether the drugs had been purposely taken. Some 327 people committed suicide with the aid of controlled drugs, and 147 injecting drug users died from AIDS in 1995. Of over 14,000 AIDS cases reported in the UK between January 1982 and March 1997, some 880 (6%) probably acquired the virus through injecting. Of these, 630 had died by the end of March 1997. Of the 602 deaths in 1995 resulting from drug dependence or non-dependent misuse of drugs, about 53% used morphine-type drugs (including 19% involving methadone) and about 7% used volatile substances. Fifteen per cent of those who died were under 20 and about four fifths of these deaths were of people aged under 35.

Table 3.4 Summary of drug-related deaths, by year of registration, UK, 1988–95

Underlying cause of death	1988	1989	1990	1991	1992	1993	1994	1995
Drug dependence and non-dependent misuse of drugs[1]	222	245	294	307	345	322	489	602
Deaths where a controlled drug was mentioned:[2]								
Accidental	191	202	233	259	329	359	445	470
Suicide	478	433	440	459	414	352	352	327
Undetermined	302	279	262	298	280	256	246	259
AIDS	19	32	55	79	82	110	119	147
Total	1,212	1,191	1,284	1,402	1,450	1,399	1,651	1,805

Notes
1. Includes solvents and other non-controlled drugs, such as alcohol.
2. Excludes Northern Ireland before 1991. However, there are very few drug-related deaths in that part of the UK.
Source: Table 16 in Corkery (1997).

The main Class A drugs mentioned in the deaths from accidental poisoning were methadone (154), morphine (97) and heroin (60). Benzodiazepines were involved in one sixth and dextropropoxyphene in one tenth of such deaths. About a third of suicides caused by poisoning involved at least one controlled drug. These were usually Class C, particularly dextropropoxyphene and benzodiazepines (often Valium or temazepam), and Class B drugs (mainly dihydrocodeine, codeine and barbiturates) (*ibid.*).

The Advisory Council on the Misuse of Drugs (ACMD) (2000) examined questions arising from drug-related deaths. They did not define what they meant by 'drug-related deaths' but examined the statistics and the methods by which these statistics were compiled. They concluded:

> The current system for collecting and reporting on drug related deaths in the UK stands in need of considerable amendment and strengthening. There is valuable experience on which to build but the fact remains that at present the system for generating data on drug related deaths in Britain cannot provide information of the quality needed.

The ACMD made six major recommendations. These are as follows:

1. The establishment of a national reporting and surveillance system for HBV and HCV (hepatitis B and C), together with repeat national sample surveys on the virus and the status of clients attending drug treatment agencies.
2. Toxicological screening to be ordered by coroners in England and Wales when there is reason to believe controlled drugs were involved in the death.
3. Better recording by coroners and their Scottish counterparts on the role of drugs in deaths.
4. Agreement to be reached on a consistent ICD code to be used in drug deaths.
5. Further support on international comparisons of mortality rates.
6. A new system, appropriately resourced, for data collection on drug-related deaths.

How and to what extent these recommendations will improve matters is to be seen. Clearly the problem is serious. With a total number of deaths associated with substance abuse of about 1,800 per year, where about 80% of those were under the age of 35, this is little short of a tragedy. We ought not fall into the trap of believing that, because these data have shortcomings, we should ignore them altogether (the ACMD recognised their failings), but even on this rough and ready guide one wonders why more attention is not given to this. As far back as 1968, Thomas Bewley showed that the death rate of heroin addicts was 28 times that for the commensurate age group so we ought not to be surprised at the current figures – which, incidentally, appear to show a welcome proportionate decrease. Drug taking has always been a high-risk exercise and these figures confirm it or, as one heavy user said, 'Drug addicts go to a lot of funerals'.

Sentencing and the treatment of drug offenders

This broad overview of the number of offenders, the manner in which they were sentenced and some of the health risks involved sets the scene for a wider discussion on the sentencing practices of the courts. As shown in Figure 3.3, only about 10% of drug offenders are sentenced to immediate custody, and about the same number is placed on probation, with rather more (but falling numbers) being fined. Most drug offenders never appear at court but are cautioned by the police, having admitted their offence. Here I want to look at the courts' four major sentences (as shown in Figure 3.1): probation, the fine, caution and imprisonment to determine the offenders' contribution to drug-related crime reduction. First probation, which (as shown in Figure 3.1) accounted for about 8% of drug offenders in 1997 and was the least used of the four major sentences (for these purposes, cautions are called a sentence).

On the face of it the probation order would seem an obvious method of dealing with drug offenders. It is primarily rehabilitative in approach, concerned to assist with the welfare of the offender, with facilities to assist in treatment and with officers who have knowledge of local facilities. In practice, the probation order appears not to work well with drug users: supervision can be patchy and the type of treatment offered does not always appear to have much impact. For example, in a study on the Inner London Probation Service the results were anything but clear cut or favourable to the probation service. When asked what had been the greatest help overall in tackling drug use, most of the offenders in the population who were on probation mentioned factors other than probation. However, in doing so, most of those interviewed felt their probation officer had played a part in securing this help (Hearnden and Harocopos, 2000). Or again, over two thirds of respondents felt the probation service's relationship with drug users could be improved. Many judged their officer to have little understanding of drug issues and terminology so that probationers who were not prepared to discuss fully or divulge drug use said it was easy to mislead their officer – a matter that is of deep significance when we come later to discuss the Drug Treatment and Testing Order (DTTO). On the other hand, the offenders who were interviewed said they did not necessarily think their officer's knowledge needed improving, regarding it as sufficient that their officer could refer them to a drugs specialist either within the probation service or elsewhere (*ibid.*: 3). There was some success in reducing drug use whilst on probation but it seemed too often that the demands of the drug were more powerful than the demands of the probation officer.

There is little doubt that the probation service is in the front line when it comes to dealing with drug offenders. The study quoted above shows that a significant minority of the Inner London Probation Service (ILPS) case-load has consistently been identified as problem drug users. Data from the ILPS Drug and Alcohol Demonstration unit suggested that, in 1989, around 1,800 (20% of the caseload) fell into this category (*ibid.*). In a study by Claire Nee and Rae Sibbitt for the Home Office (1993), the con-clusions were depressingly similar: that there was substantial variation among probation services in terms of the kind of response made, the effectiveness of the responses, the number and range of drug agencies available, and the relationships with these agencies. Nee and Sibbitt (*ibid.*: iv) say 'in many ways the responses appeared inadequate; probation officers had not been trained to recognise drug misuse and drug programmes did not always have the support of management'. Of significance in matters relating to the conditions of treatment that can be attached to a probation order, Nee and Sibbitt (*ibid.*: *iv*) say 'once they had made a referral probation officers were usually unable to get feedback from drug agencies as a result of the agencies' policies on confidentiality'. As will be shown in the next chapter, the probation service has learnt its lesson from this. Under the DTTO, those undertaking the treatment are required to report directly to the probation officer and to be responsible to the probation service.

Within the probation service there remains ambivalence about the need to control drug users – casework mingled with a harm-reduction approach sometimes being seen as more appropriate than one based on abstinence and control. This ambivalence produces all sorts of problems and uncertainties when it comes to securing and enforcing treatment. The criticisms made of the probation officers in this respect are sometimes more unfairly directed at them when they should be directed at those doing the treatment. Treatment providers often fail to co-operate with the probation service for reasons that are sometimes difficult to determine, perhaps because they do not want to be involved in court proceedings or, worse, that they do not want to inform the probation officer of the patient's failings as this 'might damage the relationship with the treatment provider'. To which the obvious retort would be that the relationship is not very strong if it cannot stand that measure of honesty.

Those sentences that offer the best opportunities are those of a probation order with a condition of treatment. Briefly, the Powers of the Criminal Courts Act 1973 permits the court to attach a condition of treatment to a probation order (which may be as an inpatient or outpatient) if the court is satisfied on the evidence of a duly qualified medical practitioner that the offender's condition is such as requires and may be susceptible to treatment but is not such as to warrant detention in hospital under the Mental Health Act 1983. (There is an apparent confusion here that turns out to be resolved thus: a person on a probation order with a condition of treatment can be detained in a hospital but, unlike those patients detained under the Mental Health Act, his or her condition will not be severe. Whilst on probation he or she has the same rights whilst in hospital as an outpatient to refuse treatment and to discharge him or herself. That, of course, may lead to a breach of probation but if a refusal to undergo treatment is reasonable, having regard to all the circumstances (s. 6 (7) Powers of Civil Courts Act 1973), no breach would be implied. The main advantage of this type of probation order is that treatment can be given to offenders whose condition is not so severe as to warrant detention in a hospital under the Mental Health Act. This treatment can also be given for those forms of mental disorder that fall outside the Mental Health Act, such as alcohol and drug misuse.

There seems to be general agreement that what is commonly called the 'psychiatric probation order' – or, more accurately, a probation order with a condition of psychiatric treatment as essentially determined by s. 3 of the Powers of Criminal Courts Act 1973 – is under-used, undervalued and under-researched. As far as can be seen, the high point of the order was in the mid-1970s when approximately 1,000 outpatient and 500 inpatient orders were made – 'approximately' because, surprisingly, there were few accurate national statistics on the orders made. By 1987 it appears the figures had dipped to 870 and 150, respectively, and, by the late 1990s, dropped even further (of course, these figures are not just for drug offenders but for all offenders on the probation order with a condition of treatment, some of whom may not use drugs).

It is difficult to explain the lack of interest. It may have something to do with a general reluctance on behalf of psychiatrists to accept patients on an order and a similar reluctance by the probation service to negotiate with psychiatrists about resolving existing tensions. The courts, too, seem to have lost interest or perhaps have simply gone along with the prevailing climate. No one seems to know. Only one detailed research study has been undertaken, and that as far back as 1980 (Lewis). This study looked at the use and effectiveness of such orders. The conclusions were generally favourable, with Lewis arguing for greater use, especially among the less severe mentally disordered. Sadly, the study produced little general interest and has hardly been referred to again.

The Criminal Justice Act 1991 attempted to revive this type of probation order by placing community treatments at the centre of the criminal justice system. For example, s. 9 allowed the court to require the offender to comply, during the whole or part of the period on probation, with such requirements as the court considered desirable. The 1991 Act seems not to have improved things, with the decline continuing. It is difficult to know how that decline can be reversed.

In addition, there are 'bail and arrest' referral schemes that, strictly speaking, are not part of probation but are often run by the probation service. These constitute a catch-all group and are available where an offender requires assessment or treatment and an early investigation of the options. These can be provided through the bail scheme. Bail schemes may also involve the services of a consultant psychiatrist. The accommodation is usually in local bail hostels. If the offender is on police bail, the police may choose not to prosecute if the offender is being successfully diverted and treated. Sometimes the police will refer to the Crown Prosecution Service (CPS) for advice (NACRO, 1993: 15).

There are various types of arrest referral schemes, some of which may involve nothing more than supplying the offender with an address to seek assistance or accommodation; others involve treatment agencies attending the police station and offering advice on treatment. Yet others offer incentives contingent on receiving treatment. Much is made of these schemes, with the potential for diverting drug offenders out of the criminal justice system (although the caution does that successfully), but there is little information on the number of such schemes or on their effectiveness.

Secondly is the fine. Figure 3.1 shows that the use of the fine has fallen in the last decade, from just under 40% to a little above 20%. The interesting feature is not the decrease in use but that the fine is used at all. It clearly has no place for street drug users whose lifestyle makes them unsuitable for that type of sentence or for the serious trafficker. It may have more of a place for a possession offence where the drug involved is not Class A and the charge involves a small amount (e.g. cannabis or perhaps even a similar amount of ecstasy).

How, then, to account for its use? The key is found in Table 3.1 (and in Figure 3.3), which show the principal offences and the sentence. Table 3.1 shows that the drug most likely to lead to a prosecution was cannabis (86,086 in 1997), followed by amphetamines (13,354) and then by ecstasy-type drugs (4,164). In contrast, the number of prosecutions for drugs such as heroin and cocaine are relatively small – 8,759 for heroin and 3,369 for cocaine in 1997, making 12,128 (i.e. fewer than for amphetamines). It is reasonable to assume most of these offences were for possession, given the data in Table 3.1. What this table shows, then, is that most drug offences are for possession i.e. for a drug that does not normally carry a severe penalty and, presumably, this is why the fine is used.

However, the implications go beyond this and extend to matters surrounding policing (discussed in Chapter 7) as they raise questions about the effectiveness of policing for example, how is it that most drug offences are for the possession of a small amount of cannabis? They also raise questions about introducing drug courts into Britain. Could we introduce drug courts to include this group of offenders who would otherwise expect only the minimal punishments? And they also raise questions about the type of drug policy we might wish to pursue: are we correct to use up the court's time for these relatively minor offenders or should sentencing policy be more severe to produce a more deterrent effect?

There is no information available as to the effectiveness of the fine for drug offenders, neither in terms of reconviction rates nor as to whether the fine was paid. Compounding, which is a fine in every respect except it does not involve a court appearance, can be imposed by HM Customs & Excise and has remained steady since 1987. There is no information on the effectiveness of this, but payment is made direct to the customs service at the time the drugs are discovered. The numbers of offenders given the fiscal fine (for Scotland only) were comparatively small. The fine carries no treatment requirements.

Now to deal now with the caution. Table 3.1 and Figure 3.3 show that, as the use of the fine has declined, that of the caution has increased – so much so that it is reasonable to suppose the caution has replaced the fine at this lower end of the sentencing tariff. Briefly, there are two types of cautions: the informal and the formal. The first is given in the form of a warning, no record is made of the incident and no further action is taken. The formal caution is different. It arose in the late 1940s with juveniles in Liverpool where it was found that children who were made subject to the juvenile court proceedings did rather worse in terms of reconviction than those who did not go to court. Hence the formal caution, usually given by the police but without the involvement of the court. The caution is a pragmatic device aimed at cutting down court appearances and avoiding reconvictions. It is a peculiarly British device, hardly used outside the UK. It is cheap, effective and thought to be especially useful for juveniles, although it is increasingly used for adults. Formal cautions (like informal cautions) carry no treatment provisions, although there is nothing to stop the police from advising those cautioned where they can receive treatment, should they so wish.

Table 3.1 shows how the use of the caution for drug users has increased dramatically in the decade 1987-97. Almost half the drug offenders were cautioned in 1997 – this up from about 25% in 1987. The ACMD (1994: para. 7.6) saw cautioning as a 'particularly appropriate way of dealing with minor drug offences', adding that 'the effect of cautioning in reducing re-offending remains in question', although for most first offenders the likelihood of re-offending appears no greater than after conviction by the court (*ibid.*). It defined cautioning thus:

> In England and Wales the police may formally caution an arrested offender instead of initiating prosecution by the Crown Prosecution Service. The procedure is not used in Scotland. Although the practice of formal caution has statutory recognition it is nowhere

defined in legislation, and is essentially an administrative act based on the discretion the police have in whether or not to prosecute offenders (*ibid.*: para. 7.2).

A major problem is the variation in the rates of cautioning throughout Britain: some police forces caution on a first offence only, others do not caution if the offender has a previous drug offence and some do not caution for supply. At one level, of course, this offends principles of natural justice: equals should be treated equally. At another level a national policy might be inappropriate and is recognised as such by many police forces, who said they wanted to operate a policy related to the conditions in their area. They would not want to caution a drug user in an area where drug use is rare as they say it sends the wrong messages but, where drug use is common, a caution might be more appropriate. Home Office Circular 18/1994 (*ibid.*: para. 7.36) encourages greater consistency between police forces and tries to meet other criticisms that cautions are a soft option. The circular also discourages the use of cautions for the most serious offences. To what extent that advice is heeded is difficult to say, but the ACMD were correct to say they were convinced of the value of cautions in dealing with drug offenders (*ibid.*: para. 7.1) and, accordingly, we can expect their use to continue.

Finally comes imprisonment. The use of imprisonment has remained relatively steady over the last decade and currently (1998) runs at about 9% or 10% of the total of drug offenders. There was an aggregate increase of 4% over 1997 compared with a 19% increase over 1996. These increases do not affect the proportion of drug offenders sentenced to immediate custody as they match the rise in drug offenders generally. Imprisonment is used less for possession and more often for trafficking offences defined in Table 3.1 as the production of drugs, unlawful supply and possession with intent to supply unlawfully, and unlawful import and export. The longest sentences are awarded to the most serious traffickers.

Generally, the main aim of imprisonment is to punish according to individual and general deterrence, retribution and rehabilitation. Treatment is part of a rehabilitative framework and is provided in prisons alongside mandatory drug testing. The latter was introduced in all penal establishments in England and Wales by March 1996 is primarily a deterrent against using whilst in prison but, if provided alongside a treatment programme, it can be beneficial.

There are three main reasons why treatment programmes should be run in prisons. The first is to provide treatment for those who say they want it – prison provides an opportunity to give treatment, and that opportunity should not be missed. Secondly, treatment programmes help reduce the extent of drug use in prisons generally. Thirdly, treatment in prison also provides a means by which dug users can plan for their release (most relapses occur soon after release). Determining the effect of these programmes is impossible with current data sets: there are no measures of the numbers of drug users in prison generally so it is not possible to estimate the impact of the programmes, let alone compare one programme with another. Nor is it clear what criteria should be used to measure the impact of programmes or to determine to what extent incarceration itself was of greater importance than the treatment. Reconviction, and perhaps continuing drug use, are the only measures generally available but these are not always valid measures and are rarely reliable.

The range of programmes for prisoners must of necessity be limited – whether due to the available facilities or the length of stay of prisoners (treatment programmes in whatever setting should last at least 3 months). In an American study of over 100 jails providing treatment, it was found that few had comprehensive services, most had poor screening facilities and few were linked in any systematic way to community agencies on release. The services provided which varied greatly in content and, one suspects, also in quality were available only to a small proportion of inmates who should have been receiving them (Peters, 1993: 47–49; Weinman and Lockwood, 1993). Most of the treatment consisted of a mixture of group therapy and psycho-educational approaches within therapeutic community settings, often determined by the interests and qualifications of the staff and the amount of time allocated to this rather than other requirements. Similar results were found in prisons in Britain where John Burrows *et al.* (2000: 3) reported that the provision of drug services throughout prison establishments was uneven and where prisoners reported that the treatment often depended on what was available rather than what was appropriate to their needs.

There is little doubt treatment services are required. Burrows *et al.* (*ibid.*) report that drug taking among prison populations prior to incarceration is high, with use in the 12 months before entering prison ranging from 40% to about 70%. Findings from self-report studies show that many continue to use drugs whilst in custody. Many (66%) cited heroin as their main drug and said they had used it everyday in the 30 days before being sentenced. In addition, a third said they took crack and a half took cannabis. Overall most were polyusers (*ibid.*: p. 2). The researchers also noted that the primary means of identifying prisoners with drug problems is when they themselves seek help. However, many are reluctant to do this as it means the authorities know they are drug users and the prisoners fear they will be targeted during their sentence –

for additional searches, etc. These are some of the impediments to receiving prison treatment. Add to these the increasing numbers of prisoners with a coexisting mental disorder and dual diagnosis (about 11% in US jails, according to the US Department of Health and Human Services (1998)) and the problem is huge.

What is particularly disturbing is that some prisoners reported that their detection and punishment had adversely affected their use. In a sample of 148 prisoners, Edgar and O'Donnell (1998) found that 37 claimed they did not use drugs whilst in prison. However, of the remainder (111), almost half (53) said they had not changed their drug taking whilst in prison; 4 said they had tried heroin for the first time and cut down on cannabis use; 7 reported altering their pattern of consumption, taking less cannabis but continuing to use heroin; and 17 out of the 111 said they had reduced their consumption (i.e. not stopped). An outcome of mandatory drug testing (MDT) is that many prisoners will spend longer in custody at a significant cost to the prison service. Edgar and O'Donnell (*ibid.*: 4) report that, in 1997, about 159,000 days were added to prisoners' sentences as a direct result of MDT roughly equivalent to 360 prisoner years or about £7 million in additional running costs. A criticism of MDT, at least from the prisoners' point of view, was that not enough attention was given to identifying serious drug use and directing prisoners to treatment, and rather too much on deterrence.

The US Department of Health and Human Services (1998: 4) talk of what they call 'obstacles to effective post release transitions' – in other words, problems about providing adequate through-care facilities. The obstacles, they say, are substantial, with most coming from the structure of public sector systems, such as fragmentation of the criminal justice system, community providers' lack of attention to offender issues and funding barriers. John Burrows *et al.* (2000: 3) paint an equally dismal picture for Britain when they say 'Drugs throughcare provision is characterised by structural impediments where delivery is restricted by disputes over professional boundaries, areas of responsibility and fragile funding. Successful schemes are typically the product of one or two charismatic individuals and unusually strong interagency partnerships'.

The prison service is clearly alive to the problem and its 1998 strategy is aimed at providing an equitable provision of basic and enhanced specialist services to meet low-level, moderate and severe drug problems. In practice this means developing what is called a Counselling, Assessment, Referral, Advice and Throughcare Service (CARATS) within and across the prison service, with greater emphasis on the inputs of the treatment services. At the same time, security is strengthened and drug testing continues: the usual mixture of carrot and stick is in evidence (see Duke (2000) for a discussion of prison policy).

It is doubtful if prison in particular, or the criminal justice system generally, is able to manage its drug users successfully, even though a considerable number of them are in prison. Some, those convicted for trafficking, are unlikely to be drug users and more likely to come from the organised crime syndicates described in Chapter 6. They pose particular control problems, their sentence being wholly for retributive or for deterrence reasons and likely to be lengthy. Rehabilitation, whatever that might mean to drug offenders generally, is not likely to be available for this group and nor will there be treatment whilst in prison for these traffickers. Yet there are many other drug offenders where the principles of rehabilitation do apply; treatment is needed and supervision is required.

No one wants to underestimate the difficulties. Some drug offenders are reluctant to disclose their drug use when first taken to police stations or when subject to a report from a probation officer, believing this may result in a longer sentence, especially if a woman and certainly if pregnant. Nor are they the most rewarding offenders to deal with. For some, the concept of rehabilitation does not apply – not because they are not worthy candidates for a rehabilitative approach but because rehabilitation assumes they were once 'habilitated', and that assumption may be unwarranted. They may never have received the basic skills (social, technical or otherwise) in the first place. Many are unemployable, reaching their mid-twenties never having had a proper job. Their life experiences have largely been shaped by periods in prison and the drug scene, where interpersonal violence and the demands for instant rewards are commonplace. Supervising these offenders is always going to be difficult, whether inside the prison or on discharge. Yet all too often these are the offenders who cause enormous expense to the criminal justice system and who take up a disproportionate amount of resources.

Sentencing drug users

Looking at the numbers of drug offenders and the number and length of sentences passed tells us little about sentencing policy, about changes in policy or about the practices of the courts. Drug offenders, as defined in Table 3.1, are only a small proportion of offenders with a drug habit appearing before the criminal justice system. Countless others, where the Index offence is not a drug offence, appear regularly. For some, the court will not know there is a problem and, if it does, it is not clear whether or not it should consider the drug problem when passing sentence. Secondly, even if we knew of all the drug offenders, the numbers of offenders sentenced to each specific sentence are insufficient to identify a sentencing policy; at the very least we would need to know the ratio of sentences to offences – that is to say, we need to know the years of prison time, the amount of the fine, the period of probation, etc. That answer would give only a crude figure because it would ignore other key factors such as previous convictions, the amount of the drug involved and so on. We are left, therefore, able to do little more than describe the sentences themselves, examining the changes over time and inferring likely trends.

The principal rationales for sentencing are no different from for any other offender; there are no special defences for drug offenders and no particular reasons to deal with drug offenders outside the usual justifications for imposing sentences on any other offenders. Sentencing involves a mixture of legal principles, moral assertions, theoretical justifications and legal precedents that can occasionally be reduced to the concept of a tariff – that is, a rough and ready guide based on a common law tradition about what a particular crime is worth as far as a sentence goes. To say one crime is worth a more severe sentence than another is to invoke a multitude of arguments about proportionality, deterrence and rehabilitation – plus a mixture of mitigating circumstances that can include the nature of the offence, the way it was committed and the character of the defendant. In this respect sentencing drug offenders is no different from sentencing others: the sentence will contain the same components. For example, there will be a need to deter others from committing the offence, to deter the individual from committing the offence again, to sentence the offender because he or she has committed an offence and therefore deserves to be punished, and to offer a form of rehabilitation whilst being punished. Finally, the court will take account of any mitigating circumstances that may or may not include the offender's dependence on drugs. (This may not always work to the offender's advantage as the court may think this is a self-inflicted condition that justifies a heavier sentence than would be the case otherwise.)

However, in one respect drug offenders *are* different. It is increasingly recognised they need to be sentenced according to principles of rehabilitation rather than deterrence or retribution. This has occurred because of the links with treatment: 'treatment works' is a recurring theme to be found in later chapters of this book. Rehabilitation was a dominant philosophy of the 1960s and 1970s but was largely discredited – to be replaced by a just deserts model that draws on retribution as its intellectual inspiration. The basis of a rehabilitation philosophy is that offenders require help not punishment where help is usually provided through some therapeutic intervention or by medical services.

The paradox of the present position is evident: the treatment of drug offenders resurrects the theory of rehabilitation and with it all those arguments that were left behind when the just deserts philosophy became dominant. Rehabilitation has within it a set of apparent contradictions; it is regarded as too soft when drug offenders are given treatment in the community rather than being sent to prison and too harsh when they are detained in prison for treatment longer than they would otherwise. For those conducting treatment, rehabilitation places them in an increasingly powerful position, for they will be asked to decide when the drug offender is ready to be discharged. They will also be asked who will be given treatment, what will be given, the cost, the length of time it is likely to take and, above all, who is suitable. They will have their say about who is to be let into treatment and who is to be excluded.

Currently, rehabilitation as a dominant theory of sentencing is held back by a shortage of treatment services. There are about 500 drug treatment agencies in England and Wales (Royal College of Psychiatrists 2000) and these have a relatively minor part to play within the criminal justice system. Emphasising the importance of rehabilitation could change that, especially where it involves a greater level of co-operation between treatment services and criminal justice. Were that to happen, it would herald a return to a rehabilitative philosophy with all its attendant problems although, it is hoped, it would be resurrected in a form that avoids the failings of the past. It is highly likely that the extent of a rehabilitative influence will increase as the demands for treatment also increase.

At present, much energy in Britain seems to be taken up with less important pursuits, such as whether drugs (mostly cannabis) should change from one class to another (typically from Class B to Class C), or whether ecstasy should change to Class B from Class A. The argument for doing so is that a more accurate 'hierarchy of harm' will help target policing and also will help to allocate prevention and treatment resources more effectively. Whether that will be so remains to be seen for, as will be shown later, policing drug offenders is more haphazard than this. Most prosecutions, especially for cannabis, occur when the offender is arrested for a non-drugs offence and is found to be in possession of cannabis. Few offenders are targeted for possessing cannabis, although more may be for possession of ecstasy. Reclassifying them, however, is not likely to make much difference to the drug problem – especially as most are cautioned or fined. More likely the reclassification argument is part of a wider demand for decriminalisation or legalisation and has little to do with sentencing, policing or public policy.

Of the many aspects of sentencing which are important, there are two that need to be emphasised as likely to be of significance for the future. First, that drug offenders in Britain rarely go to prison for possession but are very likely to do so for illicit supply. Secondly, that the links with treatment mean that sentencing is closely aligned to a rehabilitative philosophy. In the first, the development of treatment facilities must become increasingly community based and, in the second, the emergence of rehabilitation as a driving force behind sentencing will need to be considered in order to avoid the defects of rehabilitation that were glaringly obvious when rehabilitation last assumed a measure of dominance. I shall refer to these points again in later chapters.

Chapter 4

Coercive treatment and mandatory drug testing

The previous chapter set out an overview of the facilities available within the criminal justice system for dealing with drug offenders. In this chapter the aim is to look more closely at treatment within the criminal justice system that, for these purposes, means coercive or enforced treatment. This examination will take place alongside a more detailed look at mandatory drug testing. It is interesting to note that, from the mid-1990s onwards, British governments have shown an increasing willingness to fund and thereby increase the range of treatment facilities for substance abusers and, correspondingly, have shown a willingness to increase drug testing. They have done so because they recognise that treatment provides one of the few options for containing the drug problem, coupled with a belief that it breaks the link with crime. Drug testing is included because it is thought that, without that backup, treatment will fail. Drug testing is the building block of treatment within the criminal justice system and needs to be considered carefully.

Briefly, the background to the various government initiatives is as follows. In 1995 *Tackling Drugs Together: A Strategy for England 1995-8* was produced for England (those for Wales and Scotland were produced about the same time) (Ministerial Drugs Task Force, 1994; HM Government, 1995; Welsh Office, 1998). *Tackling Drugs Together* (HM Government, 1995) committed the government 'to take effective action by vigorous law enforcement, accessible treatment and a new emphasis in education and prevention' (para. 1.3). There were no details of the treatment programme in these strategies but promises were made these would be provided in a later task force report. The emphasis in *Tackling Drugs Together* was on re-organising local services, including replacing them with Drug Action Teams.

The later task force report (Department of Health, 1996) assessed the range of treatment services and commissioned some research; its terms of reference included 'a comprehensive survey of clinical, operational and cost effectiveness of existing services for drug misusers'. The National Treatment Outcome Research Study (NTORS), the biggest study of drug treatment ever conducted in Britain, showed there were considerable benefits in bringing drug users into treatment. However, the rates of improvement were less than in the USA (Gossop *et al.*, 1997; 1998). NTORS followed the progress of 1,100 drug misusers through treatment and concluded there were no 'magic bullets' to cure drug problems. In a review of treatment using NTORS data, the conclusion was that drug abuse was a chronic relapsing condition that required treatment to fit the client's needs. Drug treatment that embraces social care and support as well as clinical intervention can be effective in reducing drug-related harm, but most substance misusers require several attempts at treatment before noticeable success occurs (Gossop *et al.*, 1997).

In 1998, a second drug strategy was introduced by the newly appointed Anti-Drugs Coordinator, entitled *Tackling Drugs Together to Build a Better Britain; The Government's Ten Year Strategy for Tackling Drug Misuse* (HM Government, 1998). This largely reiterated the themes of the 1995 document whilst adding performance targets for drug reduction for the next decade. Finally, in 1999 guidelines on the clinical management of drug users gave advice to the medical profession about how best to implement the drug strategy. However, by 2001 (June) the post of Anti-Drugs Coordinator had been abolished and the Drugs Czar given a part-time job as an international adviser. The centre of the government's strategy moved from the Cabinet Office to the Home Office, presumably on the grounds that policy had traditionally come from the Home Office and that two centres of policy-making produced unnecessary duplication.

Treatment was endorsed and emphasised as a desirable platform in the government's aims to reduce substance misuse. This policy was based on extensive statistical evidence, which suggested 'treatment works' - that Britain already has one of the most developed and widespread sets of treatment services that *must* be of help in any treatment-based strategy. Already legislation has been introduced that requires some drug offenders to submit themselves to treatment – this in addition to facilities already in existence. The Drug Treatment and Testing Order (DTTO) provided for under ss. 61–64 of the Crime and Disorder Act 1998 (and drug testing in prison carried out under s. 16A of the Prison Act 1952) links the treatment services with the criminal justice system in ways that require them to work according to criminal justice requirements. The new

Criminal Justice and Court Services Bill currently before the House of Lords (2001) extends government thinking, where it says: 'Identifying drug misusing offenders at every stage in the criminal justice system is now a prime objective of the crime reduction strategy and will make an important contribution to the overall drug strategy' (House of Commons, 2000: para. 28.

Under Clauses 40–42, 48, 49, 51 and 52, additional powers are given to require offenders and alleged offenders to be drug tested at various points in their contact with the criminal justice system. These are at a cost of national implementation of £45.5 million, of which £20 million will be police costs (paras. 133 and 134). Clearly this is where the government is putting the funding. There will also be the Drug Abstinence Order requiring the offender to refrain from misusing Class A drugs and to undertake a drug test on instruction, as well as introducing pre-sentence drug testing.

Why are these additional facilities required? There have long been facilities to treat offenders under a probation order, perhaps with a condition of treatment as an inpatient or outpatient. However, these facilities appear not to have been taken up, for reasons that have not always been understood. Briefly, the Criminal Justice Act 1991 tried to boost the use of treatment under a probation order and gave courts powers to impose treatment as part of a sentence of probation – as it was then called. It was rarely used. The Home Office Probation Inspectorate said this was because:

- The Home Office and Probation Services adopted a neutral stance declining to issue guidance.
- Probation officers did not believe coerced treatment would work so were reluctant to recommend it in their pre-sentence reports.
- Sentencers lacked information on the treatments available.
- Within the criminal justice system treatment providers were un-enthusiastic about operating coercive systems.

The result is new legislation where the overall effect is to make a shift towards more forms of treatment (some of which are coercive) and away from the earlier approach, which is still beloved by many of the treatment services – that treatment should at all times be voluntary. This is not the place to discuss the philosophy of treatment (see Bean and Nemitz, 2002 for a discussion on treatment generally), but the government has clearly been influenced by the American research that proclaims in unequivocal terms that treatment is successful (Anglin and Hser, 1990).

Yet behind the slogan 'treatment works' lies a range of difficult questions. First, there is a group of empirical questions, such as with whom does treatment work? Can successful treatments be given over a single period or do they require subsequent treatments even after the success of the first? Is a single type of treatment appropriate to all patients? Then there are questions about the principles of treatment. What are the aims of treatment? What should be the remit and to whom should treatment be given (it clearly cannot be given to everyone who takes drugs)? Finally, there are a group of questions specifically surrounding treatment within the criminal justice system, such as: what are the aims of treatment in criminal justice? Do they or should they differ in a qualitative sense from those provided outside the criminal justice system that is, can treatment be effective if the offender is coerced or does it always need to be voluntarily? The questions to be dealt with here centre on the links with the criminal justice system and the corresponding matter of coercion. Others of a more general nature are considered in another volume more directly concerned with treatment generally (see Bean and Nemitz, 2002).

The aims and nature of treatment

The treatment of substance abuse, whether in or out of the criminal justice system, uses a mixture of traditional medical interventions, including treatment talk, which is likely to dominate treatment programmes. In the early stages when the offender enters the programme, the focus tends to be narrow, perhaps centring on detoxification or other forms of withdrawal. As treatment progresses it becomes more inclusive i.e. more therapeutic, taking in wider aspects of the drug takers' lives. The Royal College of Psychiatrists (2000: 155) sets out the aims of treatment: they are to prevent and reduce harm resulting from the use of drugs. The Royal College says this definition includes social, psychological or physical harm, and may involve medical, social or educational interventions. It also includes prevention and harm reduction – prevention presumably applying to everyone but harm reduction for those who are chronic substance misusers (*ibid.*).

The straightforward definition provided by the Royal College differs in content hardly at all from that found in most standard texts on the rehabilitation of offenders, although it differs in form in that, rarely, are definitions as succinct as this. This is to its advantage as it spells out the treatment aims in a clear unequivocal manner – a quality rarely found in textbooks on treatment. More likely there will be a discussion or, rather, a description of the nature of drugs and addiction, then it will move to questions of assessment followed by an examination of measures of intervention usually including a discussion on the range of treatments and the special types of problems encountered with a final section on follow-up and outcome. The central questions will be neatly bypassed, such as what should treatments aim to achieve, and for what reason?

Within the drugs field the language of treatment is predominately medical. There is little to suggest, however, that treatment is aimed at curing an 'illness', although the patient's condition may, during the withdrawal period, be akin to this requiring expert medical intervention. The model of addiction most favoured in Britain, including that by the Royal College of Psychiatrists, is a socio-behavoural one; an alternative, the disease model, has little support outside the rather narrow confines of AA/NA (Alcoholics Anonymous/Narcotics Anonymous), who provide programmes such as the '12 steps' or other self-help groups.

Treatment has, and will continue to be, thrust into prominence for two main reasons. First, there has developed a wider understanding of the links between drug taking and crime, initially promoted during the late 1980s when drug cases began to escalate dramatically alongside an ever-increasing crime rate, particularly property crime. Within this research studies confirmed what many had suspected: that large numbers of offenders on arrest were testing positive for a range of drugs, claiming they were committing crime under the influence of drugs (Bennett, 1998). Overwhelmed by this increase in drug use and the apparent criminality it produced ('apparent' because, as shown in Chapter 1, the links with crime are more tenuous than at first appears), the government's response has been to increase the range and numbers of treatment programmes. This, it expects, will provide relief from the so-called revolving door of crime, where drug users endlessly move between the courts the criminal justice system and the world of criminality. The NTORS is a clear example of government interest (Gossop *et al.*, 1997). Of course, not all drug users are part of the revolving door syndrome, but those who are create the biggest problems.

Secondly, treatment has been revitalised by the growing belief that treatment works. This is more alive in America than Britain where there is not the complement of research data to verify it, but it has been picked up in Britain nonetheless and the NTORS study goes some way to redress the balance. Research has not always made clear how treatment works, with whom it works or whether some treatment modalities work better than others, but there has arisen the popular belief it does work. Perhaps the slogan has been accepted because it provides the only way of dealing with a problem almost out of control: treatment provides a life-raft and gives hope against an otherwise relentless increase in drug use. Whether this is the case so or not, treatment (and the expected success it will bring) is imbedded in the popular image, and governments are prepared to invest heavily in treatment programmes.

Linking treatment services with the criminal justice system

It seems axiomatic that any increase in the treatment services will be directed towards the criminal justice system, for this is where the government sees the problem at its worse and, consequently, is likely to spend its money. Governments no longer live in that world where they hope the drug problem will magically go away; they recognise its enormity and the cost it brings, socially and otherwise. That would suggest, whether the treatment services like it or not, that there must be a closer working relationship with them and the criminal justice system. In the USA this has already happened. In the 1980s there occurred a so-called 'paradigm shift' where the treatment services and the criminal justice system agreed a development programme and strategy about how best to implement it. This included decisions about who should and who should not be treated, about the best way to move forward and about how to remove existing barriers to co-operation. It meant sharing beliefs and accepting a new set of aims and objectives. In practice, the changes were almost all one way: the criminal justice system shifted its position hardly at all. That 'paradigm shift' has not yet occurred in Britain but it cannot be long before it does.

A likely implication of a closer working partnership is that the treatment services will lose some of their independence and, with it, their more theoretical approach to treatment. A possible outcome is that treatment agencies will be subcontracted to the criminal justice system, providing treatment to offenders on court orders, whether at the pre- or post-sentence stage. This is already happening under the DTTO, but the change is likely to accelerate in the short and long term as governments seek new ways to control drug offenders. Treatment agencies will also have to face demands to evaluate their work. Whilst most agencies have been able to avoid this type of scrutiny hitherto, an effect of this scrutiny will be to bring about an erosion of some cherished beliefs and a corresponding change in some of the assumptions underpinning their work.

One established cherished belief likely to come under threat is that which asserts treatment ought only be provided if the patient seeks it voluntarily (this was one of the first casualties of the 'paradigm shift' in the USA). This view, which like so many others has been promoted and sustained with little or no research evidence to support it, has become one of the shibboleths of the treatment world. It is based on a set of assumptions that suggests the patient must give of him or herself fully and freely to a treatment programme or it will not be successful. A coerced patient will be a failed patient. A closer look at what is meant by coercion or enforced treatment and what constitutes coercive or enforced treatment is therefore required.

The coercive or enforced treatment of substance abuse

Much confusion centres on the term 'coercion' as if there is something sinister about the fact that offenders are coerced. Yet coercion (or enforcement) is a *sine qua non* of the criminal justice system, being one of its essential features. Treatment agencies operating within the criminal justice system must expect to work within a coercive apparatus; that some appear to try to operate otherwise shows they misunderstand the nature of their task. It is not, therefore, whether coercion is acceptable for, by definition, coercion is part of criminal justice; the question is, or should be, what should be an acceptable level of coercion and what should be the powers of those able to coerce? What should be the boundaries of a coercive regime?

As far as coercive treatment is concerned, two major legal forms of coercion can be identified, each with its own subtypes:

1. Those involving *civil* commitment. The agencies undertaking civil commitment usually include the courts sitting as a civil court, created government agencies (including the police) and a medical agency.
2. Those involving *judicial* commitment. This occurs where commitment is a condition of a sentence, as in a probation order or compulsory after care. Imprisonment for the Index offence is not included in this category.

First comes civil commitment. There are no provisions in Britain for the civil commitment of substance misusers. The Mental Health Act 1983 expressly forbids the inclusion of drug addiction as a category of mental disorder, although a mental disorder resulting from drug abuse could warrant compulsion. The first Brain Committee report (Department of Health, 1960) considered introducing civil commitment provisions for substance abusers but rejected it, and the Review of the Mental Health Act 1959 (which led to the Mental Health Act 1983) noted that government advisory bodies said it was incompatible with current thinking to regard drug dependence and drinking problems as a form of mental disorder:

> These conditions are increasingly seen as social and behavioural problems manifested in varying degrees of habit and dependency. However, it is recognised that alcohol and drug dependency can be associated with certain forms of mental disorder. (Department of Health, 1978: para. 1.29)

However, the distinctions have increasingly become blurred. Substance abuse is frequently found in mentally disordered patients and mentally disordered patients are frequently found to be substance abusers – the so-called 'dual diagnosis' patients. Moreover, substance abuse can mask or mimic disorders, making diagnosis difficult and treatment equally so. None the less, as a general proposition, the Brain Committee were correct to make and establish the distinction and the recent review of mental health legislation was also correct to leave things as they are.

Civil commitment has been used extensively elsewhere. In a United Nations' survey of 43 countries, 27 had civil commitment provisions for substance abuse (Porter *et al.*, 1986). In America, civil commitment was introduced early in the twentieth century when users were referred to so-called narcotic farms and, later, to hospitals (as in Lexington, Kentucky). It was used again in the 1960s in California and New York, again through the civil law, based on assumptions that, whilst some drug abusers are motivated to treatment, others are not. Accordingly, a mechanism had to be established to deal with the less motivated users – what was called 'rational authority' – but which Inciardi *et al.* (1996: 28) say was a euphemism for appearing not to be punitive yet able to exercise mandatory control. The California programme permitted commitment for up to 7 years – without, of course, having convicted the drug user of any offence. In New York it was similar.

Few civil commitment programmes have been properly evaluated, including those in America. Inciardi (1988) says of the New York programme (that is, where such evaluation as there was existed) that it was an abject failure. This, he says, was not because the idea was wrong but because it was poorly funded, had poor treatment facilities, appointed untrained staff, had a poorly developed after-care programme and lost public support, leading to a wave of bad publicity. Anglin and Hser (1991) evaluated the California programme and concluded that civil commitment was an effective way of reducing narcotic addiction, yet added this conclusion should not necessarily lead to immediate implementation. It was useful for bringing users into treatment, but it was not treatment, and could not take the place of treatment (Leukefeld and Tims, 1988; Anglin and Hser, 1991). Anglin and Hser (1991) believe that drug abusers should be given greater encouragement to enter treatment voluntarily and, unless funding is provided to create new programmes or to extend existing ones, the coercion of an individual into drug treatment may make the situation worse.

There are, of course, civil rights questions to be asked about civil commitment. People in Britain rightly object to the notion that a person can be detained without having been convicted of a criminal offence because he or she abuses substances. (In Britain there are, incidentally, fewer qualms about compulsory detention of the mentally ill without due process of trial.) It may be true that the extent of abuse makes a user a danger to him or herself as death rates are high. So, too, are they amongst motor cyclist or young car drivers, but are these people to be detained also? The justification for civil commitment in the USA is based on considerations about health/economics (that is, detention is justified because of the expected cost to the public health services if left untreated). Of course, the same could be said for anyone engaged in dangerous pursuits, from skiing to working as a steeple-jack. The more serious point, however, can be made with those who care directly for children, including pregnant women, where substance abuse can seriously damage the physical and mental health of those in their care.

The second type of commitment (judicial commitment) is used extensively in Britain as shown by the given data in Chapter 3. This involves committal to treatment by a court order and, whilst the offender is given a choice about accepting the order (as in the DTTO), in practice this choice is illusory, resembling more of a Hobson's choice than a real choice. Judicial commitment has existed for some time through the probation order and it is now to be extended through the DTTO (through parole and for offenders in prison). There is little doubt this is the area for future development where, increasingly, it will envelope all within the criminal justice system – perhaps extending to those who work within the system, prison officers, probation officers, etc.

It is within judicial commitment where critics, many of whom are from the treatment services, see judicial commitment as coercive and, by implication, wrong. They see it as standing in stark contrast to voluntary treatment, which, they say, by definition, is not. This assumption is at best misleading and at worst simply wrong. It produces a *coercion* v. *voluntary* dichotomy that fails to take account of the possible shades of meaning within each of the terms. For example, judicial commitment does not mean the drug abusers always feel coerced into treatment; some may enter willingly and be glad of the opportunity to be offered the options. Nor does it mean that coercion from the courts is the only source of coercion; greater coercive pressure might have come from elsewhere, family, friends, employers, etc., which may be more powerful and influential than anything from a court.

It makes more sense to talk of different levels of coercion operating at different points on a contuum and coming from different sources. Take the court and the legal system as an example. De Leon (1998) suggests that the court offers different levels of coercion, able to invoke a range of options based on different degrees of severity (Farabee *et al.*, 1998). First, de Leon (1998) says, there is *legal referral* that operates according to an explicit procedure where the offender is referred to treatment according to a sentence of the court or by some other formal practice as in probation or parole. Secondly, there is *legal status*, where the offender is referred according to an administrative device as with bail or arrest referral schemes. Finally, there is *legal pressure*, which refers to the extent to which the offender experiences discomfort over the potential consequences of non-compliance such as where the court makes clear that failure in treatment is likely to lead to a long prison sentence. Legal pressure is the form most likely to be regarded as coercive but, even then, coercion might not be excessive for example, some offenders might regard a prison sentence as a less fearful option than a spell in a treatment programme. Moreover, levels of coercion may vary within programmes: some probation orders with a condition of treatment may appear coercive but, in practice, the treatment agencies rarely report shortcomings and failures, including failure to attend for treatment that, to all intents and purposes, means the offender does what he or she likes.

Or consider social and family coercion. Family coercion could be seen as qualitatively different from the coercion of friends and employees – being more likely to be sustained and with longer-term consequences. It might also be more effective in driving offenders into treatment. It is more useful, then, to see coercion as existing where the offenders enter at a certain point and stay or leave at the same or different points. The source of referral does not determine the level of coercion, although it might (O'Hare, 1996).

To concentrate for a moment on *legal pressure* as this is likely to be the mainstay of the opposition to court-based programmes, the assumption has been, wrongly as it turns out, that the level of coercion will be high. Assume, however, that it is. Does this warrant opposition to providing treatment under those circumstances? Not in terms of ethical or jurisprudential matters. Courts have traditionally been permitted to require treatment as part of punishment and have been allowed to impose conditions attached to sentences. As far as research results are concerned the answer is an unequivocal 'no'. In fact, the research evidence, albeit American, points to the conclusion that the circumstances under which an individual is exposed to treatment are irrelevant. The important point is that the drug user should be brought into an environment where intervention occurs; the more routes into this environment the better, even if they include coercive routes. Treatment outcomes are not based on the reasons for entering treatment but the length of time remaining in treatment. That is to say, the longer the period in treatment, the better the outcome. And, of course, it is easy to see how that makes sense: the longer a person spends in treatment, the greater the number of options there are so that the greater the possibility the choice will be to be abstinent (Anglin and Hser, 1991).

Of course, the initial motivation to enter treatment may be less high for many brought before the court, but motivation to enter the programme is less important than retention: considerable research demonstrates a direct relationship between retention and post treatment outcomes (Lipton, 1995: 46), how an individual is exposed to treatment seems irrelevant. What is important is that the narcotics addict must be brought into an environment where intervention can occur over time (Anglin, 1988). It is the length of exposure to treatment that powerfully predicts patient's success, which occurs no matter what the treatment setting. Taking an overview of a number of studies two major findings emerge. The first is that the length of time in treatment is the most reliable indicator of post- treatment performance so that, beyond a 90-day threshold, treatment outcomes improved in direct relationship to the length of time spent in treatment. Secondly, that coerced patients stayed longer and, therefore, treatment was more successful. Weaknesses occur where the offenders do not experience consistency or uniformity about the treatment demands; outcomes are higher where they know the rules, where the rules are enforced fairly and consistently, and where there is appropriate pressure to meet treatment demands. Coercion, then, might turn out to be irrelevant except in a moral sense; success seems to have less to do with coercion and more with how the regime is operated and the length of stay.

In practice the enforced (coerced) treatment of drug users appears to sit uneasily on the shoulders of many treatment agencies. They seemingly prefer to treat only those patients who are apparently sufficiently motivated to enter the treatment programme voluntarily. Given the otherwise consistent research findings, might it not be time to rethink that ideology, doing so in a way that permits a more receptive approach to new ideas and that allows a more flexible approach to the problem? To remain within the existing boundaries might produce a measure of certainty, albeit misplaced, but it does not provide much of an opportunity to move forward. As things stand at present, the courts and the treatment services talk past each other, yet the point made by Anglin and Hser (1991) is a sound one: that Members of both systems need to move away from adversarial stances and towards collaboration to produce the desired behaviour change in drug users. The suspicion is that if the treatment services do not make the appropriate move, they might well be the ones who are coerced, this time to accept the enforced patient. Already their hand is being forced; the DTTO is on the statute books and, were the American-style drug courts to be introduced into Britain, they would eclipse existing provisions.

Mandatory drug testing

Mandatory drug testing is not confined to the criminal justice system; certain occupational groups are routinely tested for example, airline pilots, and athletes whilst some employers insist on testing their employees. It becomes a moot point about which occupational groups should be tested; train drivers, perhaps, or bus drivers even? Or anyone working in a highly skilled occupation, or anyone where public safety is concerned? If so, the list is endless.

That apart, the theory behind mandatory drug testing is based on the proposition that, with the development of cost-effective technology, we can now intervene more appropriately in drug users' lives (Wish and Gropper, 1990: 322). Without mandatory drug testing it is suggested there is no possibility the courts (which, in Britain, also means probation officers) will be able to know the extent of the problem. Self-report studies are valuable as they provide useful information and give some data on the extent of drug use, but they are not always valid in that they do not give the whole picture. There is evidence that, when drug users are questioned about their drug use, especially at the time of arrest, they understate it, although they will often correctly admit the extent of lifetime use or use in the distant past (*ibid.*: 325). Drug testing is used to detect and provide that information which otherwise would be absent. Carver (pers.com. 1999) goes further and says that without this information the justice system is unable to obtain quick, accurate information on the offender's drug use, so that the court environment is one in which the offender can remain in denial with no immediate consequence for continued use: 'In a very real sense the criminal justice system becomes an enabler for the addict. The judge is in the dark, the defendant knows the judge is in the dark, and the con game continues' (*ibid.*: 1). He goes on (*ibid.*) to ask: 'Is it any wonder then that the justice system is viewed as ineffective in dealing with the underlying addiction that fuels the problem? Is it surprising that there is widespread scepticism on efficacy of treatment and rehabilitation?'

Drug testing can also be used as a deterrent to future use or, equally, to verify compliance with conditions of release – which will in turn deter future use. Deterrence in drug testing operates as in all other forms of deterrence: it deters the individual and it deters others, although the evidence suggests it works best when it is tied in to a treatment programme. The aim as far as drug treatment is concerned is to monitor treatment and to provide accurate, up-to-date information on the extent of use.

Basically there are five methods by which drugs are tested. These are through urine, through blood (of which hair testing is a variant), through saliva, through perspiration and through eye testing. All have their limitations and none gives a measurement of the amounts taken. Urinalysis is the most commonly used but new developments in eye testing are the most interesting (eye testing measures the intake of drugs through eye movements). Some have a so-called 'short window of opportunity' (the time when drugs can be measured) whilst in others this is longer – perspiration is longer than urinalysis. Drug-testing systems are becoming increasingly sophisticated and, in some cases, correspondingly expensive, although relatively cheap versions are coming on to the market. The aim nowadays is to reduce unit costs as tests can be quite expensive.

Generally speaking, the offender is first given a screening test and, if positive, is usually given a confirmatory test. Screening tests provide rapid results, are inexpensive and have an accuracy level of about 97 or 98%. Confirmatory tests are more expensive but give a greater level of accuracy. The most common screening test is that which tests for urine, and the most common confirmatory test also uses urinalysis but tests for more drugs and does so under more controlled conditions. Operating these tests requires considerable skill, with numerous pitfalls to be avoided, both legal and technical. The procedures must be sufficiently foolproof to minimise arbitrary or erroneous decisions, at least to the extent that it is feasible to do so. Ensuring a completely error-free process is the aim, albeit a distant one, but a positive drug test can lead to deleterious results, including incarceration or other restrictions on liberty. Accordingly, drug-testing procedures must be as reliable and valid as possible. Moreover, since drug testing (urine testing, that is) is relatively new and largely untried in Britain, the possibilities of legal challenges are considerable. As far as possible tests should be undertaken in laboratory conditions and never with poorly trained assistants.

Two types of errors are likely. The first creates false positives. These occur when a test result indicates positive for a given drug when that drug is actually absent in a urine sample or present in concentrations below the designed cut-off level. The second creates false negatives. These occur when the test result indicates a negative result for a given drug yet that drug is present in the sample. What constitutes a false positive or false negative can be largely determined by the cut-off level for the test, defined as the concentration of a drug in urine. This is usually in nanogram per millilitre (ng/ml) and it is used to determine whether a specimen is positive (at or above the cut-off level) or negative (below the cut-off level) for the drug in question. The point at which the cut-off level is set is critical to the results: a cut-off level set too low will produce false positives; one set too high will produce false negatives.

Some errors can be produced by defects in the equipment, others by failure to use correct procedures. In the first there are errors where some common licit drugs cross-react with the urine sample to produce a set of positive results that are wrong. For example, codeine, pholcodine (found in some cough syrups) and even poppy seeded bagels will produce positive results on some tests, especially so for saliva tests. Ephedrine (found in some cold medications) can cross-react with amphetamine, whilst urine samples containing enzymes are able to mimic others to produce false positives (Meyers, 1991: 298).

Other errors are more about the way the system is used. One commentator (Wish, 1988: 151) says from his experience in using urine tests in offender populations that the problems of false negatives are much larger than false positives – laboratories simply fail to pick up the drugs. He says his studies show that even when a person admits to taking a drug 1 or 2 days before the test, this is discovered in only 70–80% of the cases. Moreover, most tests fail to identify the quantity of the drug taken, its purity and its time since ingestion.

Then there are administrative errors. These can produce false positives and false negatives. These are much more common and much more difficult to control – at least those described above are well known and expected. Robert Blanke (cited in Meyers, 1991) puts it this way: 'The most difficult errors to control are administrative ones. Labelling errors, spelling errors, transposition of number, all can lead to a correct test result being assigned to the wrong subject. In fact most laboratories have learned that these occur more frequently than errors in testing procedures'. Contaminating the systems and producing temperature variations causes other sets of administrative errors that can also produce false positives. Meyers (1991) says the very ease of performing these tests belies the care with which they must be undertaken, and the consequent reliance on persons who are not trained to laboratory standards may lead to an underappreciation of the dangers of cross-reactivity and the importance of other potential threats to their accuracy. He cites the case of *US* v. *Roy* (1986), where the defence introduced log sheets that reflected the sloppy and careless operations of the system in the Superior Court. Claims for accuracy of 97% can only be achieved in ideal laboratory conditions, which are rarely met outside. Errors in prisons produce false positives ranging from 46–13% (Meyers, 1991).

The use of a confirmatory test is one way of reducing errors. Generally speaking, confirmatory tests are used after the initial screening test is recorded as positive, although some confirmatory tests have been used when the results are negative. Not all courts are able to have a confirmatory test, especially when the testee is in the criminal justice system and will be tested regularly, perhaps weekly, in which case a second screening test is likely to be used alongside a diagnostic interview (Wish, 1988: 151). When tests are to trigger further investigation or to determine whether a person is involved in drugs, a confirmatory test is not usually seen as necessary but will more likely be necessary when the offender is in a treatment programme (*ibid.*). Things are different outside the criminal justice system, as a confirmatory test is more likely and the consequences more immediate. For example in one reported case in the USA, a private employee was fired because he tested positive (i.e. as a false positive) and he received $4.1 million damages against the laboratory (cited in Meyers, 1991: 288). Offenders in the criminal justice system have a greater chance to set the record straight than an employee but, nevertheless, errors in whatever form and for whatever reason are damaging.

Then there are problems surrounding the officials supervising and manning the tests. These officials will quickly find that clean urine is a valuable commodity, worth a great deal of money to those able to market and sell it. Within the drug-testing world there is a trade in clean urine. As early as 1986 a case was reported of an American defendant who allegedly bribed an employee to have his urine results reported as negative when they were actually positive (see *The Washington Post* 12 July 1988). This is but one of a number of examples where officials have been open to bribery. In Britain, the prison service insists that two prison officers are present when urine samples are taken in prison (this, incidentally, would be regarded as wholly unsatisfactory in some circles for there still remains the possibility of bribery at a later stage, such as at the pre- and post-analysis stage). What is needed is a system that virtually eliminates human interventions so that the opportunities for bribery are eradicated; that is, to produce a system that is fully automated, which excludes transcription errors and is not open to falsification by corrupt officials. The American system operates under the slogan that 'if the system is not foolproof, don't bother testing'.

As in the world of sport, those who test positive will always seek to discredit the system and, unfortunately, drug-testing practices with offender populations undertaken away from the laboratory will be no exception. Clearly, training programmes are required and set to a high level if the system is to be free of accusations of bias and error. The fear is that too little training is provided and, where it is, it is not at the appropriate level (i.e. undertaken up to that required for laboratory conditions). Once in the criminal justice system, offenders lose many of their rights: convicted offenders in prison can be subject to searches of an intimate nature, as can someone on probation or parole. Moreover, British customs officers have unrivalled powers to search someone on the basis of reasonable suspicion of an offence being committed, as so do police surgeons under the Police and Criminal Evidence Act (PACE): 'reasonable force can be used if necessary to take non-intimate samples' – which include urine (Codes of Practice (PACE) 1984: para. 5.5, as amended by s. 58 of the Criminal Justice and Public Order Act 1994). All of which suggests that the balance is already tipped towards those doing the testing so that the least the offender should expect is that the tests will be as free from error as possible. From a rather cursory examination of existing procedures, it is not always certain this is so.

One of the questions likely to exercise the courts is the extent to which it is proper for a government to order random drug testing in the absence of reasons to suspect a person of using drugs. As a general rule, courts have held that mandatory drug testing is permissible when it serves a special need of government. So, for example, in America (in *Skinner* v. *Railway Labor Executive Association* (489 US 609 1989)) government testing was justified because there was a special need to maintain the safety of the railway system. In another case, this time involving customs officers (*National Treasury Employers Union* v. *von Raab* 816 F2nd 170 5th Circuit 1970), the court held the government has a special need to maintain the integrity of its border to ensure public safety. In both cases the demands of government were said to outweigh individual privacy. The argument was that certain employees in the public sector have a reduced expectation of privacy because they are required to produce high levels of public safety, and that their health and fitness are important aspects of their jobs. Or, alternatively, that officials such as customs officers should reasonably expect scrutiny into their probity and fitness. Similar arguments have been used in Britain, where it has been suggested there should be mandatory testing of airline pilots, police officers or members of the armed forces (*The Times* 14 June 1997; *The Sunday Times* 15 June 1997).

There is still that other tricky problem about knowing how to interpret the results. Put simply, what does a positive test mean? One obvious implication is that every individual who tests positive for drugs runs the risk of incarceration, especially if already on probation or parole. Even if incarceration is not imposed it is likely there will be some other restraint on liberty, whether it be requiring the offender to report more frequently or simply to provide additional samples. (What has concerned a number of American commentators is that drug testing has led to an increase in the prison population as more offenders on probation or parole have tested 'dirty' and thereby violated their probation or release conditions. An increase in the prison population under these circumstances may be neither cost-effective nor part of the overall strategy, but it becomes an unintended consequence of a vigorous testing system.) Assume an offender on a treatment programme is required to be tested weekly. In the first week, he or she tests positive for heroin, cocaine, cannabis, amphetamines and ecstasy. He or she does so again in the second week but says he or she has reduced the amount. In the third week, he or she no longer tests positive for heroin and cocaine but does so for cannabis, amphetamines and ecstasy, and this pattern is maintained for three more weeks when he or she no longer tests positive for amphetamines. What then? Assume this pattern continues and the best that can be hoped for in the next few weeks is that things do not get worse, then is the offender to be reported to the court, taken off the programme or what?

The fashionable answers would be that progress has been made and we should be satisfied with that, or that the drugs being currently taken are not dangerous and, anyway, should be legalised. The unfashionable answer is that officials making these decisions ought not to be required to decide what is and what is not lawful. Parliament (in its wisdom) has decreed that certain substances are illegal and the officials' job is to enforce that. It is the Benthamite distinction that insists 'is' should be distinguished from 'ought'; it is not about the law as it ought to be but what the law is that is the deciding matter. Moreover, failure to deal with substance abuse (whatever the form or type) is as presented in these tests is a *de facto* way of legalising the drug and thereby undermining Parliament's wishes.

Part of the muddle we get ourselves into is that we are unclear about what we are trying to achieve. Are we trying to achieve abstinence or harm reduction? If the latter, then it is difficult to see how this can be achieved within the criminal justice system. Harm reduction might be an appropriate response for non-offender populations or may be used as a strategy to progress towards abstinence at a later date (drug users are rarely able to become abstinent over night), but it cannot be an end for offender populations. Harm reduction allows the use of less harmful drugs in preference to those that are more harmful. That means the criminal justice system is required to turn a blind eye to continued use and use that is unlawful. The alternative (abstinence) is more logical and straightforward: abstinence means the offender stops all drug taking and so, by definition, stops breaking the law. That, after all, is what a court order should involve. Abstinence, however, is not a fashionable proposition nowadays, but it has the obvious virtue of making treatment goals compatible with the goals of criminal justice and it avoids the confusions involved in clinging to a harm-reduction philosophy. It might be an advance that an offender stops injecting heroin and smokes cannabis instead, but that cannot be the sole aim of drug treatment systems working within a criminal justice setting. That must be compliance with the law.

Questions about who should see the test results are no less easy to resolve. A positive test can produce the stigmatising effect of being labelled on the court record as a drug user. Clearly, sets of regulations are required to determine who should or should not have access to test results if only because most people would equate a positive drug test with being a drug user – perhaps even a persistent one – although the proportion of offenders who are found positive and are seriously involved in drugs is unknown (Wish, 1988: 152). Protecting the rights of the offender in this respect is never going to be easy. The history of pre-sentence reports (PSRs) in Britain is testimony to that, when PSRs find themselves in all sorts of establishments with all sorts of people having access to them, even though they were prepared for the court. This raises the point about the dangers of making test results available to employers or potential employers and the even more difficult question of whether there should be a duty to do so if employment involves matters of public safety, such as being in the transport industry (train driver, perhaps).

Finally there are questions about drug testing using urine samples, about which lawyers refer to as 'search and seizure'. In 1989, the US Supreme Court held that urine tests compelled by the government constitute a search under the Fourth Amendment. Traditionally, only those tests that necessitated an actual physical intrusion, such as a blood test, were afforded Fourth Amendment protection. In a famous case (*Skinner* – see Meyers, 1991: 420) Justice Kennedy said:

There are few activities in our society more personal or private than the passing of urine. Most people describe it by euphemisms if they talk about it at all. It is a function traditionally performed without public observation: indeed its performance in public is generally prohibited by law as well as social custom.

The Court held that urinalysis is a search because it implicates expectations of privacy. It does so in the act of urination and in the subsequent analysis of the urine specimen. Urine analysis could reveal highly personal information about the testee (e.g. such as pregnancy, epilepsy or diabetes). As far as the English legal position is concerned, urinalyses also constitute search and seizure and for similar reasons to the USA. That is urine, is 'of possessory interest' and its analysis can reveal features of the person's life. An aggravating factor is that it is necessary to ask additional personal medical information before the sample is given; otherwise the test results could be interpreted wrongly (e.g. such as whether or not the testee is taking other medication). And because these personal questions need to be asked, urinalysis becomes increasingly intrusive. What appears, then, on the face of it to be a relatively straight-forward exercise (that is, testing for illegal substances) turns out to be highly complex with issues far beyond that of the tests themselves.

Conclusion

I have tried to untangle some of the knots we have tied for ourselves, especially in the fields of coercion and drug testing. There are many examples of sloppy thinking surrounding these topics that have led to numerous problems and, it is hoped, in this chapter some have been eased. In the next chapter an examination will be made of some instances where coercive treatments and drug testing have been introduced, with the question being asked as to what effect these new provisions will likely have on the solution to the drug problem. It is also asked where these proposals are likely to lead us in the future.

Chapter 5

The Drug Treatment and Testing Order and drug courts

It was noted in Chapter 3 that relatively little use had been made of the arrangements under Schedule 1A (6) of the Powers of Criminal Courts Act 1973 (as inserted by the Criminal Justice Act 1991) to impose treatment as part of a sentence. The findings of the Home Office Inspectorate as to why there had been a failure to make use of these services have been given earlier, but two of those findings need emphasis:

1. Reluctance on the part of probation officers to make such proposals in their pre-sentence reports, based on the view that coerced treatment is unlikely to be effective.
2. A perception of a lack of enthusiasm on the part of treatment providers to operate mandatory programmes.

The implied criticisms by the Home Office were that the probation service retained an outdated view that coercive treatment was unacceptable in moral terms, or not likely to be effective, illustrating again the alliance of probation with traditional social work values – an alliance not to the government's liking. One result of this is a new order, the Drug Treatment and Testing Order (DTTO), introduced in the Crime and Disorder Act 1998 (see ss. 61–64). It is the government's flagship and will, according to the official government publication, solve many of the earlier problems by strengthening the courts' powers. Its aim is to toughen up the probation response to drug abuse and to require the offender to undergo treatment, either as part of or in association with an existing community sentence. It will be targeted at serious drug misusers and aimed at reducing or removing the amount of crime committed to fund their drug habit (Home Office, 1998a). The government identifies two crucial differences between this and earlier provisions: the DTTO will review the offender's progress through a court review hearing and drug testing will be mandatory. It adds, somewhat darkly and prophetically, that 'The success of any new legislation will depend on the availability of treatment and the resolution of cultural differences between the criminal justice system and treatment providers, underpinned by strong inter-agency arrangements' (*ibid.*: para. 4). What the government calls 'cultural differences' I have called 'ideological differences' – it is the same point with different terminology.

Briefly, the legal provisions are that, under s. 61 of the Crime and Disorder Act 1998, the court by or before which the offender is convicted may make a drug DTTO. This will require offenders to undergo treatment for their drug problems, either alone or in tandem with another community order. The DTTO lasts for not less than 6 months and not more than 3 years, and includes the following requirements and provisions:

> A Drug Treatment and Testing Order shall include a requirement (the treatment requirement) that the offender shall submit, during the whole of the treatment and testing period, to treatment by or under the direction of a specified person having the necessary qualifications or experience (the treatment provider) with a view to the reduction or elimination of the offender's dependency or propensity to misuse drugs (s. 61).

The section also gives the courts powers to test and states:

> A drug treatment and testing order shall include a requirement (the testing requirement) that, for the purpose of ascertaining whether he has any drugs in his body during the treatment and testing period, the offender shall provide during that period, at such times or in such circumstances as may (subject to the provisions of the order) be determined by the treatment provider, samples of such description as may be so determined.

The order is for offenders over the age of 16 years (*ibid.*). They will be supervised by the probation service, and supervision includes provisions for the order to be reviewed at intervals of not less than 1 month. Under s. 63, the offender is required to attend a review hearing, although if progress is maintained the order can be amended so the offender need not attend. Where treatment is not satisfactory or the offender commits another offence, the court may consider the order within the meaning of s. 6 of the Criminal Justice Act 1991, that is, it may sentence the offender again for the offence for which he or she was made subject to the original order.

Section 62 requires a DTTO to include a treatment requirement stating whether the treatment will be residential or non-residential. It must identify the treatment provider and include a testing requirement with a specified frequency of drug testing. Treatment providers are required to give each offender the minimum number of tests required by the court and to submit the results to the supervising probation officer, who will report them to the court. The offender must report to a probation officer as required and notify the probation officer of any change of address. This is in line with probation orders generally.

The model for the DTTO is that of the American drug court, although nowhere is there any public recognition this is so. The DTTO uses the three central platforms of the drug court: first, treatment is provided by outside agencies, called treatment providers in the legislation, itself an American term; secondly, treatment is backed by drug testing; and, finally, treatment is reinforced by supervision, which in this case includes that of the probation service mixed with frequent court appearances where progress is reviewed. However, differences between this and the drug court are immense, not the least because in the DTTO these features are poorly integrated. In practice, the DTTO turns out to be a weak carbon copy of drug courts, lacking certain essential features necessary to make the system work.

Take two examples: drug testing and the review hearing. In the first there are questions to be asked about the link between drug testing and the treatment programmes. Some American commentators say that positive urine tests should always be backed by other information (progress in the treatment programmes, etc.). Experiments in Texas where drug-testing programmes were introduced without the necessary treatment backup showed how it failed. The conclusion was that drug testing was a poor deterrent on its own; it works best as part of a wider strategy where it is incorporated into a programme.

It is doubtful if that measure of integration exists within the DTTO. This is due to a number of reasons, one of which is a lack of clarity in the guidelines (Home Office, 1998a) on the drugs to be tested. For example, the *Guidance for Practitioners Involved in Drug Treatment and Testing Order Pilots* (Home Office, 2000) says that, 'The index drug or drugs (i.e. the drug most closely implicated in the offender's criminal behaviour) should *always* be tested for. Treatment providers and supervising probation officers should consider in addition if it would also be valuable to test for the presence of other illicit drugs'. If the supervisor does not know which drugs are being taken, it is difficult to see how treatment can be properly assessed. A lack of clarity or, rather, a lack of urgency, pervades the system.

Another is the manner in which the results are obtained. The *Guidance for Practitioners* (*ibid.*: para. 5) says that 'Test results should be returned to the treatment provider within 5 working days of dispatch'. Most judges in the American drug courts have the results sent to them immediately or within 20 minutes. They say delays allow the offender to manipulate the system whilst decisions based on past events are of little significance to current treatment requirements. The aim in American courts is to integrate test results into the programme immediately; the judge and the supervisor need up-to-date information if supervision is to be meaningful. Delays of up to 5 days would be regarded as unacceptable.

Then there is the rather vague manner in which the review is to be conducted. Under review hearings (s. 63 (1) of the Crime and Disorder Act 1998), we are told in the *Guidelines* (Home Office, 1998a: para. 8) that the aim is to examine progress under the treatment programme. Here it is said these are not breach proceedings but a unique opportunity to assess the effectiveness of the sentence (*ibid.*: para. 7). The order can be amended at the hearings depending on progress or lack of it, and the court will have reports from the probation office. One obvious problem is that there is no guarantee the offender will appear before the same bench of magistrates; indeed, it is highly likely he or she will not and, again, continuity is lost. The *Guidelines* (*ibid.*: para. 8) say that where this occurs 'it is vital that magistrates are made aware of the history of the order, particularly what was expected in the time immediately prior to the present review'. Damage limitation, perhaps, but hardly satisfactory given the nature of the exercise.

A second problem concerns the style of the review hearings. On the one hand, whilst in very broad principle they follow the style of drug courts, they lack the sense of firmness of purpose drug courts possess. Drug courts may have an informal style but this is deceptive if informality is seen as being lax or lacking in strength. In Britain, for example, the bench is encouraged to acknowledge success and to be firm in seeking explanations for missed appointments. It is also encouraged to permit active participation by all concerned and there is to be no format for the hearing (*ibid.*: para. 9) – presumably individual benches may vary in their approach. But there the matter ends. In contrast, the drug court has all the informality, allows encouragement and blame to be accorded and has enormous variations in practice. The difference is that they act quickly and forcefully against any shortcomings and they *require* all involved to be present. For the DTTO, the *Guidelines* (*ibid*.: para. 6) say: 'It is also expected that in the vast majority of cases either the probation officer or a drugs worker would attend the hearings to assist the court'. In drug court, sanctions are imposed immediately; DTTOs have breach proceedings at some later date.

In addition there are the ethical and jurisprudential questions of testing, which seem to be ignored in the DTTO. As said earlier, erroneous results place the offender in jeopardy, as indeed do all positive tests. Everyone who tests positive for drugs within the criminal justice system runs the risk of incarceration or some other punitive decision. In the USA, drug-testing laboratories that report erroneous positive test results to the court are civilly liable to defendants injured by the erroneous information. One wonders what would happen if the same threat existed in Britain under the DTTO.

Errors also occur when the samples are contaminated. These can arise in numerous aspects of the testing procedures, as are shown daily in the way athletes have successfully challenged their particular drug-testing systems:

> False positive results are also caused by contamination of samples or equipment, improper calibration, inadequate maintenance of the equipment, temperature variations, or failures in the chain of custody system. The very ease of performing these tests belies the care with which they must be done, and the consequent reliance on persons who are not trained to laboratory standards may lead to an under-estimation of the danger of cross reactivity and the importance of other potential threats to the accuracy of the tests (Meyers, 1991: 299–300).

As for testing 'up to laboratory standards', there is little hope this will be achieved in Britain. The *Guidelines* say that:

> The sample should be divided into two containers in front of the offender, who should be asked to sign two labels for the sample containers. These should be affixed to the two containers in his/her presence. One portion of the sample should be offered to the offender ... [who] ... should be advised to refrigerate the sample immediately if they wish to undertake independent testing. The remaining portion should be split again and one portion refrigerated to be dispatched for confirmatory testing. The remainder should be frozen and retained for one year in case of judicial review or challenge (*ibid*.: para. 10).

The American system aims to produce a drug-testing system free of all possible errors, and that means reducing the possibility of any human contact, whether with the offender or the drug-testing equipment. In Britain as reported in the evaluation of the DTTO, there was a certain laxness when it came to supervising urine tests. Sometimes offenders were handed the container and allowed to give a sample in the privacy of a lavatory; in one probation area, however, there were no facilities for supervised testing (Turnbull *et al.*, 2000: 36). The possibilities of error, of providing false samples, of corrupt officials, as said earlier, there is a trade in clean urine are endless. It is difficult not to conclude that, in Britain, the rules and regulations for this part of the DTTO fail to provide the necessary protection, whether for the offender or the person doing the testing. The order could well produce trouble for all concerned, whether from the court of appeal or elsewhere.

The pilot studies

Before they were introduced nationally, the DTTOs were piloted in three areas, Gloucestershire, Croydon and Liverpool. Inexplicably, the government decided to introduce DTTOs before the evaluation was completed, suggesting that a political decision had been reached rather than a criminological one. Had the government waited they might have been able to iron out some of the problems thrown up by the evaluation. The results of the pilot were not wholly convincing. It is difficult to summarise them all but the main ones are as follows: the use of drugs in the offender population, urine testing, interagency working and the supervision of offenders whilst on the order.

First comes drug abuse. This appeared to be the most successful feature, at least on the face of it. Offenders substantially reduced their drug abuse, at least at the beginning of the order, and the 6-months' follow-up confirmed this. Of those who completed or nearly completed the order a similar pattern emerged: a number said they were drug free and crime free, except for cannabis use. However, without a comparison group, it is difficult to state to what extent the DTTO was responsible for the change and, with the small numbers interviewed, it is difficult to draw firm conclusions. None the less, on the basis of these results and many were based on self-report data which are not the best from which to draw conclusions, the DTTO made some impact on the use of some drugs.

Secondly is urine testing. The frequency of urine testing varied markedly between the pilot areas. The evaluators thought that testing needed to be integrated fully with treatment programmes, with testing regimes tailored to the objectives set for individual offenders. They suggested a minimum standard – twice per week for the first 3 months of the order with discretion to reduce this to a minimum of once per week after that period (Turnbull *et al.*, 2000: 85–86). Croydon administered the test three times a week throughout the order, Gloucestershire averaged two tests per week and Liverpool about one.

There seemed to be little to suggest a standardised approach was being used for the testing procedure, and observation was not always undertaken with care. The evaluation reported as follows:

> Before administering the test DTTO staff asked drug using offenders if they had used drugs. It was not uncommon for drug using offenders to admit to drug use, in which case staff recorded a positive result without testing, in order to save money. Croydon was the only site where urine sample giving was observed routinely. Observation was frequently undertaken in Gloucestershire although there was emphasis on an offender being observed if falsification of a sample was suspected. Of the comparison sites only the STEP programme routinely observed the provision of urine samples. The Hastings programme had no facilities for supervised testing: PASCO and Fast Track occasionally observed the provision of urine samples (*ibid.*: 36).

Thirdly is interagency working. All three teams struggled to develop an effective model of interagency working, in spite of training for team members at all pilot sites. The evaluation said that: 'although interagency relationships improved at all three pilot sites only the Croydon team resolved conflicts and disputes sufficiently thoroughly to be operating as an effective team whose whole was greater than the sum of its parts' (*ibid.*: 53). One wonders how it was possible to run an effective programme in these circumstances. Interagency co-operation which is always difficult in any circumstances is likely to be additionally important in a project such as this where responsibilities for tasks need to be made clear, and where processes are outlined to review supervision goals.

Finally comes supervision. Supervision, another critical component suffered in similar ways to that of interagency working in that guidelines, such as there were, appeared not to be clear or, if they were they, they were not appropriately implemented. The evaluation says the teams had different expectations: 'The three sites had widely differing approaches to warnings, breaches and revocations. In all three sites offenders quite often failed to meet the conditions of the order. The main form of non-compliance was failure to attend but … many continued to use illicit drugs especially near the start of their order (*ibid.*: 80). Again it is difficult to see how such a situation arose. From the offender's point of view, these variations violated the basic principles of natural justice in that one team, the Gloucestershire team, applied much stricter requirements about drug abuse and attendance and produced the highest revocation rate at 60%. This compared with Croydon at 40% and Liverpool at 28%. For the probation officer, it highlighted levels of uncertainty about the object of the exercise as, apparently, teams found it quite difficult to give precise definitions of breach criteria (*ibid.*: 42).

The general conclusion as reported in the evaluation is not one that leads to a measure of confidence in DTTOs. At best, the failings can be explained by reference to the uniqueness of the programme, the expected teething troubles that were bound to arise and the lack of preparation – which was clearly not adequate. The alternative explanation is less charitable and points to a failure in training, preparation and planning, which should have been resolved earlier. The obvious question is, therefore, if this was the outcome for the pilot stages, what is to be expected now that the DTTOs are made nationwide?

Given these failings, how are we to interpret the results? Considerable time has been given to an examination of the DTTO if only to show how, without training and providing built-in safeguards, failure is inevitable and immediate. The testing procedures were not adequate to produce valid results and the data on drug use were based largely on self-report information, especially at the end of the order. It is difficult to see how credence can be given to these results given the shortcomings of the data and the processes involved in their production. At best it seems the data should be treated with caution. Can we assume, then, that the failings in the procedures will be ironed out in the national implementation? Probably not, as many are not failings or shortcomings due to a lack of preparation but structural failings created by the isolation of organisations from each other and from their reluctance to change traditional ways of working. The solution in part involves the creation of a new organisation along the lines of the Treatment Alternatives to Street Crime programme (TASC) (discussed in the final chapter) and of a new type of DTTO that breaks from the past and does not bring with it a set of ideological presumptions that are barriers to change. One of these could be drug courts.

Drug courts

In 1987, Chief Judge Wetherington alarmed at the ever-growing numbers of convicted drug users appearing at the Miami courts sent Judge Klein on a sabbatical year to come up with a solution. The result – in 1989 – was the first American drug court or, rather, the first drug court to use the approach known as the 'Miami drug court model'. Other drug courts existed, but their aim was to process drug users more speedily through the system, these are called fast-track administrative courts. The Miami model is different: it is a slow-track treatment court where the aim is to provide court-based treatment programmes to treat the offenders' addictions. From a relatively modest beginning in 1989 there has been, in the space of a decade, a burgeoning growth to well over 400 'Miami' drug courts (or simply drug courts henceforth) in every US state, as well as in Australia, Canada, the Republic of Ireland and Puerto Rico. It is proposed to introduce drug courts into Scotland in 2002.

Drug courts arose for three main reasons. First, the existing system was not working. The early efforts to speed up the process for the large numbers of drug offenders appearing before the courts (the so-called 'expedited case management courts') merely produced a faster, more efficient system by reducing waiting time between arrest and conviction. Paradoxically, this had the reverse effect; these courts hastened the offenders' progress through the revolving door from courts to prison and back to the courts. Other attempts to deal with the problem fared no better. The so-called 'build-out' approach, which meant building more prisons to deal with more and more offenders produced no relief. All that happened was that the prison population grew exponentially with an alarming increase in costs. As one Miami drug court judge said: 'Before the Miami drug court began the strongest prisoners slept on mattresses, the weaker on the floor and the weakest standing up' (pers. comm.).

A second reason was the link between drug taking and crime. As in Britain, the research evidence shows that large numbers of American offenders tested positive for drugs at the time of arrest, and many claimed their criminality was a direct response to their habit. In the circumstances it was reasonable to infer a direct link – with more certainty where the drug users were street addicts. The crack cocaine epidemic of the late 1980s and beyond produced large numbers of offenders charged with possession offences, especially from the inner-city areas. Efforts to reduce crack cocaine use became a high priority.

Thirdly is the courts themselves, especially the judges, who were critical of legislation that redefined the criminal codes and escalated penalties for drug possession and sales. The 'three strikes' policy restricted judicial action, as did other sentencing guidelines, so that judges increasingly saw themselves tied into a sentencing straitjacket. They believed these guidelines produced no tangible results, except perhaps longer sentences and, where they did not, offenders were simply moved through the system in ways that did nothing to reduce their drug taking on discharge. The 'three strikes' policy invariably produced sentences of 30 years or more, sometimes for a relatively small amount of cocaine, and many judges saw this as neither sensible nor productive. Drug court became a judge-led movement where judges wanted a more humane, effective programme that dealt directly with the problem of drug abuse.

These features alone did not account for the popularity of drug court, the shape of its programmes and the ethos surrounding it. For that there needs to be an assessment of drug courts as a social movement, which is beyond the scope of this book. There are, however, a number of aspects worth highlighting. First, drug courts operate according to an abstinence model, which sits easily within the compass of the earlier prohibition movement. There is also within the drug court system a strong evangelical approach that is part of an American cultural worldview not used elsewhere. Thirdly, drug courts operate under a free-market model where the offender is expected to pay towards the treatment and where the aim is to return the offender to being 'a productive member of society' – terminology rarely used outside the USA. The European perspective is suspicious of abstinence, preferring harm reduction, is suspicious of evangelism and is unused to talk in terms of a 'market model of treatment'.

Yet for all these criticisms drug courts have produced the largest number of clean addicts to be found anywhere; the drug court movement is burgeoning and, at present, unstoppable; and it has attracted inter-national interest and acclaim. Evaluations of drug courts are promising but not as hopeful, as was thought earlier. As less tractable offenders enter the programmes, rates of compliance and graduation will decline and recidivism will rise. This is an inevitable feature, especially as the earliest drug courts dealt with less serious offender groups. None the less, drug courts still achieve their aim of reducing levels of addiction and are more successful than any other programme.

Drug courts have also been introduced into the juvenile justice system, and there are similar courts for drunken drivers, domestic violence offences, for mentally disordered offenders and for 'dead-beat dads'. More recently, drug courts have moved into the prison system where pre-parole prisoners are placed on a drug court programme and, if successful, are granted parole. It has been said we should expect only one good idea in criminal justice per decade; that being so, drug court makes up for two.

Drug courts are not a homogeneous group and, within the Miami model, there are differences. Some courts place offenders on a diversionary or quasi-diversionary programme; others are post-adjudicatory, that is, the offender is sentenced to a drug court programme after conviction. Some drug courts deal only with minor offenders, others will not take offenders with convictions for violence, and still others will take only those charged with a possession offence. As the movement develops, so the population of offenders has become more varied, but one of the main criticisms is that, too often, the drug courts have concentrated on low-level offenders (Gebelein, 2000). It is interesting that the Australian approach has been to target the persistent drug user and high-level offender.

The National Association of Drug Court Pofessionals (NADCP) lists the following as the 10 key components of drug courts. These are taken from its document, *Defining Drug Courts; The Key Components* (NADCP, 1997), where each component is explained, followed by performance benchmarks, some of which will be given here. These key components provide the most useful means of examining and explaining drug courts.

1. *Drug courts integrate alcohol and other drug treatment services with justice system processing.* This is one of the most important of the components as it sets out the mission of drug courts, which is to stop the abuse of alcohol and other drugs and related criminal activity through a co-ordinated team approach that includes all the court personnel and the police, alongside community organisations such as education services, housing, etc. Drug court operates on the basis that the criminal justice system has the unique ability to influence a person shortly after a significant triggering event, such as an arrest, and thus to persuade or compel that person to enter and remain in treatment. This mission statement repeats the point made in Chapter 4, which is that research indicates that a person coerced to enter treatment by the criminal justice system is likely to do as well, if not better, than one who volunteers.

One of the many innovative features of drug courts is that the court supervises the offender. Elsewhere, the offender is handed over to another criminal justice agency such as the probation service, who decides on the nature of control and treatment. Often that agency will itself subcontract some or all of that control and treatment to another agency – perhaps psychiatry, where the subcontractor is required to report to the probation service on the offender's progress. That they rarely do this is another criticism of the traditional approach to treatment, irrespective of the type of treatment or the type of offender. In drug court, the court retains supervision and control and directly employs the treatment providers. This means hiring and firing according to the demands of the programme. The treatment providers work for the court, as do those involved in drug testing including the probation officers. In drug court, judicial control is pervasive, with the judge at the centre of the programme – this being a way of using the status and power of the judge to impose the programme on the offenders.

2. *Using a non-adversarial approach prosecution and defence counsel promotes public safety whilst protecting participants and the due process of rights.* Drug court makes much of the importance of the team approach where, it is claimed, in order to facilitate an offender's progress in treatment, the prosecutor and defence counsel must shed their traditional adversarial courtroom relationship and work together. This, of course, is easier said than done, or rather when it is done it may work to the detriment of the offender's rights. Drug court has provoked intense criticisms in some quarters by shedding the non-adversarial methods and opting for a team approach (Boldt, 1998; Bean, 2001b). As it turns out, the prosecuting attorneys seem to experience fewer problems than for the defence, for the former has a duty to protect public safety by ensuring that each candidate is appropriate to the programme. That is relatively straightforward. The defence counsel, on the other hand, is required to seek a not-guilty verdict or, if not, the most lenient sentence, as well as protect the offender's due process rights. According to the NADCP, the defence counsel does this by advising the offender on the nature of the drug court one of the benchmarks for this component, while encouraging the offender's full participation in the programme. But what happens if the defence believes a successful rebuttal of the charges can be achieved, or that it would be possible to receive a more lenient sentence than in drug court? Should the defence go for that and forgo the possibility of the client receiving treatment for his or her addiction? These questions have never been answered satisfactorily by the drug court movement, nor can they be for they centre on a subsidiary question about priority. That is, should priority be given to the offender's rights or to his or her welfare?

3. *Eligible participants are identified early and placed promptly in the drug court programme.* The period after arrest is seen as a critical time for an offender, who conveniently gives drug court a window of opportunity for intervening and introducing the value of treatment. Judicial action, taken promptly after arrest, capitalises on the nature of the arrest. Entering the drug court typically takes place as soon as possible after being convicted,

and the programme itself will usually begin within 24 hours of coming before the drug court judge – this is one of the benchmarks to be achieved. The offender enters drug court after being found guilty of one of the accepted offences: 'accepted' in the sense it must be one of the types of offences and offender the drug court will take. Instructions will be given immediately about reporting to the court usually three or four times a week at this stage, followed by the first of many regular drug tests when the offender will be promptly allocated to a treatment programme. Generally speaking, the programme will last for 2 years and, if the offender successfully completes it, he or she will have the original charge dropped and possibly have it taken off the file. This is important, especially for those subject to the 'three strikes' policy. In exceptional cases, as in the Superior Court at Washington, DC, successful completion will lead to a 2-year probation order.

4. *Drug courts provide access to a continuum of alcohol, drug and other related treatment and rehabilitation services.* Drug court claims that treatment experience begins in the courtroom and continues throughout, making it a comprehensive therapeutic experience. On entering drug court there will be an initial screening and evaluation period, lasting about 24 hours, after which the offender enters the programme. Successful completion, however, requires more than abstinence. The Delaware drug court, for example, not only requires 4 months of abstinence but also that the offender meets the other demands of full employment, etc., in order to graduate. Different criteria operate throughout, but abstinence plus full employment are likely to be the most common. However, treatment also includes dealing with co-occurring problems such as mental illness, primary medical problems, HIV and sexually transmitted diseases, homelessness and domestic troubles, some of which may include domestic violence. It will certainly expect to be long term for, unless these other factors are addressed, success in treatment will be impaired.

5. *Abstinence and the use of alcohol and other drugs are monitored by frequent drug testing.* Drug testing is an essential feature of the programme, as accurate testing is seen as the most objective and efficient way to establish a framework of accountability to determine the offender's progress. Those who do well that is, do not test positive, advance in treatment and fulfil other requirements, such as hold down a job and become a productive tax-paying citizen – drug court is more than about being drug free it is about being fully rehabilitated, and will be allowed to report less frequently. Drug testing is almost always through urinalysis, and the

results are made available immediately. One of the benchmarks is that failure to comply, that means testing positive and missing treatment appointments and court appearances will produce immediate sanctions. In some courts the local police give a high priority to those who fail to attend and are in breach of the programme. Another benchmark is that drug testing must be certain – the samples must not be contaminated. Alcohol is invariably included as one of the drugs to be tested as NADCP argue that alcohol use frequently contributes to relapse among individuals whose primary drug of choice is not alcohol. Contracted laboratories are held accountable to established standards.

6. *A co-ordinated strategy governs drug court responses to participant compliance.* An assumption behind drug courts is that addiction is a chronic relapsing condition so that becoming drug free is a learning experience in which failures, especially in the early stages, are to be expected. None the less, sanctions are imposed for continued drug use, and responses increase in severity for failure to abstain. In contrast, if the offenders complete the programme successfully they are rewarded. This may involve praise from the judge, encouragement from the treatment staff or ceremonies in which accomplishments are recognised and applauded, or there may be an award of a diploma or some other means of official recognition at the graduation.

Drug courts have what is called a co-ordinated strategy to deal with non-compliance, which will often involve short periods in prison. State legislation permits these multiple sanctions, which are almost unique in common law jurisdictions. Normally there will be no more than one sanction imposed for each offence and, when that punishment is served, the offence is expiated. The exception is on a probation order where it is possible for the offender to be dealt with on more than one occasion for breaking the conditions of the order, but it would be very rare for that to occur more than once.

7. *Ongoing judicial interaction with each drug court participant is essential.* The judge heads the team, which includes the prosecuting and defence counsel, the police and all other officers of the court. This team approach is another of the innovations of drug courts, which was traditionally absent in the adversarial system where collaboration and co-operation are at a minimum. Competition is more common. In drug courts, all work together for the common good – stopping the offender from taking drugs. The origins of the team approach can be found in the TASC (Treatment Alternatives to Street Crime) programme, which itself emerged from research showing that treatment was more effective in settings in which

legal sanctions and close supervision provide incentives for offenders to conform with treatment protocols and objectives (Lipton, 1995). To operate successfully, there had to be a team offering co-operation rather than a number of agencies pulling in different directions. However, TASC unlike drug courts did not seek to fuse the criminal justice system with the treatment services but to provide a bridge by supplementing traditional adjudication with treatment services, usually through diversion.

8. *Monitoring and evaluation measure the achievement of programme goals and gauge effectiveness.* From the outset, drug courts have been evaluated. Evaluation is often a condition of funding, where process and outcome evaluations are built in to the programme. (Process evaluations are concerned with the way the system operates, and outcome evaluations are about the successes, achievements or failures of the programme.) In spite of this, only a small number of evaluations have been sufficiently rigorous to meet acceptable standards, and most have varied in quality comprehensiveness, the types of measures used and the appropriateness of comparison groups (Balenko, 1999: 7). Initially, the drug court movement claimed results that have not been validated, and some of the earlier claims have had to be scaled down. More realistically, later evaluation results are consistent with some, but not all, of the earlier findings that is, drug courts continue to engage drug offenders in long-term treatment, providing more regular and closer supervision than received by those in other forms of criminal justice supervision in the community. Drug use rates and criminal activity, as measured by urine test results and recidivism, are reduced while participants are on the programme. In the evaluations of outcome that use a control group, post-programme rearrest rates and drug use, the rates are lower than for those who drop out or are terminated from the programme (*ibid.*: 4). The overall conclusion is that drug courts are more successful than any other drug-involved prevention activity, and cost evaluations suggest that, for every US$1 spent on drug court, there is a saving of US$7 in the criminal justice system.

9. *Effective drug court operations require continuing interdisciplinary education.* Those working in drug court, at whatever level, are expected to participate fully in the training programmes. One reason is to bridge that gap (noted in Chapter 4) which exists between criminal justice and treatment personnel. Criminal justice personnel need to be familiar with treatment goals and the many barriers to successful treatment, whereas treatment personnel need to be familiar with criminal justice account-

ability and courtroom operations. All need to understand and comply with drug-testing procedures. Drug court operates best when a spirit of commitment and collaboration is promoted, and this can be achieved through education and training programmes – which should always take place before the drug court is up and running and where, as a benchmark, attendance is regarded as essential, whether at the outset or later.

10. *Forging partnerships among drug courts, public agencies and community-based organisations enhances drug court effectiveness and generates support.* Most communities are proud of their drug courts, believing they offer a serious attempt at dealing with an otherwise intractable problem. One of the lessons learnt by the earlier drug courts was to seek and obtain support from the media, especially in the formation stage, as opposition from the media was a severe detriment to their success. Accordingly, drug courts have learnt to promote themselves and to present themselves favourably to the local community. Federal funding has rarely been sufficient so that drug court judges have had to raise monies themselves (selling lottery tickets was not unheared of, alongside other popular activities). Promoting and producing public support have been an important way of securing funding and help to restore faith locally in the criminal justice system.

Some additional comments

The 10 points listed above cover much of what constitutes drug court. They do not, however, convey the flavour of the court, the dramatic intensity that is often present and the interactions between judge and offender (for a full description of the drug court and its personnel, see Nolan (1998)). The drug court in James Nolan's terms produces personalised justice and, with it, a set of attendant dangers. There is little doubt that drug court has raised again the spectre of rehabilitation that was widely discredited in the late 1970s and which has appeared again under a new guise and different banner. The emphasis on treatment, the belief that treatment breaks the link with crime and the transformation of the judge to a type of judicial social worker have helped push rehabilitation to the forefront (for a critique of this, see Bean, 2001a). But anyone who has experienced a drug court in full swing will know how easy it is to be pulled along on that tide of enthusiasm. Drug court workers believe in their crusade, for a crusade it certainly is.

It would not be impossible to introduce drug courts into Britain, but it would need a political commitment and require the courts and their appropriate government departments to be persuaded of the need to be innovative. Opposition would be expected from the probation department, who would find itself marginalised with a less dominant part to play than under the DTTO. In drug court, the judge is doing what the probation service does, and much more. As one drug court judge said: 'There is nothing the probation service can do that I cannot do, and I can do a lot more than the probation service' (pers. comm.). The voluntary sector might also find it difficult to work in drug court, although initial reservations in the USA diminished when voluntary agencies saw the work was worth while and profitable. There is little doubt that drug courts would produce stresses and strains on the existing system, but there will always be such stresses with radical change and drug court is nothing if not radical. Its supporters talk of reinventing justice and, to some extent, this is so.

The judge is an integral part of the court structure – it is the unique power of the court and the status of the judge that drive the system along. Attempts to weaken the system by handing over responsibility for treatment to, say, psychiatrists or probation officers emasculate it to the point where it ceases to be a drug court. There is no one else able to command the same respect as the judge or to have powers to enforce the order in that way. Judges promote a type of regime that mixes sympathy with control; no excuses are accepted for not reporting or for returning to drugs, whether it be a family bereavement, doing overtime or the car breaking down. (One drug court judge urges new offenders on the pro-gramme to call all their family together as from the judge's experience, most will die during the treatment programme – *some more than once!*) It is not unusual for a drug court judge to have a caseload each day of over 80. Burn-out rates are high and, when a drug court judge steps down, it is not always possible to find another sufficiently motivated to continue and, without a highly motivated judge, drug court does not work well (Gebelein, 2000).

Drug courts and the DTTO: a comparison

Too often claims are made that a drug court has been introduced in Britain when the 'drug court' in question turns out to be nothing of the sort. Or demands are made to introduce 'drug courts' when there seems little understanding of what this means. Sometimes the so-called 'drug court' places the offender on probation and the offender returns occasionally to the court to report on progress. Or the 'drug court' involves a few probation officers who have found a group of treatment agencies willing to take an interest in treating drug offenders. These are not drug courts in the sense in which the term is used here: they are traditional courts using probation orders with bells and whistles attached.

Table 5.1 compares selected features of the two systems, although it needs to be emphasised that, within the Miami model, there are differences between drug courts, and sometimes between states as well as within a state. Differences are usually about the type of offenders, the length of the programme and the manner in which the original conviction is retained on file. They do not differ in their basic methodology.

The table compares the two systems and, incidentally, shows the types of changes necessary were drug courts to be introduced in Britain or, for that matter, in any common law jurisdiction. It is not simply about bolting drug courts on to the existing system but of making structural changes to

Table 5.1   Drug courts and the Drug Testing and Treatment Order (DTTO): a comparison

Drug court	DTTO
Aim is abstinence. That may include alcohol	Aim is harm reduction, especially heroin or cocaine
Treatment providers are employed by the court	Treatment providers work through the probation service
Judge conducts the supervision	Probation service conducts the supervision
Adversarial system replaced by team approach	Adversarial system remains intact
Judge can impose multiple sanctions	Court restricted to breach proceedings defined in legislation
Drug test results sent to the judge immediately	Drug test results take up to 5 days before arriving at court
Courtroom procedure is less formal	Formal procedures remain in tact
Offender may be required to pay for treatment	Treatment is part of NHS provisions
Drug court judge concentrates on drug offenders	Judges retain full control over a range of offenders
Probation service has only a minor part to play	Probation service is central to the order

the way the courts operate. However, Britain, with its common law system, would find the changes less dramatic than were it to have a Roman law system. The differences between the DTTO and drug courts are considerable and show, first, in the ideologies and aims of treatment. In the drug court it is abstinence; in the DTTO it is harm reduction.

The second major difference is that the court employs the treatment providers. This is a radical departure from existing practice with profound implications, whether at the criminological, jurisprudential or political level. Treatment providers in Britain have traditionally been employed by voluntary agencies or the major national agencies such as the National Health Service (NHS). Working for the court would be a new experience, where some professionals especially those in medical and allied practices might find it difficult being employed by a judge or panel of magistrates. Some psychiatrists, for example, have said they could not accept such forms of employment; on the other hand, some directors of voluntary agencies say they would welcome the opportunity, seeing the introduction of drug courts in Britain as a new, challenging, profitable experience.

The third major difference is that the judge conducts the supervision. Judges in drug courts have invariably made themselves knowledgeable about addiction and its associated effects, and have become experts in their way. They may not be entirely suited for the social work role they are required to undertake but there is little doubt most conduct themselves with confidence. They have been prepared to break the mould and engage in activities not always to the liking of some of their colleagues. Their position is not without some justifiable criticism and, were drug courts to be transferred to Britain, their British counterparts may not be expected to engage in the more extreme activities, nor may they want to. On the other hand, a few changes might be welcomed.

The fourth difference produces the most controversy, for this changes the complexion of a common law adversarial system of justice that is deeply ingrained in the ways things are done. To a large extent, claims by drug courts to be 'reinventing justice' are hyperbolic, although there is no doubt they have made things different. Operating as a team changes judicial roles and produces a loss of procedural rights, as well as the protection those rights provide. The question for the offender is how much he or she is prepared to trade off or forgo rights when there is the prospect of being drug free. For the judicial system, the key question is how far is it prepared to go in the direction of that 'team' approach? Legal restrictions can be imposed on drug courts and the powers of the judge could be limited, or it could be allowed an unbridled development. The latter would not seem a sensible option.

Fifthly, there is the question of multiple sanctions. Were drug courts to be developed in Britain, legislation would be required should they operate on the Miami model. Multiple sanctions, the key to drug court success are not permitted under current legislation, yet without them drug court becomes not much more than an extended type of probation order.

Tests results are given to drug court judges immediately. Under the DTTO, delays of up to 5 days are to be expected. The difference is critical if decisions are to be made about the offender's current position and, if they are not, one wonders how they can ever be effective.

The courtroom procedure in drug court is less formal than likely to exist in the hearing for the DTTO. Offenders in drug courts believe the informal contact with the judge is an important ingredient to their success. Some drug courts operate more like a legal circus; others are more muted in their response. There is no evidence to suggest one is more successful than the other, but offenders are clear that personalised justice, in some form, is important to them.

Some drug courts require the offender to pay for his or her own treatment on the basis he or she produced his or her problem and should pay for it to be removed. Their view is that it is not the state's business to pay through its citizens' taxes for a self-inflicted disease. The European perspective is more corporate and unused to this rampant individualism. Given the manner in which many American ideas have arrived in Britain, usually first being considered outrageous and unacceptable, how long, one wonders, will it be before this one is accepted? Drug court is what it says – a separate court with a specially appointed judge who hears drug court cases only when the drug court is sitting. There is no court set aside for offenders on a DTTO.

Finally, in drug court the probation service has a minor part to play, but under the DTTO the probation service is central. Opposition to drug courts is likely to continue to come from the probation service, who would be a major loser. On the other hand, treatment services would be the major victor, albeit employed by the court, for they would have increased funding and would assume a dominant position in the new drug court structure.

Clearly, the DTTO is the government's flagship in dealing with the problem of drug abuse and crime. It has within it certain flaws and, as such, it will, in my judgement, be a failure. I say this more from sorrow than anger, yet the omens were not good at the start: the pilot results were hardly satisfactory but the government pressed ahead, none the less. Everything one hears about the way it operates confirms that pessimistic view. It will be another example of doing too little too late and, in part, of not grasping the nettle about coercive treatment. It is also another example of a fudge and of having an eye on the professionals so as not to make too many changes, not to spend money and to tinker with existing institutions rather than reform them.

There are, of course, other models of treatment but the drug court remains a persuasive one other countries are using, but Britain with the exception of Scotland is left with a system already outdated and creaking at the seams. It is not only that the DTTO will not work. It is that time and energy have been given to it that should have been directed elsewhere. The DTTO leaves too many pertinent questions unanswered, including: what types of actions are likely to produce the best results when tests are found to be positive? Will testing work more effectively on certain types of offenders than others? Can strategies be developed for estimating a person's risks on the basis of drug-test results? These are the types of questions we should be asking, but they must remain for the future – at least until we have sorted out the current predicament. No one suggests that drug courts are free of blemish but they have produced a more coherent and considered approach than the DTTO and should have at least been considered.

Drug courts in Scotland and Ireland

Scotland is ahead of the rest of the UK in that the first pilot drug court is scheduled to begin in Glasgow in the autumn of 2001. Its history is interesting. A working group entitled 'Piloting a Drug Court in Glasgow' was established in February 2001 on the initiative of the Scottish Justice Department. The remit was 'to make proposals to the Scottish Deputy Minister for Justice and report by Easter on a model within existing legislation of a Drug Court and on the arrangements for its operation in Glasgow Sheriff Court by the Autumn of 2001'. The timetable was commendably tight, allowing 2–3 months to prepare a report and a further 6 months to complete preparations.

The working group proposed that the objectives for the Glasgow Drug Court should be to:

1. reduce the level of offending behaviour;
2. reduce or eliminate offenders' dependence on or propensity to misuse drugs;
3. examine the viability and usefulness of a drug court in Scotland using existing legislation and to demonstrate where legislative and practical improvements might be appropriate.

Point 3 is interesting because the aim in Scotland is to produce a drug court within the existing legislative framework and then see which new features are needed. The working party concluded that, in comparison with other courts generally, drug courts have been successful in engaging and retaining offenders in treatment services; that drug courts provide closer and more intensive supervision; that criminal behaviour is lower; and that drug courts save money.

The court will operate in the same way and with the same authority as other courts. There will be the same range of powers and the same sentences will be available. These are a probation order with a condition of treatment, a DTTO, a concurrent DTTO and a conditional probation order, and a deferred sentence. What it will do is impose on these sentences the principles and practices of drug courts. This is what makes it so interesting because it has adapted the drug court model to the Scottish system. In addition to the usual conditions of probation, etc., the Scottish drug court will require the offender to:

1. submit to treatment with a view to the reduction or elimination of dependency on or propensity to misuse drugs;
2. conform to the directions of the treatment provider;
3. agree to be tested for drugs;
4. attend review hearings;
5. abide by any such additional conditions as may be inserted.

It could be argued that the court can already act in this way under the DTTO so that the drug court is doing little more than a DTTO. But that is wrong; it is doing much more. It is taking the Miami system and recasting it to fit the Scottish experience and, in so doing, introducing many distinguishing features. These are as follows:

1. It has a specialist bench consisting of a sheriff who will develop a considerable measure of expertise.
2. A multi-agency team who will oversee the operation of the drug court.
3. Regular and random testing of all orders, including probation.
4. Regular review of the offenders' progress.
5. A multi-disciplinary screening group and interagency working.
6. Fast-track court procedures to get the offender into treatment quickly.
7. Initiation of breach proceedings by the bench.
8. Use of summary sanctions at reviews.

Point 1 is new. Point 2 is also new but does not go so far as giving the team the powers and responsibility of the American system. Point 3 constitutes a departure from existing practices, as does point 4, and point 5 moves close to the American team approach. Point 6 is not new except the existing system is slow, but point 7 certainly is new. Point 8 is interesting. The aim here is to seek legislative change to allow multiple sanctions to be introduced so the offender can be dealt with on breach of the order and the order be allowed to continue.

The Glasgow drug court will take some of the so-called hard-to-treat users. It is thought about 8,000 drug users in Glasgow could benefit from the drug court, which will be able to take about 150 users per annum. The age group will be 21 years and over, but the mean age is expected to be higher – there is a steep upward failure rate in American drug courts for those under 28 years. When it comes into operation late 2001, it will be the first drug court in the UK.

Ireland already has a drug court. It began in January 2001 in Dublin and, in the first 4 months from January to May 2001 there had been 22 referrals. The Dublin drug court team consists of two probation officers, a liaison nurse, two community workers and an educational assessor. Cases are referred from other courts and then assessed. If the offender is suitable, and the Irish court takes those who have failed under voluntary programmes as well as serious offenders, the offender is sent to drug court. The programme lasts for 2 years (Haughton, 2001).

The Dublin court is a bail bond court that is it operates with the offender on bail. Being on bail, the offender can opt out at any time; he or she has not been sentenced but, whilst on bail, must abide by the conditions of bail. The Irish Bail Act says it is a breach of conditions of bail if the offender is no longer of good behaviour, and this is what gives the court its powers. This is another example of the way in which drug courts can be adapted to local conditions yet retain the spirit of a drug court.

The intention in Scotland and Ireland is to take the hard-to-treat and serious offenders. This is based on the assumption that, if drug courts have anything to offer, they should be able to deal with those offenders who cannot easily be dealt with elsewhere. It will be interesting to see how matters develop, especially in Scotland.

Chapter 6

Trafficking and laundering

For our purposes, trafficking is defined widely. It includes the distribution of illicit drugs by large-scale operations, which can and often do cross national boundaries, as well as the small-scale syndicates that distribute drugs at the local level. All operations at whatever level pose questions for law enforcement, government policy or the local communities on which they have a deleterious effect. Each distribution system has its own methods and practices, posing distinct problems that require different strategies.

This chapter will not examine the nature of production, although the circumstances in which drugs are produced can have an effect on distribution. The aim here is to examine some central features of trafficking. There is a large amount of information available on trafficking, especially for South America, but less for South East Asia or elsewhere. Much less is known about the production and distribution of the precursor chemicals necessary for the manufacture of such drugs as heroin and cocaine. A great deal of the research is American, concerned with American matters, especially relating to cocaine trafficking which has dominated American drug policy for two decades.

Trafficking – an overview

The geographical areas of production are worth listing for they show where trafficking occurs and the different types of organisations used to distribute a variety of drugs. Briefly, coca leaf is produced extensively in Bolivia, Peru, Venezuela and Brazil, although for these purposes Brazil is the least important producing country. Invariably, the coca leaves are sent to Colombia in the form of coca paste to be refined into cocaine hydrochloride. 'Crack' (the base form of the salt, cocaine hydrochloride) is almost always produced in the consumption areas. Unlike other illicit drugs, which grow in almost all geographical regions, world coca production is limited to the Andes, with Peru (60%) and Bolivia (20%) being the major producers.

Afghanistan currently accounts for almost 75% of the world's illicit opium supply (MacDonald and Mansfield, 2001). Much of the remainder is from the traditional growing region of the Golden Triangle (Burma, Laos and Thailand). Significant amounts, however, are grown elsewhere, such as in Iran and Turkey. There is firm evidence that heroin production is also occurring in the Andean region with the Colombian cartels moving away from cocaine (*Drugs Intelligence Trends* (The Colombian Heroin Connection) 1992). There, the 1970s were characterised by an increase in cannabis trafficking; in the 1980s it was cocaine; in the 1990s, heroin is the major concern. In 1991 and in the first quarter of 1992, Colombian authorities destroyed a total of 3,500 hectares of poppy fields and three heroin laboratories (*ibid.*). With maximum market share of cocaine, the move is now to increase heroin production, and high levels of purity are already being achieved. Whether this means a major shift in the world markets is difficult to say, but it is interesting to note that the price of heroin in Puerto Rico continues to fall. There are about 80,000 heroin addicts in Puerto Rico, giving further evidence that heroin is available in that region (Drugs Enforcement Agency (DEA) pers. comm., 1994).

Cannabis is produced worldwide. Estimates of cannabis production suggest that world production is increasing, in spite of intensive crop-eradication programmes. Unfortunately in countries such as Belize or Jamaica, where crop eradication has occurred, the dealers have shown a readiness to transfer to cocaine (*ibid.*). Manufactured drugs are also produced worldwide; ecstasy was until recently mainly produced in Amsterdam (Bean, 1994) but local British factories are now operating. LSD is manufactured throughout the industrialised countries, with production moving as factories are closed down. This is also the case with methamphetamine, whilst 'ice' a distinct form of methamphetamine is almost exclusively manufactured in North Korea and distributed through Hawaii, but it is penetrating deeper into the US market and may soon appear in Britain (Bean, 1991b). How much has already arrived is difficult to say, as the British market is still monopolised by cocaine.

Trafficking and traffickers differ according to the drugs being smuggled, the source of production and the local distribution (Dziedzic, 1989). An early important text (Cooper, 1990) that concentrates on the economic forces that drive the drug trade shows that drug dealing was then worth an estimated US$500 billion per year. Moreover, Cooper (*ibid.*) shows that the traffickers are flexible and effective, especially when set against some rather ineffective and outdated forms of interdiction, especially in the Caribbean region and some parts of Europe, and that in spite of the occasional successes by law enforcement. Given the size of the drug market it would not be an exaggeration to say the drug trade is the largest and most successful form of criminal activity ever developed (*ibid.*). Later European research confirms this (Ruggiero and South, 1995).

Once the drugs have crossed the local customs area into their final destination, such as Europe or the USA, their value increases dramatically. Table 6.1 gives the figures for cocaine provided by the DEA (pers. comm., 1994). It is suspected they have not changed greatly over the last decade or so as far as the street price is concerned, but even if they have the point remains that the price in Colombia bears no relation to the price on the streets.

The figures for opium are no less impressive. The total value of opium production in Afghanistan at so-called 'farm gate' prices at harvest time was estimated at US$183 million, or about US$35 per kg. By the time it had passed through customs in the UK, it was estimated to be worth US$25,000 per kg (MacDonald and Mansfield, 2001: 3). The massive increase in the price at each stage of the operation shows how the end price bears no relation to the cost of production: the distribution costs are the heaviest. Peter Reuter (2001) adds to this by calculating that a pilot who demands US$500,00 for flying a plane with 250 kg of cocaine is generating costs of about US$2,000 per kg, less than 2% of the retail price of each kg.

Moving against the drug cartels, especially in South America, involves serious economic and political costs, including for governments as the drug industry has accumulated significant political influence (Lee, 1989). The resulting concentration of wealth and coercive potential in the hands of drug cartels, especially in Colombia, has led to a severe threat to that

Table 6.1 The value of cocaine whilst en route to users (in US$ per kg)

Leaving from Guajala (Colombia) in an air drop	300
Arriving at the US border	3,000
Into the USA	12,000
Distributed to users	20,000

Source: DEA pers. comm., 1994.

and some other country's national and regional security. Whilst it is clear the drug producers, the farmers, growers, etc., receive only a small percentage of the vast profits, to what extent these cartels threaten Western security is not yet known, but already there are disturbing signs of their influence on smaller economies within the Caribbean. A massive inflow of drug money into economies such as the Bahamas was immensely destructive, where the government in the early 1990s had considerable difficulty, meeting immense pressure from the traffickers, on the one hand, and the American government on the other who wanted rid of the traffickers. Damage is not restricted to the economic environment; it extends to the political institutions where the proliferation of sophisticated weaponry among traffickers, and the ease with which they undermine democratic institutions, is commonplace. This is so whether in South America, South East Asia or elsewhere, but it is in Latin America that all these factors are most often combined (Dziedzic, 1989).

In Colombia the situation is by now almost beyond repair (MacDonald, 1989), but Venezuela and Ecuador increasingly attract trafficking, and cocaine production is extensive, making them additionally vulnerable. One of the many difficulties for national governments is that traffickers have appeared to assist local industries although, of course, their assistance quickly turns out to be catastrophic. In one of the most carefully documented studies in Peru, Morales (1989) shows that coca production and the processing of its derivative alkaloids have become major Peruvian growth industries, the ramifications of which reach into the heart of Peru's political life, its law enforcement and its judicial systems. In the long term, Morales believes the net effect will create conditions producing greater levels of social and political impoverishment than hitherto. Peter Reuter (2001) is, however, more optimistic. He claims that the land under coca cultivation fell in Bolivia and Peru from 150,000 acres in 1992 to 60,000 acres in 1999 (*ibid*.: 21). Of course, all figures must be estimates but Reuter believes crop-eradication programmes have had a measure of success in parts of South America.

A study of the long-term effects of the narcotics industry in all societies, including Western Europe countries, would need to include selected political and social institutions, especially those centring around finance. It would need to determine the extent of the traffickers' current influence, and then show the likely impact in the short and long term. The US experience suggests that Western European institutions are strong enough to be impervious, although to what extent they can remain so must be difficult to judge. The amount of drug money available must always be a threat to institutions, however large.

Again, in Morales' study of Peru (1989), he notes the extent of dependency on the lives of peasants and workers whose livelihoods are closely linked to the production of cocaine. It was they who resisted attempts by governments to introduce alternative cash crops in the region. Peasants and workers have traditionally supported the drug producers, seeing them as providing an income higher than that expected in crop-substitution programmes. Healey (1989) found similar results in Bolivia, where support for coca-leaf production came from well organised peasant unions closely tied to the national labour movement. So too in Pakistan, where resistance to opium crop-eradication programmes is legendary. These studies tell us a great deal about the impact of drug production on local industries and, for that reason, could easily provide a model for a study on the impact of the drugs trade on local areas in Britain and elsewhere i.e. of the dependency of local landlords, traders, etc., on local drug markets. There are differences, to be sure, but they are sufficiently isomorphic in their structure to suggest one could usefully act as a model for the other.

Generally speaking, more is known about South American traffickers than those from South East Asia or elsewhere. However, MacDonald and Mansfield (2001) report that, in Afghanistan, although the agricultural conditions for growing opium are conducive throughout, opium is not grown nationwide. They say the labour requirements are demanding so that the producing areas depend heavily on a type of share-cropping where women and young children are actively involved in weeding and harvesting. Farmers growing opium are given preferential access to credit, thereby ensuring harvesting and continuity in terms of production. Whilst the Taliban authorities in Afghanistan have passed an edict banning the use, production and sale of opium, and cannabis, implementation of this edict has been problematic (*ibid.*: 5).

Colombian trafficking operates largely in cartels that are best characterised as a federation of multiple independent groups that, when necessary, forge multiple alliances. They are not centrally organised although some cartel members are more powerful than others and offer leadership when required. The cartels function much like legitimate businesses, with sections concerned with distribution, sales, financing, product promotion, security, etc. They tend to compartmentalise their organisations into production, transportation, distribution and money laundering. Yet unlike legitimate businesses, the cartels cannot resort to the courts or other legitimate enterprises to sort out disputes over product quality, to collect debts or resolve other matters. Instead, they rely on bribery, extortion and violence to achieve effective and efficient production and distribution, to avoid arrest and to make a huge profit (Florez and Boyce, 1990). South East Asian heroin traffickers seem to be slightly less sophisticated in their business methods, preferring to remain more individualist, but are no less reluctant to resort to extreme levels of personal violence when required (Lo *et al.*, 1991). In Britain, Turkish traffickers control much of the importation of heroin, with the drugs coming into Britain from Afghanistan via Turkey.

There are probably four major cartels in Colombia: the Medellin, the Cali, the Bogota and the Northern Coast cartel, although some see the Northern Coast and Bogota as one and the same. The Medellin cartel has had the most publicity, but the Cali cartel is larger, more efficient and certainly more business-like, although recently unconfirmed claims have been made that the Cali cartel has been broken up. Almost all the cartel members in Colombia are known to the DEA and the FBI, as are their movements and their major business associates. By all accounts the traffickers were, or are, small-time gangsters, unsophisticated yet with an easy recourse to violence. Their lifestyles are ordinary and their tastes crude. They have a shrewd organisational sense that allows them to know whom to employ, how to obtain the best financial advice and how to enforce discipline. The DEA and FBI have developed an extensive portfolio of cartel members, and consistently and persistently apply to the Colombian government for their extradition. Rarely do they succeed (DEA pers. comm.).

Generally speaking, we can distinguish between cartel members, traffickers and dealers, although sometimes they are one and the same. Cartel members usually own the drugs whilst the traffickers transport them, acting as middlemen between the cartels and the more local dealers; sometimes the cartel members hand the drugs over to the traffickers, sometimes not. These high-level traffickers usually work directly with the cartels but mostly outside national boundaries, and are responsible for transporting the drugs, having purchased them from the cartels, some of whom may be cartel members in their own right. The traffickers and dealers, especially those from South East Asia, are mostly men, approaching middle age or older, have excellent organisational skills, have established connections often with organised crime syndicates or are prepared to work closely with organised crime, and have capital to invest. They also have a willingness to take large business risks. Their activities exist within a highly competitive market that is populated by individual entrepreneurs. These traffickers change as enforcement strategies change or as they tire of the corrupt practices endemic to the illegal trade (Chaiken and Johnson, 1988). Some may be intermittent traffickers, as in South East Asia, active perhaps once in every two or three years whilst others who may not be involved for a period of time seem drawn back to it. There is, it seems, some compulsive and highly attractive element about high-level trafficking, which seems to generate levels of excitement not found elsewhere (Lo and Bean, 1991).

Alongside the cartel members are the financial advisers, mostly people from Europe who emigrated to Colombia before or after the Second World War. Typically, these are sophisticated professionals with a detailed knowledge of financial markets and financial institutions. Culturally and socially they have little in common with the traffickers and regard themselves as superior. Yet they are as central to the operation as the traffickers, for money and drugs are but two sides of the same equation. Without the financial advisers there would be no trafficking, and without trafficking there would be no financial advisers: both create the profits for, without profits, there would be no drugs (*ibid.*).

Cocaine is typically transported from the Guajala peninsular in Colombia or from Venezuela, using at least four major methods. These are as follows:

1. In containers where the drugs are sent direct to selected ports.
2. By air drops to selected Caribbean locations.
3. By sea to selected Caribbean locations.
4. By small-time couriers.

Most of the earlier trafficking was done in containers, and this seems to be the most successful form – at least from the perspective of the traffickers. The Port of Miami randomly selects 1 in 100 of all containers passing through and subjects them to detailed examination. These are in addition to those selected as a result of information from undercover activities, informers and the like. It takes a small team about 2 weeks to examine each container. Corrupt employees within the port working for the traffickers will know in advance which containers have drugs and will remove the drugs before they are searched. This is another example how traffickers find ways of undermining attempts to seize illicit drugs. The drugs may have travelled in a number of different containers, perhaps leaving Colombia, going round Cape Horn and Ecuador before passing through the Panama Canal en route to Miami. The aim here is the same as with money laundering: to leave a trail that cannot be followed.

Large amounts of drugs are sent by air to be dropped into the sea somewhere off a favoured island in the Caribbean, where they are picked up traffickers are able to use the most sophisticated equipment, usually Global Positioning Systems or GPS purchased indirectly from the US military and stored until they can be moved to the USA, Europe or beyond. Peter Reuter (2001) says most air drops are of 250 kg or more. Using the global positioning device, the claim is that the drugs can be dropped within 6 ft of the target area. Corrupt local police will be paid to look the other way, as will others including senior politicians, who will all be paid in cocaine, and the drugs will find their way into the network as required. Air drops are probably less successful than containers as US radar is very effective in the Caribbean region.

Local fisherman using small craft are able to ship quite large quantities of drugs from Colombia to the Caribbean islands the shortest route takes about 5 days. These boats are difficult to detect by traditional radar, they are low slung and fast, and the local peons see drug transportation as more profitable than fishing. The aim is to avoid the patrols by the Royal Navy and others, especially from the USA, but, by all accounts, there is no shortage of volunteers willing to transport the drugs in what remains a hazardous exercise given the size of the boats and the distances to travel. Some go as far as Jamaica.

The fourth method of transportation is by local couriers who will transport small quantities but, given the numbers operating, will when added together produce a large total aggregate. The major aim may have less to do with the amounts transported and more to do with testing out new routes to be later evaluated by the traffickers. Tourists, too, can be effective couriers, helping to promote new routes and new markets or sustaining existing ones. Too little attention has been given to this group. Also, European nationals and former nationals returning to see relatives or coming home to Europe for other reasons, including seeking medical treatment can help to establish new networks e.g. Suriname to Holland and so on. Again this is an under-researched area that needs closer attention. Couriers, or 'mules' as they are often called, from Nigeria or Jamaica are small-scale traffickers bringing small amounts of heroin into Britain – one of the major effects being to increase the female prison population in Britain (see Chapter 9).

Traffickers tend to sell to their own ethnic or cultural groups, believing these to be the only ones to be trusted. They will sell the drugs to Jamaica but insist on transporting them. Accordingly and as expected, Spain is the major destination for trafficking from South America to Europe (Gillard, 1993), but Jamaica is a main staging post for drugs on their way to Britain, as are some Caribbean islands such as St Martin for transfer into France and Holland. St Martin (an island in the Caribbean) is owned jointly by France and Holland. There are no customs posts between the two parts of the island and no customs posts between the island and its European counterparts. Accordingly, traffickers getting their drugs into St Martin find no difficulty in getting them into France or Holland and, once there, to send them around Europe. This is another example where political systems favour the traffickers.

Numerous methods are used to conceal the drugs and to ship them to their destination. Two famous cases involved drugs packaged as fruit. In May 1999, Interpol Madrid reported the seizure of 550 kg of cannabis concealed in tins of tomatoes. This seizure was similar to that in Essex, where 2,061 kg of the drug was seized, again in tins of tomatoes (NCIS, 2000). Traffickers invariably deal in specific drugs, but some high-level dealers are more generic. For example, a Belgian national was intercepted driving a lorry importing drugs through Dover. In the lorry were 20 kg of ecstasy, 200 kg of base amphetamine, 2 kg of cocaine, 9 kg of herbal cannabis and 1 kg of cannabis resin (*ibid*.: 32). Or again, an operation in Nottingham resulted in the seizure of cannabis, amphetamine and ecstasy with a street value of £1.6 million (*ibid*.: 16). Traffickers and dealers will easily switch commodities, depending on the profits. In Britain, large numbers of drug dealers are moving into cigarette and tobacco smuggling. The profits are as good, the operational arrangements less difficult and the likely sentence if caught much less severe – an expected sentence of 3 years for multi-million pound tobacco trafficking is not uncommon, whereas for a Class A or Class B drug producing similar returns they could expect at least 10 years.

It is difficult to evaluate interdiction practices. Most of the research evidence is American (Reuter, 1988) and there are few comparable British studies. The American studies show that many traffickers are simply not sighted nor their couriers detected. Based on data relating to seizures, these studies invariably conclude that 'we do not have the data to support conclusions about how successful we are now, what impacts our efforts have, or what the situation might otherwise be' (Home Office, 1986). It seems that the systems perform well once a trafficker is detected – but, again, the data supporting this are not all that strong and many improvements are required (Reuter, 1988). Reuter (2001) notes that the US policies are heavily supply-side orientated: that is, the primary aim is to restrict the availability of illegal drugs. He notes that the federal government and other departments together spent US$35 billion annually on drug control in the year 2000, up from the US$10 billion annually of the mid-1980s (*ibid*.: 16).

The general conclusion is that seizing drugs before they enter the country has little impact on drug use within the country, unless the seizure is a monopoly seizure, as with, say, Operation Julie, which was not an overseas operation but none the less is instructive in this respect. Operation Julie closed down a large LSD manufacturing site in Britain and, as this was a monopoly supply site, it effectively stifled LSD consumption in Britain and elsewhere for many months. A likely impact of some successful interdictions is that they will affect domestic consumption and, sometimes, local drug production (Reuter, 1991). For example, production may be shifted to other sites, some local, some not. Those drugs having a direct substitute effect are likely to lead to shifts in production so that successful interdiction of heroin, for example, can lead to a growth in methadone production. It is unlikely that one successful interdiction, however large and impressive, will greatly affect consumption or price. Drug production is cheap and losses can be easily restored (Bean, 1995a). Indeed, Reuter (1991: 22) notes that whereas it would cost US$10,000 to ship one kilogram of cocaine from Bogota to Miami, a legitimate private company would charge only US$100 to ship the equivalent legal amount: 'It is hard not to attribute the differential to law enforcement.' This is, of course, one measure of the success of supply-side interdiction, as in a legal regime cocaine would sell for US$5 per g (*ibid.*).

This is not to say interdiction is a failure or that efforts should be directed elsewhere. What it means is that the best that can be expected is to disrupt and seriously interfere with trafficking so as to inconvenience the traffickers in every way possible. It also sends out an important political message that governments are not prepared to give way to trafficking and that they will devote extensive resources to that end. The expansionist model of consumption asserts that the American market is almost full, and that Britain (along with other Western European countries) provides the means by which the existing market can be expanded. Moreover, the amount of land area given over to cultivating the coca leaf in South America has increased to such an extent there is a need to look for new markets to take up the growth in supply (i.e. drug use, at least for cocaine, is supply led) (Stutman, 1989). For other drugs such as heroin or ecstasy, a different theory applies, perhaps more demand led. The expansionist model implies that trafficking to Britain will increase over the short term, which means that interdiction policies will continue to be required.

International co-operation

The methods of transportation and the means by which drugs enter national boundaries and are transported to other counties differ widely. One means by which interdiction can be improved is through international co-operation. There is evidence to suggest that some forms of international co-operation are increasing, but existing formal and informal mechanisms of co-operation need to be strengthened and developed if the investigation and prosecution of international trafficking is to be improved (House of Commons, 1990; Bruno, 1991; Anderson and de Boer, 1992; Birch, 1991; 1992). The prospects of Europe without internal frontiers, plus the need for information sharing between countries, are the driving forces for greater co-operation. Increasingly, high-level traffickers live in one country and direct operations in another, with the drugs imported and sold in the third.

As far as Britain is concerned, there are three main areas in which formal co-operation against trafficking takes place, not including the extensive co-operation between Britain and America, which continues in the Caribbean, as well as elsewhere, such as in Turkey and the Far East. Here, we are concerned mainly with formal European co-operation. There have been a number of developments in international co-operation. First there is the Schengen group. Initially this included all EC countries other than Britain, Ireland and Denmark, with Greece having observer status. The government has decided to apply for 'partial but significant' membership of the Schengen group and implementation by 2002 is expected. Secondly there was a development described by the National Criminal Intelligence Service (NCIS) as 'significant', which was the agreement of the European Convention to allow Europol to store criminal intelligence (NCIS 2000: 37). Europol has no executive or operational powers and no capabilities to gather evidence; it is an intelligence-based organisation able to offer services to operational teams in the EU (*ibid.*: 39). The UK has a designated National Unit for Europol, with four officers seconded as liason officers. Thirdly, there are the international activities, such as the International Intelligence Branch (IIB) which consists of the drugs liason officers' (DLOs) network in Europe that is based at The Hague. All are seen as contributing to the increasing international nature of drug trafficking, and the annual reports of NCIS and the National Crime Squad (NCS) are full of examples of where co-operation was successful. Nicholas Dorn (1993: 19) talks of the way attempts at co-operation are 'increasingly linked through information systems [, are] rapidly converging in their methodologies and [are becoming] more slowly harmonised in terms of their general rules'.

Yet how much co-operation actually occurs is not known. Clearly, some takes place but it is uncertain how much and it is not clear how effective it is. Attempts are made to understand the nature and extent of the barriers against promoting co-operation further. One possibility is to produce larger, centrally directed organisations leading to 'some super Europol' (Birch, 1992); another is for a more pragmatic approach that improves arrangements for co-operation between existing agencies without taking away their independence or unique role (*ibid.*). Sadly, the history of co-operation at the national and international level has not always been good, sometimes showing spectacular rivalries between agencies (the early years of the DEA and its rivalry with the FBI being the most dramatic), with gross inefficiencies in and between the international community. Policing at the international level has often been a hit and miss affair dominated by national interests that seem rarely to be transcended to allow full co-operation to occur (see particularly US General Accounting Office 1990 for a description of such rivalries). There is, it seems, rather more co-operation in Europe than elsewhere, with some evidence to suggest things are going quite well, but this still remains below what is or should be required with some European countries reluctant to provide more than token assistance.

Drug dealing in Britain

The expansionist model of drug use that sees Britain as an overflow from America promotes a view of drug dealing in Britain as having a static triangle or pyramid with a big, Mafia-type organisation sitting at the top controlling the market. Dorn *et al.* (1990: 203) conclude otherwise: 'There is no person, no Mafia, no cartel organising the market overall. Rather a large number of small organisations operate fairly autonomously of each other in a manner that may be described as disorganised crime.' Such a view has support from Peter Reuter's seminal American study (in Reuter *et al.*, 1990: 23): 'The old images of highly centralised and controlled drug distribution systems have largely disappeared in face of growing evidence of competitive violence and the failure of individual organisations to endure a dominant position.'

In a later study (2001: 18) he rather modifies this and says 'There are probably just a few hundred people with significant roles as importers. Roughly 400 tons of cocaine enter the US each year and since some criminal organisations handle 10 tons or more annually not a lot of importers are needed.' He seems to have moved closer to the point made by Johnson *et al.* (1990) who suggested that larger and more hierarchical organisations will emerge in the retail crack trade as it matures. Reuter, back in 1990 disagreed:

> Two factors make this outcome unlikely. First without the ability to buy large scale corruption from law enforcement agencies, the leader of a large organisation is at risk from his employers, any of who can turn informant. Second the erratic behaviour of so many

heavy drug users in the crack trade makes for a particularly difficult management problem: successful long term entrepreneurs are likely to be those able to select a small number of reliable subordinates (p. 24).

In Britain the notion of the large-scale trafficker operating within national frontiers has been promoted and sustained largely by the police. Organised trafficking, say Dorn *et al.* (1990: 203), has helped create a near consensus within the Association of Chief Police Officers (ACPO) that some degree of centralisation of policing was needed. Moreover: 'the function of the National Drugs Intelligence Unit, its role in piloting the broader National Criminal Intelligence Service, and the elevation of the intelligence centre over local operational teams effectively bequeathed Britain a national detective agency along the lines of America's FBI' (*ibid.*). They ask: what more is needed to promote further the myths of the big trafficker?

If there is no central control organising the market, what is there, then? The general conclusion seems to be there are large numbers of small independent organisations:

This analysis of the returns to participation in the drug trade is not much complicated by the existence of monopolistic organisations. In most cities entry into the drug selling business seems relatively easy, requiring little capital or skill beyond which is acquirable through familiarity with the trade and its members. Low level dealers are not apparently subject to systematic extortion by broad-based criminal syndicates (Reuter *et al.*, 1990: 24).

This is so for America as for Britain. Drug markets, it seems, are fluid, made up of many diverse trafficking enterprises that change their *modus operandi* over time. Of course, all are organised, if only to pursue strategies designed to make a profit, collect debts, sell the drugs and keep as far away from the enforcement agencies as possible. But that does not mean being organised in the sense of there being one overarching structure that controls trafficking in Britain.

I said in an earlier paper that there were about 4,000 people in Britain able to move quite large quantities of drugs (but not all at the same time), and about 100 gangs in London operating in the drug world as reasonably high-level dealers (Bean, 1995a). In the absence of any evidence to the contrary, I see no reason to revise these figures. This in contrast to the USA, which has about 200,00 involved in cocaine retailing, some on a part-time basis (Reuter, 2001: 18). Dorn *et al.* (1990) have produced a typology of trafficking firms within Britain, which, they suggest, may not be able to represent the fluid nature of the British drug market but which, they believe, has its merits none the less. This typology is as follows:

1. Trading charities are enterprises involving an ideological commitment to drugs with profit as a secondary motive.
2. Mutual societies involve friendship networks of user dealers who support each other and sell or exchange drugs amongst themselves.
3. Sideliners are licit business enterprises that begin to trade in drugs as a sideline.
4. Criminal diversifiers are existing criminal enterprises that diversify into drugs.
5. Opportunistic irregulars are those who get involved in a variety of activities in the irregular economy, including drugs.
6. Retail specialists are those enterprises with a manager who employs others to distribute the drugs to users.
7. State-sponsored traders are those enterprises that operate as informers and that continue to trade (see Chapter 8).

Dorn *et al*. (*ibid*.: xii–xiv) look closely at these various organisations and, *inter alia*, conclude there are many mixed cases that are difficult to classify and that, generally speaking, the more amateur trading charities have been replaced by the more overtly criminal elements. None the less, this is both an interesting and valuable typology that allows a greater understanding of the way dealing operates.

Whilst there is a considerable literature showing the links between trafficking and organised crime, this is rarely grounded in hard data. Much is by law-enforcement officials or policy analysts who base their conclusion on an examination of official documents. Almost all that literature concludes that organised crime, defined to include the Mafia, the triads, etc., is deeply involved in drug trafficking. That involvement is said to be increasing and is expected to increase further (European Community 1992).

Of late, both the Council of Europe and the EC have been saying within the framework of TREVI (Terrorism, Radicalism, Extremism and International Violence) that there is an urgent need for more action to deal with organised crime. They retain a strong belief that the interdependence of national economics has helped spawn the growth of multinational crime systems that are becoming difficult to identify and control (Martin and Romano, 1992). Moreover, as Europe has a barrier-free style single market, the spectre of criminal organisations without frontiers looms large, and the Mafia, amongst others, is thought to see a golden opportunity to extend its influence – even beyond the community to east European countries (Reuters News Agency 1993).

There is another literature linking organised crime and terrorist organisations such as the IRA (Boyce, 1987), where drug trafficking provides the money to finance these operations and the drug traffickers use the terrorists to ensure the source of their supply. The end product is social disruption (Sen, 1989). One view is that, as the financial rewards of drug trafficking increase, so will drug-related terrorist activities (Langer, 1986). Another is that terrorist links are constantly being redefined and new terrorist organisations are being developed. Interpol (ICPO Interpol 1989), for example, draws attention to developments in Africa where heroin from the Indian subcontinent, intended for Europe and North America, is being funnelled through Africa by Nigerian organisations – some of whom are African terrorists.

What remains unclear is how the traffickers and terrorists/organised crime syndicates interact. At what point do they work together and at what point do they part? Boyce (1987), for example, says there does not appear to be links between traffickers and terrorist groups within the USA – although there may be a measure of co-operation before the drugs enter the country. As mentioned earlier, Dorn *et al.* (1990) also say of Britain there is little direct organised crime linked to trafficking. In contrast, Wardlow (1988: 5) says 'eliminating terrorist links will have little impact on the flow of drugs. Drug connections are established for practical academic reasons rather than ideological ones'. There is a shortage of data on those links. If, as Dorn *et al.* (1990) suggest, drug markets are fluid, then how organised crime syndicates work with terrorist groups, both of whom may also work with local distributors is an important area for future research.

The extent of anecdotal evidence linking trafficking with organised crime is more than adequate to suggest links exist, are sustained and operate at all levels. What is less clear are the terrorist links. Terrorists avoid publicity: their world is one that thrives on secrecy, ill-informed opinion and as few contacts with law enforcement as possible. Traffickers have no great political conscience about changing the world; their aim is to change their financial position within it. Working with publicity-seeking political ideologues seems not to their liking. And yet anecdotally we are told that trafficking and dealing support terrorist organisations. If so, and there is no reason to believe otherwise given the claims made by journalists and the like, it is important to know the basis and means by which they interact and the manner in which the deals are secured. Is there a go-between and, if so, who would that be? Are contacts made direct to traffickers or are they through national dealers? These are the types of questions that need to be answered.

Money laundering

The recognition that drugs and money are but two sides of the same coin marked an important change in the way traffickers were seen and dealt with. In Britain, the Drug Trafficking Officers Act 1986, amended by the 1994 Act, introduced detailed provisions for dealing with trafficking, including the introduction of confiscation orders (i.e. based on the older process of forfeiture at depriving traffickers of the proceeds of their crime). Mrs Thatcher, addressing her remarks to traffickers, said in January 1986: 'We are after you. The pursuit will be relentless. The effort will be greater and greater until we have beaten you. The penalty will be by prosecutions. The penalty will be confiscation of everything you have ever gotten from drug smuggling' (*Parl. Debates* 21 January 1986: 273).

Laundering is defined as the concealment of illicit income and its conversion to other assets so as to disguise its source or use. Laundering for the traffickers is the process used to solve the problems of large amounts of detectable cash arising from sales, which cannot at that stage be declared to the authorities. There is an extensive literature on money laundering but much less on confiscation orders.

The legislation on money laundering is complex and full of difficult moral, jurisprudential and sociological questions. Briefly, the main legislation is the Criminal justice Act 1993, which has amended the Drug Trafficking Offences Act 1986 by inserting into that Act ss. 26(b) and (c) that define the obligations to report money laundering as well as creating a new offence of 'tipping off' money launderers who are being investigated. These create new and drastic offences. 'Tipping off' is disclosing to any other person information or any other matter that is likely to prejudice that information (Fortson, 1996). This was introduced when police officers found local bank clerks were notifying their investigations to the money launderers. As the police moved in the front door the teller went out the back and made the phone calls. Hence it is now an offence to 'tip off'.

Section 26(b) places an obligation to report money laundering. It says a person is guilty of an offence if:

(a) he knows or suspects that another person is engaged in drug money laundering,
(b) the information or other matters on which the knowledge or

suspicion is based came to the attention in the course of his trade, business, profession or employment, and,

(c) he does not disclose this information or other matter to a constable as soon as is reasonably practical after it comes to his attention.

American legislation imposes a duty on persons to report – in effect to the police – transactions and other information on the basis of suspicion held relevant to a possible contravention of the drug trafficking legislation. That for England and Wales imposes a duty to report suspicious circumstances related to money laundering, but this applies to all persons and not just to those working in financial institutions. The amount of the transactions about which those in America must report varies but, in some states is $10,000 or above.

International co-operation in relation to money laundering is becoming extensive: the 1988 UN Convention against Illicit Traffic in Narcotic Drugs and Psychotropic Substances, the 1990 Council of Europe Convention on Laundering, Search Seizure or Confiscation of the Proceeds of Crime, as well as the 1991 Council of Europe Directive on Prevention of Use of the Financial System for the Purpose of Money Laundering (Gilmore, 1991). Collaboration is seen as essential, given the movement of funds and the complex processes involved in money laundering.

Such assistance by way of formal treaty obligations is a major weapon to fight the traffickers. The Financial Action Task Force is a major step forward in this respect (FATF 1990). Article 3 of the UN Convention against Illicit Drugs (1988) requires parties to establish as criminal offences *inter alia* the international conversions or transfer of property knowingly derived from production or trafficking for the purpose of concealing or disguising the illicit origin of the property, or assisting any person involved in production to evade the legal consequences of his or her actions. Parties to the convention are required to make laundering drug money a criminal offence. However, there are European countries that have signed but still not ratified the convention, and many Caribbean countries, amongst others that have neither signed nor ratified. Nor has the EC directive on money laundering been enacted in the domestic laws of all community states. The directive requires member states to introduce a mandatory supervision-based reporting regime applicable to all credit and financial institutions (see Gallagher, 1990).

The problems about co-operation in the money-laundering field are not dissimilar to those relating to policing. One view is that co-operation is largely cosmetic, another is that it is in its early stages and is developing slowly (FATF 1990). As far as providing information is concerned, one of the most important innovations in EC co-operation is the development of the commission's European Monitoring Centre for Drugs and Addiction (EMCDA). This body has comprehensive documents relating to laundering, involving the powers of the council, the commission, the European Parliament and the courts of justice, which involve official discretions, decisions and even the written questions that were asked (European Community 1993). One of the major problems relating to co-operation at the international level is that money laundering is international in scope. As the EC noted: 'Internationalism of economies and financial services are opportunities which are seized by money launderers to carry out their criminal activities, since the origin of these funds can be better disguised in an international context' (EC *Explanatory Memorandum* I (i) Document E, Chapter IV (ii), p. 243). The EC (through the Financial Action Task Force) goes on to say, in respect of the problems of co-operation, that:

> Many of the current difficulties in international co-operation in drug money laundering cases are directly or indirectly linked with a strict application of bank secrecy rules with the fact that in many countries money laundering is today not an offence and with insufficiencies in multilateral co-operation and legal assistance (*ibid*.: Document B, Chapter 1, p. 14).

This second quotation sums up the major difficulties but, even so, substantial progress has been achieved in a relatively short period of time. Gilmore (1992: xix) argues that 'it is no exaggeration to say that in the area of drug related money laundering the landscape of international co-operation has been radically and positively transformed'.

Others would be less optimistic, pointing to the reluctance of some countries to comply (*ibid*.). By way of illustration, Levi and Osofsky (1995: 40–41), speaking of the British police, say their relationships with HM Customs are far from smooth for, among other things, they have different priorities. Customs are concerned with seizures, the police with developing informers. Herein lies the seat of the difficulty, for if co-operation cannot easily take place within national borders, it is even less likely to take place across national borders.

There are a number of bibliographies that include the major national and international declarations, and one of the best is that provided by Gilmore (1992). Similarly, there are a number of collections describing the methods and nature of money laundering and the practical ways in which money launderers could be defeated (Gallagher, 1990). Apart from international and national co-operation, Parlour (1994) who also includes a review of useful handbooks on the subject suggests that the methods that seem to be recommended include the following:

1. More staff training to make staff aware of the nature and importance of money laundering.
2. The importance of staff knowing their customers and their customers' backgrounds.

There are also extensive bibliographies on money laundering – the United Nations in Vienna has one of the best of these.

A great deal of the literature is descriptive, setting out the ways in which money launderers operate and the environments in which they flourish. These include poor-quality exchange controls, bank secrecy laws, unregulated casinos and money-changing bureaux, and offshore financial services that, when combined with minimal disclosure requirements, provide a highly facilitating environment. There are also the beginnings of another literature on the role of the civil courts and what the civil courts could do to trace and recover laundered money, especially where banks are involved in involuntary laundering and the money needs to be traced (Birks, 1995).

The money launder is faced with one central question: how to return the money to the owners of the drugs in a currency they can use. Or if not, how to invest it in countries and forms that will produce a safe (i.e. will not be confiscated) legitimate return. Drug trafficking is cash intensive and, increasingly, governments aim to confiscate that cash. How best to launder is the aim of all launderers. Typically, money laundering goes through three processes. These are called placement which also involves smurfing, layering and integration, although in practice there is overlap and the processes are far from discrete.

Placement

Placement is the initial stage in the process. It involves placing the cash into the major financial institutions of the selected economy. There may (and often is) an even earlier stage where the money is taken out of one country to be placed in another, but this does not affect the main point that the launderer is seeking to place large quantities of cash into the retail economy. The placement stage for the launder is the weakest link in the money-laundering chain and is the point where detection is most likely. Where (as in the USA) there are limits to the amounts of monies that can be deposited in a bank for a single deposit, 'smurfers' make deposits ($1 below the legal limit allowed) in various different banks. A 'smurfer', therefore, is someone who conducts financial transactions in sums below the threshold amounts. (In one interesting case a smurfer was caught with a number of caches of monies to be deposited. He told the police, correctly, that the monies did not belong to him. When the police compounded the monies, the smurfer wisely asked for a receipt. He would have to convince his immediate superiors he had not kept the monies himself.)

There are numerous ways in which placements can occur, some more sophisticated than others. The most obvious involves using a form of bank structure that produces bank deposits in such a form as to evade the threshold currency-reporting laws. This may involve making numerous deposits in many different banks before bringing them all together in one central bank account. The easiest as far as the launderer is concerned is to place all deposits in one bank with the complicity of a corrupt employee, who will accept the deposit without question or, better still, find a bank whose ethos is corrupt. Alternatively, the launderer could buy into the securities and commodities markets, again with the help of insider traders. Or he or she might purchase large expensive items for cash (such as precious metals, precious stones, works of art, boats or property) or play the casinos in the expectation of winning legitimate money. All these activities are the early stages of a paper trail aimed at disguising the true source of ownership.

Layering

Layering involves separating the illegal proceeds from the source by creating complex layers of financial transactions designed to disguise the audit trail. Once layered into the financial system, detection becomes increasingly difficult. The favoured method is to convert cash into monetary instruments (such as money orders, bonds and stocks) and then move them elsewhere. This allows the use of electronic funds transfers – probably the most important element in the layering process as they offer the advantage of speed, distance and increasing anonymity – to move the instruments anywhere in the world. Deposits of cash may be similarly converted into material assets, which can then be sold or exported and the proceeds held in another form.

Integration

Integration is the final stage in a process where the aim has been to create a paper trail that is increasingly impossible to follow. The methods used will involve the most sophisticated forms of financial transactions, usually through 'shell' companies that trade but that have been set up for the purpose of acting as front companies and where the launderer may even pay tax using bank cheques drawn on the company account. Shell companies may also be used, say, to buy and sell property that eventually leads to a sale which appears to legitimise the company's funds. False import and export invoices will be used in other transactions where documents overvalue the transactions. Most of all, were the launderers to get the help of a bank with secrecy laws able to protect the launderer, this bank would be the focal point of all transactions.

These are but a small number of examples of what has become a highly specialised form of criminality yet they demonstrate the range of money-laundering activities undertaken. The destructive nature of money laundering shows itself whenever a small company is taken over by the launderers and converted to their aims. So imagine a small company is trading as a boatyard, making, selling and repairing boats. This is bought by the launderers and listed as one of their companies. It then has a slow but increasing amount of laundered cash passed through its books and, on the face of it, appears to be a wealthy company growing at an exponential rate. But in fact the lifeblood of the company has been drained away and it becomes nothing more than a route of convenience for vast sums of laundered money produced elsewhere. Here is where the impact of money laundering is important; it might not be economically destructive in the whole scheme of things (it is just one company after all), but multiply this a number of times, especially in third-world countries, and it becomes a different matter. The means by which laundering distorts economic activity is beginning to be well understood; the difficulty is to persuade key organisations such as banks and professional organisations to co-operate.

Whilst the methods involved in laundering are interesting in themselves, the implications of attempts to control money laundering are sometimes forgotten. The study by Mike Levi (1991) is a notable exception. Levi analysed the development of police–bank relationships, principally in the UK but also elsewhere within the context of money laundering. He found that we have moved from a situation of national control over bank secrecy to an emerging new international order in which most, though not all, countries are pressurised into taking greater measures to reduce bank secrecy where money laundering is suspected. In Europe, banks are being turned into an arm of the state by being required to keep detailed records and to inform the police where they suspect, or even where they ought to suspect, that monies banked are the proceeds of crime. It is difficult not to conclude there is a surfeit of material on how to deal with money laundering and a shortage of material such as that given by Levi on the implications. In our eagerness to defeat the traffickers we sometimes forget that changes are being introduced, the implications of which have not been fully realised.

Confiscation orders

The literature on confiscation orders is slim by comparison, yet claiming and recovering the proceeds of drug dealing are as important as developing strategies for dealing with money laundering. Surprisingly, confiscation orders have received little attention from philosophers of punishment (Levi and Osofsky, 1995), yet the justification for confiscation is often cited as a way of compensating society for behaviour that is socially unacceptable (Mitchell *et al.*, 1992; Bin-Salama, 1996).

If conversations with high-level drug dealers are anything to go by, the confiscation order is what they fear the most. They say they can do the 'time' even if this amounts to a long sentence of 8 years or more. What they dislike the most, however, is when their families have to leave their leafy, wooded, five-bedroomed suburban houses and their children taken from private schools and sent to comprehensive schools, with their families living in local authority accommodation. If that is so (and it is said too often to suggest otherwise), we need to pay more attention to the powers and impact of confiscation orders and to use them more vigorously.

However, important issues are raised by the legislation on confiscation orders, some of which are jurisprudential but others of which are more directly related to social science. Critics of compensation orders point to the dangers of allowing courts to seize property, without what is referred to as the 'due process of law' for, in this case, the courts have considerable discretionary powers in the making of an order (Levi and Osofsky, 1995). The social science questions are more about the impact of this legislation on the drug dealers, and about the way in which the property is collected. For example, there is a wide discrepancy between the assets restrained by the court and the amount collected. Under the Criminal Justice Act 1988 the total assets restrained as of 31 December 1994 were £9,258,742.00, but the assets confiscated amounted only to £527,419.00. Or, again, under the Drug Trafficking Act 1994, the total assets restrained as of 31 December 1995 were £3,815,707.75 but the assets confiscated were only £795,451.74 (data from government confiscation statistics, 1995). However, recently there has been a considerable improvement. The figures for 2000 in England and Wales show that 334 prosecutions were made against 550 defendants. The total assets recovered on which there are restraining orders amounted to £15.5 million, whilst during that year assets totalling £10.0 million were collected.

The Drug Trafficking Act 1994 and the Criminal Justice Act 1988 govern the legislation. These give law enforcement the authority to investigate and the Drug Trafficking Offences Act 1994 gives them the tools to do so (the Proceeds of Crime Act 1995 slightly amends the investigative process). The Central Confiscation Bureau, part of the Crown Prosecution Service (CPS) operates the system and, once an order is made, the CPS hands details over to the local financial investigation officer (usually a detective constable), whose task it is to collect the assets. One of the reasons there has been an improvement is that these financial investigation officers are better trained than hitherto; earlier, the task was given to a police constable who was told to 'get on with it' (Bin-Salama, 1996). There is still the problem of motivating the police to be more enthusiastic. The CPS loses interest once they pass the information over to the police, and the police see asset collection as another burden placed upon them. There would be an even greater incentive if the police in Britain were allowed to use the money collected for law enforcement and research purposes, as happens in America. None the less, the improvement in assets seized is encouraging as it means things are moving in the right direction.

Chapter 7

Policing drug markets

Figures 7.1–7.3 provide data on the drugs seized by the police (including those by HM Customs & Excise). Figure 7.1 gives the number and weight of seizures of heroin in the decade 1988–98. It shows that these have risen dramatically but that the quantities seized have remained steady. Presumably this reflects a much greater effort by the police, who are operating with increased levels of efficiency – including better international co-operation. However, the amounts seized provide the more interesting statistic; they almost certainly reflect a method of trafficking

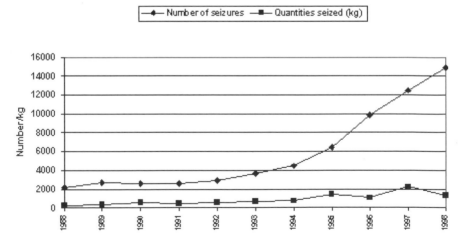

Figure 7.1 Number and weight of seizures involving heroin, UK, 1988–98
Source: *Home Office Seizures and Offenders Bulletin* and Corkery, 1999.

heroin (involving relatively small amounts of the drug) which starts in Afghanistan, moves through Pakistan to Turkey and then into Britain. It is likely the amounts involved will always be smaller than for trafficking in cocaine.

Figure 7.2 gives data for the UK in terms of seizures per million of the population. It is difficult to know how to interpret these data except to point out that Cornwall, Wales, much of south Scotland, Norfolk and Humberside along with London have the highest rates, which presumably has more to do with where the drugs were seized and less to do with where they were destined for – except, of course, London where seizures and destination are probably the same.

Figure 7.3 is interesting. It illustrates drug seizures in the UK for the decade 1988–98. It shows that over 80% of all seizures are for cannabis. On the face of it, this is an extraordinary amount, suggesting that cannabis is the priority for the police and that law enforcement is geared up to cannabis prosecutions. Figure 7.3 also shows that cannabis seizures follow or are part of the same pattern of seizures for all other drugs, the inference being that cannabis is linked in some way to the same enforcement programme, directly or otherwise.

There are, of course, alternative interpretations. It seems highly unlikely the cannabis prosecutions represent anything more than serendipity on behalf of the police. Almost all these cannabis seizures are likely to occur when an offender is arrested and taken to the police station and required to turn out his or her pockets. Cannabis is then discovered and the offender is charged with a possession offence, perhaps alongside other offences or, if not, the possession offence is the most obvious and easy one on which to secure a conviction. The second point is in the form of a question: what are the police doing all this time if the annual seizures of non-cannabis drugs are so few? What of the drug squads and the specialist units? What do they do? Are they, as John Grieve suggests, so busy collecting intelligence and having more than they can usefully handle, they do little else? (pers. comm.) Or is something additional happening that is not apparent from these data? The data show that cannabis accounted for 113,818 seizures in 1998 out of a total of 149,907 and in terms of offenders, cannabis accounted for 113,232 out of a total of 127,919. Either way the data give an interesting window on British policing.

Policing policy

In so far as there is, or ever has been, a policy for policing drug use in

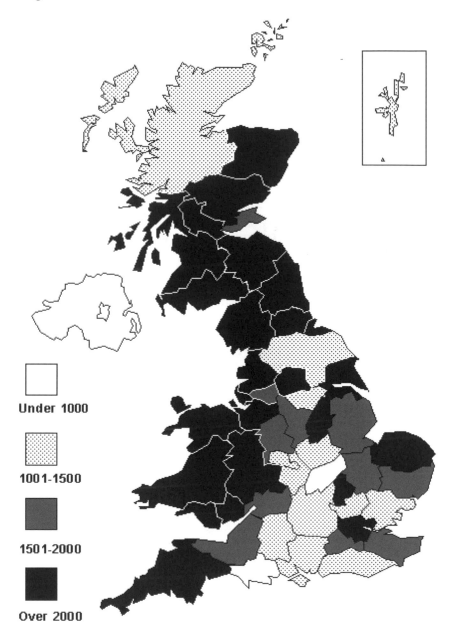

Figure 7.2 Seizures per million population, UK, 1998
Source: Corkery, 1999.

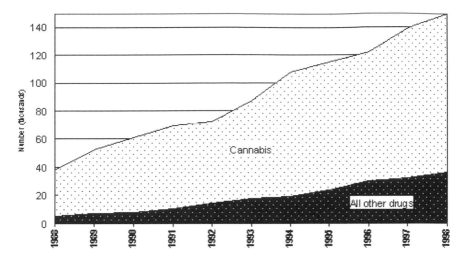

Figure 7.3 All seizures compared with seizures of cannabis, UK, 1988–98
Source: Corkery, 1999.

Britain, that policy was derived from the *Broome Report* of 1985 (ACPO 1985). That report set out the structure for tackling the supply and distribution of drugs. There was to be a three-tier strategy:

1. Regional crime squads were to address major distributions and operations at a national (and sometimes international) level.
2. Force drug squads were to target middle-level dealers and were to co-ordinate the force's intelligence on drugs.
3. Divisional-level officers would encounter drug suppliers and users in the normal course of their duties.

The Advisory Council on the Misuse of Drugs (ACMD 1994) noted that, within the Broome structure, the police were responsible for deciding how drug misuse and trafficking should best be tackled, presumably within force areas and according to local conditions. At the upper level, the police (working alongside HM Customs) would be concerned with international crime, the international trafficker and the high-level national dealer. Middle-level enforcement, according to Broome, was to be directed at the organisation responsible for trafficking within national boundaries (in the British case, this would be by the drug squads). Lower-level enforcement would be by uniformed street patrol officers. While the drug squads would be concerned with getting the so-called 'Mr Bigs', the lower-level patrol officers would be concerned with street dealers. The

ACMD (*ibid*.: 12) also noted that concerted action, other than at the upper level, was regarded as relatively unimportant.

The Broome strategy was based on the belief that drug markets operated according to a model derived from a police officer's view of the structure and importance of policing (i.e. allowing the most important traffickers to be dealt with by the most important police officers, the less important with the less important police and so on). Clearly, the model was flawed in that there was no evidence traffickers worked that way but, worse than that, it had a detrimental impact on the drug problem in Britain during its critical formative years. Street drug markets were allowed to develop and grow and, once established, were difficult to remove. The Broome model has now been discarded but not before much damage was done. It has been replaced by other models that direct attention at the low-level street markets, for these are where the drugs are sold to the consumer and where novices are recruited, whether as users or dealers.

Drug markets generally

Drug markets have certain common features. Irrespective of the size or location of the market, drugs are bought and sold like all other commodities; in that sense there is nothing unique or special about drugs. There are, of course, differences. Unlike most other commodities, drug markets are characterised by a high degree of immeasurable risk, by the inability to enforce contracts in a court of law and by the poor information about the product (Rydell *et al.*, 1996). Nevertheless they are markets with buyers and sellers and, as with other markets, subject to basic economic laws of supply and demand.

Within these markets, dealers have to secure financial transactions in a crooked world with no one else to enforce contracts. They are always vulnerable to theft and violence by greedy business associates. Protecting their transactions takes up most of their time (Bean, 1995a). Most will find it necessary to employ those who are familiar with intimidation and violence or, if not, make themselves comfortable with violence which they use to collect debts and to enforce discipline. In Britain, Dorn *et al.* (1990) describe how a new breed of criminal was attracted to the drugs world where violence was an essential part of their worldview. Whether this really was a new breed or simply an old breed with a previous history of violence attracted by the possibility of a share in the increasingly extensive profits is not known. Whatever the reason, the overall effect is to make drug markets violent places where those working in them become more frightened of other dealers than of the police. They operate in a Hobbesian world where no rules or guidelines exist, except those made by themselves to serve their own interests. The problem is that, once initiated into this world, it becomes difficult for them to accept any other.

The lack of skills required to enter as an entrepreneur and the ease of transportation of the high-profit commodity are likely to be some of the attractions. In broad outline, the drug market, like all other markets, works on credit that is, the beginner is granted credit at a certain level of interest and expected to pay back the debt within a given period of time. Failure to do so will mean certain punishment. Within this general framework there will be considerable variations in terms of the social class of the sellers, the venue and the range of credit facilities. However, the demand for repayment does not vary, and nor do the punishments for those who default.

Higher-level dealers are increasingly involved with, or are part of, organised crime. In Britain, these involve the traditional organised crime syndicates but increasingly include others bound up with ethnic or local groups. For example, Turkish organised crime syndicates (who also control the major distribution networks in the kebab houses) increasingly dominate the heroin trade in Britain. They have links with British nationals of Turkish origin. These organisations are difficult to penetrate as they remain part of a close-knit community trading only with others of the same nationality and background. The National Criminal Intelligence Service (NCIS) has a Turkish Intelligence Unit to combat heroin trafficking; this provides a co-ordination point for intelligence related to Turkish heroin trafficking in and outside the UK (NCIS 2000: 25). Triads and Mafia-type organisations are well represented amongst the high-level dealers so that, in August 1999, the Cocaine Intelligence Unit was formed by NCIS to provide an overview of cocaine trafficking in the UK (*ibid.*: 26).

There are few data on the links between these higher-level dealers and those on the streets. In America they talk of 'kingpins' – senior local dealers who presumably make that connection. Research is needed in Britain to establish those links, where it is suspected there will be marked variations between drugs and organisations. For example, Turkish importers may also be the distributors, controlling the market at all stages. In contrast, the cocaine importers may not be concerned with distribution and may hand this over to local 'kingpins.' But this is all speculation; we simply do not know.

At the lower levels, dealing will differ again according to the drug, although some dealers are polydealers willing and able to sell anything.

Cannabis is typically bought and sold from individuals who come from a broad range of backgrounds and from a wide variety of settings, from inner-city areas to middle-class institutions. Dealing tends to cover a wide range of socioeconomic groups, as it does for ecstasy, where consumption is more typically at raves or clubs (i.e. where the drugs are taken by teenagers who may be occasional rather than heavy users). Heroin, on the other hand, is very much a street drug although, as with all others, the situation changes daily so that what is typical for today is highly unusual for tomorrow. Even so, at the lowest end of the market, heroin will be bought and sold by users for whom the sale is less important as a method of generating cash than as a source for personal use. Here, the typical street seller is a user who buys an amount and uses a quantity of it before selling the surplus to others. Next day, he or she may well buy back that surplus, paying more for it than he or she sold it. At the higher end, the dealer will not be a user.

Cocaine sales differ again. Unlike heroin there is a substantial middle-class demand for the drug – the income from these users funded from largely legitimate sources. The prevalence of cocaine use is growing whereas heroin use remains more static, even if its use increases in fits and starts. Like cannabis, cocaine is bought and sold in a variety of social settings. For example, cocaine creates a demand from some who may use relatively large quantities (*ibid.*: 17). Wealthy experienced users purchase relatively large amounts in discreet transactions, usually in London (Bean, 1995a), whilst new, relatively poor users operate at street level. Cocaine has become deeply embedded into a black ethnic cultural group where its effects on the black community have been destructive. Cocaine is not, of course, confined to the black group: white users vastly outnumber black users but, from our research, its impact on the black community was seen as particularly destructive (*ibid.*).

Cocaine is usually, but not exclusively, bought and sold where poverty and other social problems are common and, in this sense, has much in common heroin. In America, Inciardi and Pottieger (1995) found that street-level cocaine dealers were deeply involved in crime – in fact, the greater the level of crack distribution the greater the level of other crime commission (*ibid.*). They concluded (*ibid.*: 253) that 'young crack dealers commonly violate not merely drug laws but also those protecting persons and property; and the crack business appears criminogenic in ways that go beyond any potential it may have as a lure into crime'. This study in Miami shows crack dealers as a separate and distinct group from heroin dealers; it is not certain whether this applies to Britain.

Drug markets are wide and involve more than simply those who buy and sell drugs. They extend into the local community where others benefit. Rarely do the major profits remain locally. Once drug markets become organised the profits are taken out of the area. None the less, some money is circulated locally and it is this that helps sustain the local drug community. In our research (Bean, 1994), we found that one of the reasons some of the local population did not oppose the drug (cocaine) market was that it helped prop up a poor inner-city area. Derelict premises were let out to rent for use by prostitutes, poor-quality fast-food outlets remained open all hours, etc. However, the majority of the local population benefit only marginally, if at all, and any disadvantages greatly outweigh the advantages i.e. where there is harassment from prostitutes, litter of the very worst kind and street-level dealers operating in front of young children. Drug markets are not pleasant places to have in one's neighbourhood. If and when a closer examination is made of the extent of the tentacles of drug markets, we may find they are even more embedded into the local economy than we thought. If so, we ought not be surprised; after all, at the macro level, drug money extends into all aspects of some national economies, so why not at the micro level too?

The impact of policing

Policing aimed at taking out the 'Mr Bigs' has been a major part of the strategy of law enforcement. It fits easily into the traditional notion of policing as 'chase and capture.' It was the dominant philosophy of the *Broome Report* where the best police would chase and capture the best criminals, the less competent would chase and capture the less competent and the least competent police the least competent criminals. This type of strategy flourishes because capturing the 'Mr Bigs' also fits with the demands of police performance indicators, which are aimed at achieving targets based on a number of arrests. They deem it to be more worthy to arrest a dealer than to prevent a number of potential users from making a purchase.

The problem is that, when caught, the Mr Bigs are quickly replaced by other Mr Bigs waiting to take over, or the captured Mr Bigs run the operations from prison. Targeting Mr Big has less impact than the police would have us believe. In a major project the King's Cross project, a number of 'Mr Bigs' were arrested. It was noted how quickly they were replaced and how little time it took for levels of dealing to return to the same levels as before. Arresting key offenders may satisfy the requirements of justice but does little to ease the drug problem, whether by assisting neighbourhood protection or reducing the amounts of drugs or numbers of drug users in the vicinity. Kleiman and Smith (1990: 84) ask: 'what essential service does Mr. Big provide to the retail dealer that someone else will not supply just as well if he is made to disappear?' Their answer is that the basic financial and personnel management skills to run a drugs operation are not in short supply, no long apprenticeships are required and new organisations can quickly take up any supply shortage created by the loss of one Mr Big (*ibid.*: 83).

To make inroads into drug markets we need greater investigative capabilities than are being used, including greater co-ordination between the investigators. The challenge may be technical but it is also about style and attitude: it is about using intelligence and combining this with high-quality research on the effectiveness of police operations. It is a salutary reminder that little research is available on the effectiveness of policing – except, of course, that related to partnerships and even that is small and directed at one or two high-profile operations. One of the few British studies was conducted by Webster *et al.* (2001) and was undertaken at the request of the Metropolitan Police on their 'Operation Crackdown' (directed mainly at crack houses in the London Metropolitan District). It concluded that the impact on local drug markets appears to be limited; there was little discernible added difficulty in obtaining Class A drugs and no change in the local price. The authors go on to say: 'Several street markets were disrupted although in some cases for a relatively short period of time. Although over 80 crack houses were disrupted our best guess is that most relocated or re-opened at the same premises within a very short period of time, weeks rather than months' (*ibid.*: ii). Perhaps a better way to start is to begin by asking: what is policing trying to achieve?

Kleiman and Smith (1990: 71) say there are four main objectives to policing:

1. Limiting the number of persons who use various illicit drugs and the damage suffered as a result (psychological, physical, moral, etc.).
2. Reducing the violence connected with drug dealing and the property and violent crimes committed by users, whether to obtain money for drugs or as a result of that intoxication.
3. Preventing the growth of stable, wealthy, powerful criminal organisations.
4. Protecting the civility of neighbourhoods and, thus, their attractiveness as places to work and live (hence making them free of the disorder caused by drug dealing, open or otherwise).

To achieve these aims, various types of police operations have been made available. Three will be examined here: street sweeping, focused crackdowns and disruption, with or without partnerships. This is not the complete list (undercover work is not included and, of course, the use of informers remains central to all policing, which is dealt with in the following chapter). None the less, these are the major models. They are not, however, mutually exclusive: modern police tactics may involve all these at some stage or at various points of an operation and/or any mixture of these, plus the use of undercover operations, etc.

Street sweeping

Street sweeping involves what it says: a massive police presence concentrating on a specific area, ideally operating 24 hours per day. Normally, drug dealers tend not to work the same hours as most police – they work different hours from patrol police officers. This may seem to be such an obvious point as not to be worth making, but Kleiman and Smith (1990) say it is surprising how many police authorities apparently do not notice this. Street sweeping is similar to zero tolerance in that, whilst the streets are being swept, all suspects are scooped into the net. Large numbers are stopped and searched and all laws, however small and insignificant, are enforced, with search warrants to deal with premises in which the police suspect there is drug dealing. Street sweeping, according to Kleiman and Smith (*ibid.*), serves all the four goals of law enforcement in that it reduces drug use, reduces crime, weakens drug-dealing organisations and protects neighbourhoods.

It is, of course, not without its weaknesses. Street sweeping closely resembles an army of occupation rather than policing by consent. Street-sweeping policing produces tensions on the streets, is expensive (police forces have to work within budgets) and raises ethical questions about being too concerned with 'victims' rather than those who are responsible for maintaining the vitality of drug markets (Dorn and Murji, 1992). Tensions may arise as a result of stop and search, about which there has been increasing criticism, especially following the MacPherson report on the death of Steven Laurence. Stop and search is often seen as having less to do with policing and more to do with asserting a form of dominance over a local population or over a specific group in that population. Street sweeping produces an enormous number of arrests, many for minor offences. However, the gains it may achieve from reducing the size of the drug market will be offset by resentment from an otherwise law-abiding population that is caught up in street sweeping and prosecuted for minor offences. The police are as likely to be accused of harassment as to be thanked for their efforts. And the drug market will likely reappear when a period of street sweeping ends.

Focused crackdowns

Focused crackdowns differ from street sweeping in that they concentrate on specific drugs, on specific streets or on specific features of the market, such as crack houses or clubs and pubs. Kleiman and Smith (1990: 89) say that eliminating drug dealing in one infested neighbourhood (thus creating an area where people feel safe) may be more valuable than reducing drug activity by 10% in each of ten drug-infested neighbourhoods. They see focused crackdowns as providing the ideal strategy where the police move slowly from neighbourhood to neighbourhood, leaving behind vigilant citizens and residual markets small enough to be controlled with minimal enforcement efforts (*ibid.*). Focused crackdowns could concentrate on a small area. In Nottingham, for example, there are two main areas where drug markets flourish. These could be dealt with by a focused crackdown, or the police could concentrate on one drug crack (no pun intended!), which is sold in a different part of the drug market and by different dealers or, perhaps, on ecstasy, which, again, is sold in a different part of the city. Focused crackdowns are likely to have stronger public support than street sweeping because the police are seen to be tackling a particular problem and a particular group rather than including everyone in their net. A focused crackdown on an area of Nottingham in the autumn of 2000 that had been plagued by firearms was given considerable public and media support and the police, after they arrested a number of dealers who had firearms, were applauded by the residents for their efforts. 'Operation Crackdown' in the London Metropolitan District was an example of a focused crackdown.

Like street sweeping, focused crackdowns are not without their problems. Dealers are likely to reappear when the crackdown is over, for they know that crackdowns do not last for ever. For them, keeping a low profile during this period is likely to be productive. Alternatively, displacement may occur, when the dealers move elsewhere – again until the heat is off. Police departments have limited resources and there are other areas of a city to cover. This is a matter of attrition for the dealers and for others who wait until the police leave before they emerge. However, Webster *et al.* (2001) saw a positive side to this. It had an impact on community safety and, in particular, on local residents. They cite a drug agency manager as saying: 'Since the implementation of Crackdown the initiative has been widely endorsed by the community. [To] a large extent Operation Crackdown is beginning to restore confidence in the police.'

Disruption or low-level policing

Disruption (or low-level policing) is about policing street dealers and markets. The *Broome Report* (ACPO 1985) wanted this lowest level to be policed by officers who encountered drug misusers in the normal course of their duties – that is to say, by ordinary beat officers with little or no experience of drug dealing. This was never likely to be successful; dealing may take place on the street but the dealers rarely carry the drugs with them leaving it to the 'stashers' and 'runners' to make the delivery. Nor does it make the best use of one of the police's main weapons – to make life more difficult for the would-be buyers and sellers. As one chief constable said: 'The policeman's biggest weapon is inconvenience, not arresting people. Some people call it harassing. But there is no way we could do our job without occasionally having to inconvenience people. If it's just to stop and ask questions that's an inconvenience' (cited in Dorn and Murji, 1992: 163).

Low-level policing aims at creating 'inconvenience' by disrupting drug markets. Unless dealers and sellers are disrupted, drug markets become difficult to dislodge and, once embedded, push the local community deeper into that world of drugs. Years after Broome there is a growing recognition that street-level policing is important and has merits in its own right. The Association of Chief Police Officers' (ACPO) drugs subcommittee, in its response to the ACMD report (1994), talk of a 'bottoms up' approach that, presumably, means concentrating more resources to identify low-level dealers and traffickers. Dorn and Murji (1992: 169), in an evaluation of street-level policing, say:

> At its most positive street [low-level policing] could be an area which holds the key not to simply the ways of reducing the extent of drug trafficking and use, but also to the quality of life of many people whose daily lives are affected by the spread of drug sellers and drug users in their neighbourhoods.

Low-level policing is about making drug dealers aware of a police presence. From my own experience, dealers are more frightened of other dealers than of the police, for they rarely see the police. If low-level policing means moving dealers to a different site – displacing them – then so be it. This is an advance. It means the new site is likely to be second best as far as the dealers were concerned otherwise they would have selected it as their favoured site, and it means it will take time to re-establish contacts. Dealing is also about creating an atmosphere of trust, which means trust in the security of the deal as well as the quality of the drug. Low-level policing helps destroy that trust and makes the drug market less secure for those operating within it. The weakness of the *Broome Report* is that it was too keen to chase and capture the Mr Bigs.

Another advantage of low-level policing is that it helps keep away the novice and casual user. If the drug market is unsafe and the point at which drugs are sold is the most vulnerable for the dealer, uncertainty will be created, and uncertainty works against the dealer. Novices expect to be guaranteed their protection, and markets that are always on the move convey a measure of insecurity that makes life difficult for the dealers. No one is suggesting that these measures solve the problem but that they offer a more coherent approach than chasing high-level dealers, busting them and then chasing their replacements. Low-level policing provides an opportunity to frustrate dealers, which, in turn, puts up the costs of drugs by forcing them to incur additional overheads. It also makes their dealing more furtive and therefore less satisfying to the customer. A uniformed police presence, posted strategically in the middle of the drug market, may be all that is required, which, incidentally, is also likely to act as a reassuring sign to the local population that something is being done.

Street-level policing, at its best, would include the partnership approach. This would involve local agencies, representatives of the local community including local government and the media (the media can, incidentally, build or quickly destroy attempts at producing partnerships). Street-level policing involving partnerships is one of the most important developments in the move against drug markets and crime. Where they exist, they have been shown to be successful (Home Office 1993). They challenge basic assumptions derived from the professionals' traditional view that an agency – usually their own – can have an impact on crime. In contrast, joint agency working is the key: the partnership model challenges the assumption that a single agency approach has an impact. The police can no more deal with drug dealing by arresting the dealers, others quickly take their place than can the probation service by providing counselling. The way forward can only be by drawing all interested parties together although, for practical purposes, the police must always have a major input (*ibid.*).

There is little doubt that, in the development of partnerships, there exists a potent weapon against local drug markets. Partnerships, which received legal impetus from the Crime and Disorder Act 1997, remain underdeveloped and under-researched. The Home Office (*ibid.*: 1) puts it this way:

Many of the measures that contribute to prevention are not within the remit of any one agency. Prevention thus depends on action by many different agencies and this will be most effective when co-ordinated by a formal partnership. Such partnerships can share and

mobilise resources, generate commitment and enable the contribution of individual agencies to be targeted to best effect. They
are most successful when served by one or more dedicated staff
skilled in developing proposals and implementing action.

There is clearly a need to develop the partnership approach and a need to
evaluate the partnerships that are being undertaken. The difficulties are
immense: getting the partnerships going, agreeing on a common
approach and, above all, deciding when the project is to be ended. The
starting point must be a shared agenda involving a common understanding of the philosophies underlying the work of different agencies.
For example, the police's experience and perception of drug users may
not correspond to that of the local residents or traders. The police are
always concerned with Mr Big and the residents with the low-level drug
sellers. Moreover, probation officers see a conflict of interest between
their wish to rehabilitate offenders and the public desire to move drug
users out of the area. It is this lack of fit between the agencies that creates
the most difficulties.

Critics of partnerships always point to the way partnerships displace
drug dealing to new geographical areas and also question the levels of
community safety during and after the project. They question, too, the
value of the changes that can be made to the nature of drug markets as a
result of the partnership approach. These criticisms are predictable;
whenever a crime-reduction project is claimed to be successful there will
always be critics who raise the question of displacement. That should not
detract from the message that the partnership approach, where it has
been properly implemented, is a potent weapon against drug markets,
showing there is nothing inevitable about drug markets, that they can be
controlled and that something can be done about them.

The King's Cross project (the results of which are largely unpublished)
is a beacon of its kind. There, the local-community drug markets were
seen as disturbing and distasteful, bringing crime usually prostitution
and littering the streets with discarded syringes. King's Cross is an area in
London where large populations pass through each day. It is also
characterised by a vigorous local population who demanded action. The
result was a programme that began with the simple but somewhat
radical assumption that a partnership approach was called for, and that
no single agency could deal with the problem on its own. Community
responses demanded a co-ordinated effort between various bodies,
leading to a partnership defined as 'an association between a number of
individuals groups or agencies to pursue a common goal' (Lightfoot,
1994).

Briefly, the King's Cross project involved the police, the local authority although, in fact, there were four local authorities butting into King's Cross, a representative of the local community and voluntary associations. The police had the largest presence but they soon found the local authorities had more powers. The local authorities could close down hotels, move bus shelters where dealers were hiding to make the sell and close all-night fast-food outlets. However, the biggest problem was to get agreement about policies, about which way to move forward and about how to represent the interests of the local population. The tactic was to decide on a strategy, make the move, arrest all the major dealers (say), and then watch to see how long it took to replace them. Alternatively it was to arrest the non-drug-taking daytime prostitutes and then measure the local reaction; then move to the next strategic point and evaluate that; and so on. The result was a highly successful project – albeit an expensive one where major lessons were learnt, one of which was for police officers to accept that a good day did not mean a 'bust' of a main dealer but that success meant dealers were not able to sell their drugs.

Low-level policing meets the four criteria listed above in that it limits the number of people using drugs, reduces the violence in drug markets, prevents the growth of stable criminal organisations and protects the civility of the neighbourhood. Or at least these were the results from King's Cross. The problem is that these conclusions are based on one project that may not be typical and it may not be possible to replicate it. We need more projects of this type and more evaluations to show how best to proceed.

Assessing the effectiveness of policing

In principle the right way to choose a drug policy for a city would be to describe the problem, invent some alternative approaches to addressing the problem, predict the costs and the likely results of each approach, and choose the least painful. Then after a while measure the results and compare them with the predictions. Unexpected results or new situations would call for changes in policy (Kleiman and Smith, 1990: 102).

So wrote Kleiman and Smith, adding that no police force has anything resembling an accurate description of the drug problem and that there is no well worked out body of theory or history of experience to allow predictions of the likely results of alternative approaches. The best that can be done is to have as many data as possible available on users, sellers and dealers, right down to street level. Then and only then can a measure be made of the impact of enforcement.

Webster *et al.* (2001: ii), in their evaluation of Operation Crackdown and, having said that disruption was minimal, go on to say that:

> The main reason for the lack of disruption to local drug markets appears quite simply to be the growing scale of demand for and supply of heroin and crack cocaine in particular. The very high profits that can be made from selling drugs means that there appears to be no shortage of people wishing to become involved. It seems that socially excluded often young people in particular are willing to take considerable risks in return for profit.

In Britain, economists such as Maynard and Wagstaff (Wagstaff and Maynard, 1988; Wagstaff, 1989) have asked important questions: about the prices at each level of the illicit drugs market, about the operation of these markets and about the extent and costs of the resources the enforcement agencies devote to drug work. Studies building on this type of research, perhaps involving more participant observation, would be needed; the more sophisticated approach comes later. Peter Reuter *et al.* (1990: 20) put it this way: 'That drug markets vary a great deal across drugs and over time points to the need for a theory of how these markets function – in particular a theory of what determines who enters the market and how much such persons earn for participation.'

Reuter and Kleiman (1986) talk of a theory based on risks, when risks affect prices. We do not know, for example, how many successful deals are completed and the risks dealers carry. It is likely that about one deal in every 80 or 100 leads to an arrest, and this irrespective of the type of drug sold. If that is so, what effect has it on dealers and prices if one in 40 deals led to an arrest, or one in 20, or even one in 10? How much extra policing would be required to change the ratio of successful deals, and would the costs be worth it? What are the effects of putting dealers in prison? Typically, the answer has been not much, yet Peter Reuter (2001) says that, paradoxically, the effect on reducing demand may be greater than on reducing supply, if only because 'It's hard to replace old junkies' who consume quite large quantities of drugs.

We have learnt much from the Broome days, which typified what Kleiman and Smith (1990: 104) refer to in another context as a collection of activities in search of a strategy. Recent developments in London show that the metropolitan police have learnt the value of disruption and of low-level policing. There police distribute leaflets to householders giving details of the latest arrests, and explain to all their tactics and the nature and extent of local policing strategies. The aim is to unsettle the dealers and not to allow them to take the initiative. This is called 'policing by disruption' and, as a tactic, is to be preferred to sitting back and allowing the dealers to set the pace. It is a long way from the data-driven policies of Kleiman and Smith but is a move in the right direction. The next chapter examines another police strategy (that of the use of informers) to see to what extent this is effective.

Policing professional organisations

There are many ways in which professional organisations police their members. The most obvious is where the organisation or professional body requires its members to conform to certain professional standards. Failure to meet those standards can result in erasure from the register of that professional organisation and the corresponding loss of all rights and privileges registration confers. Another method is where the government demands of professional bodies that they require members to accord to certain practices it may, from time to time, stipulate.

The first of these is the more common. For example, the General Medical Council will discipline members who take such substances as morphine or who have an alcohol problem. Where those physicians prescribe for themselves or their families, or over-prescribe for their patients, they may be referred to the Professional Conduct Committee of the General Medical Council who may decide to erase them or 'strike them off the register'. The activities of these physicians though important, especially in the manner in which medical practice is viewed in Britain do not in the scheme of things greatly affect the drug problem – although over-prescribing must always be a matter of concern. Of greater importance as far as policing is concerned is the second of those matters, which relates to government directions to the professional bodies.

Under the money-laundering regulations, financial institutions including professional financial operations such as in law and accountancy are required to disclose to the police and, eventually, to the Economic Crime Unit (ECU) of the National Criminal Intelligence Service (NCIS), all transactions suspected of being involved in drug trafficking. English legislation imposes a duty to report suspicious circumstances relating to money laundering and this applies to all persons, not just to those working in financial institutions. These data are analysed by NCIS and disseminated to relevant financial investigation units. In practice this means each police authority will be required to act on the information provided, although how and to what extent priority is given to this information is another matter. Nevertheless, although there is a duty on all persons to give the required information, in practice, those at the forefront will be the professionals, lawyers accountants, etc.

Traffickers, in addition to using the latest technology, also use and can afford to use the most highly paid lawyers, accountants, bankers, etc., to provide them with the appropriate expertise. These professionals give the traffickers financial advice relating to investments and setting up shell companies, etc. They also help traffickers avoid detection (US Department of Treasury 1992). Money laundering and all that is associated with it is almost wholly dependent on these professional advisers. Professional privilege and confidentially help sustain and support the activities of these professionals, with little interference, if any, from the appropriate professional bodies – or so it seems from the official figures.

Recruitment of these professionals into the world of trafficking seems fairly common or, if not, then sufficient to continue to service the drug trade. Like so much else in the field, one can only speculate on matters: there is little or no research evidence to draw upon. Recruitment of these experts is probably achieved when an able lawyer or accountant finds his or her business failing or is unable to provide for his or her own expensive lifestyle. This sort of professional becomes an easy target and, as with corrupt police officers, once recruited are unlikely to break free – at least until they cease to be of value to those who recruited them. It probably costs the traffickers and dealers little to recruit such people: a one-off payment to remove existing debts and a foreign holiday might perhaps be sufficient. The traffickers would, of course, still pay for subsequent professional services undertaken but their rewards would, none the less, be huge. As noted in the 1992 US Treasury Department report on money laundering: 'among law enforcement representatives, there was almost universal presumption that traffickers and cartel money launderers can usually afford to hire the best lawyers, accountants, etc., an advantage which provides them with additional sources of expertise' (para. 1002: 291). Or as the former US Attorney General, Meese, said: 'It takes a professional – lawyer, an accountant, a banker with all the trappings of respectability – to manipulate these sophisticated schemes' (cited in Beare, 1995).

'Manipulation' in this context means the creation and implementation of these schemes, as well as defending the suspects when charged. Beare and Schneider (1990) list some of the services provided by these professionals:

- Providing a nominee function.
- Incorporating companies.
- Conducting commercial and financial transactions.
- Managing and physically handling illicit cash.
- Co-ordinating international transactions.
- Buying and selling property.

The special privileges granted to lawyers, seen as necessary to protect the lawyer–client relationship, act as a shield and barrier against them when they engage in a variety of criminal actions (*ibid*.: 331). This is less so for accountants and bankers but even these professions have jealously guarded their client relationships, and attempts to intrude have met with resistance by the governing bodies. In the USA, lawyers are required to notify the Revenue Service about their clients; this was vigorously resisted, being seen as a step towards greater outside regulation of the profession – which, incidentally, the lawyers claimed violated their attorney–client privileges. The US President's Commission on Organised Crime asked for more 'stings' and electronic devices to break through further that otherwise impenetrable shield.

In comparison, professionals in Britain have escaped lightly. The major professions involved (law and accountancy) have successfully avoided outside regulation and, clearly, want to keep it that way. The British government sees the solution as lying within the professions' own governing bodies: the Law Society, the Institute of Chartered Accountants and the like. These bodies have considerable powers and could exert considerable influence. In Canada, the Canadian Law Society have been particularly active in this respect and are a beacon when it comes to assisting with money-laundering regulations. In contrast, their British counterparts have been reluctant to assist, and the lawyers and accountants co-operate rather less than they ought, at least if Table 7.1 is anything to go by where, over the years, the numbers of disclosures by lawyers and accountants have been rather small.

The NCIS report for 1999–2000 shows the extent of financial disclosures over the 5 years 1995 to 1999 (NCIS 2000). In 1999, the Economic Crime Unit (ECU) of NCIS received about 14,500 reports of suspicious transactions. As shown in Table 7.1, the banks provided the most, accounting for about half of all financial disclosures in 1999, with rather more in 1995 – but this seems a rather odd year, when the amount rose to nearly 63%. The NCIS report states there was a disparity between the numbers of UK authorised banks, the usual high-street banks and the number of banking institutions making disclosures. In 1999, only 125 deposit-takers reported suspicious transactions to NCIS out of a possible

Table 7.1 Disclosures by financial sector, 1995–99 (%)

Financial sector	1995	1996	1997	1998	1999
Banks	62.84	48.40	49.5	44.05	49.91
Building societies	18.95	28.67	20.7	20.49	12.61
Bureaux	4.48	6.96	17.5	19.09	20.79
Insurance	4.57	3.03	3.7	4.50	4.11
Solicitors	1.53	2.03	1.9	1.97	1.77
IFA	1.27	2.54	3.8	3.39	2.01
Credit institutions	1.53	2.03	1.9	1.97	1.77
Gaming/betting	None	1.11	0.7	1.53	2.42
Accountants	0.31	0.51	0.3	0.74	0.58
Regulators	0.13	0.23	0.2	0.21	0.25
Others	5.46	6.59	1.7	4.02	4.43
Auction houses	None	None	None	None	0.25
Asset management	None	None	None	None	0.19
Credit cards	None	None	None	None	0.12
Securities	None	None	None	None	0.56

Source: NCIS, 2000.

554 regulated firms. Furthermore, 78% of all disclosures from the banks were made by ten institutions. This represents 39% of all disclosures received by the ECU. NCIS (*ibid.*: 21) notes that 'although high street banks might be expected to be more frequently targeted by criminals to launder their proceeds, it remains a concern that some banks make few, if any suspicious transaction reports'.

Solicitors and accountants produced few disclosures. Taken together, they only amount to 2.35% for 1999 – 1.77% for solicitors and 0.58% for accountants. NCIS (*ibid.*:) says:

> The ECU continued to work with accountants and solicitors to raise the level and quality of financial disclosures that are received. Although the Unit is starting to see some signs of improvement in the quality of disclosures in this area the numbers received remain low. Education within these sectors will continue to remain a priority for the forthcoming year.

NCIS might be sanguine about the outcome and the likely beneficial effect of education as a means by which the numbers and quality of disclosures will be improved, but the history of professional regulation, especially when it is seen as restricting professional freedoms, suggests it will be an uphill struggle. Professions do not like this type of pressure placed on them and resist attempts at self-regulation when this involves acting against their short-term self-interests. Neither do they want to be seen as acting as a sort of state control system. At present they have a moral duty, say, to report a cheque fraud. Imposing a legal duty on them to report suspicious financial transactions takes them one step further along the road to becoming law-enforcement agencies. Money laundering substitutes a legal for a moral duty, and this they find burdensome.

One wonders how long the professions can continue to use such a tactic. The estimates from the G7 countries are that the drugs trade generates more than the GDP of any European country, with about £73 billion going through the world's banking system each year. We could reasonably assume that much of this goes through important financial centres such as the City of London. We could also reasonably assume we have already reached the stage where there has been permanent damage to some of our social and financial institutions. Perhaps it is this that will finally persuade governments to tackle the problem. As things stand, law-enforcement organisations such as NCIS have their own financial services departments or internal organisations that investigate financial irregularities without waiting for the professional organisations to take the lead. They can and often do secure authority to examine a company's books and to seize in order to inspect any assets that may be relevant. The NCIS annual report (*ibid.*) lists some spectacular successes in this respect and, however successful this may be, it will only be a poor substitute for what might be were the professions more accommodating.

The tribunals

There is another sense in which the professions are policed, but this applies only to the medical profession and is through the tribunal system. Tribunals have a long history, going back at least to 1926 and to the *Rolleston Report* (for a discussion on tribunals, see Bean, 1991a). The current position is that tribunals were established under the Misuse of Drugs Act 1971 and were supplemented by regulations under the Drugs Tribunal Rules 1974. Briefly, the powers of the tribunals under s. 13 of the 1971 Act are concerned with irresponsible prescribing, where physicians who prescribe irresponsibly may lose their licence to prescribe. As there are links with the General Medical Council (GMC), this type of pre-scribing will almost certainly be brought before the Professional Conduct Committee where such physicians will be charged with serious professional misconduct. This carries the maximum penalty of being erased or struck off the medical register.

The process begins as a result of routine monitoring by the Home Office Drugs Inspectorate, which has noticed irregular or the over-prescribing of certain drugs. This is followed by a visit from the drugs inspectorate. About 300 physicians are visited each year. These advisory visits usually have an immediate effect as about 90% of the physicians bring their prescribing down to acceptable levels. For the 10% (or 30 individuals or so) who do not, the next step involves an official written warning they may be taken before a tribunal. This tends to reduce that number of 30 physicians to about six or seven. At this point the Home Office will have clear evidence of irresponsible prescribing – prescriptions will have been analysed and patterns determined. These six or seven physicians will then be brought before a tribunal. They may be legally represented but, by then, their number will have been reduced to about three as the others will have asked for their names be taken off the medical register prior to the hearing. Tribunals can only proceed against registered practitioners. Under the regulations, those remaining physicians will almost certainly be given directions from the Home Office (i.e. have their future prescribing severely restricted, as well as having to go before the GMC).

Critics say the system is too protracted, with a built-in bias towards the professional physician. Moreover, these critics say the whole system is conducted in a gentlemanly way typical of assessments of middle-class deviants but quite different from the way we deal with those from the lower classes. These criticisms apart, tribunals raise other questions surrounding the right of physicians with little or no experience of drug users being permitted to prescribe at all. This applies equally to such drugs as Valium as to heroin. It is not just the gross over-prescriber we should worry about; rather, it is those physicians who prescribe more than they ought and who prescribe when there is no good reason to do so we should be concerned about. And this includes drugs such as Prozac – the long-term effects of which are still not known.

Chapter 8

Informers and corruption

Informers are not unique to the world of drugs and trafficking but their activities throw up new questions and put others into greater relief. Definitions of informers vary. The US Drug Enforcement Agency (DEA 1982: 55) defines informers as 'any non-law enforcement person who supplies information about criminal activities to a police officer'. In Britain, the Regulation of Investigatory Powers Act 2000 (henceforth RIPA) includes informers as a 'covert human intelligence source' (henceforth CHIS), defined as someone who establishes or maintains a personal or other relationship with another for the covert purpose of:

- using that relationship to obtain information or to provide another person with access to that information; or
- disclosing information obtained by the use of that relationship or as a consequence of that relationship.

A CHIS might be an informer, an agent or an undercover operator. Here we are concerned only with the informer (and not with the so-called 'public-spirited informer' who gives information, usually on a one-off basis and who does not seek a financial reward). It is the professional informer who is of interest here, who either seeks financial rewards or a reduction in sentence in exchange for information about other offenders. The *Codes of Practice on Informant Use* (published in May 1999) define an informer thus:

> an individual whose very existence and identity the law enforce-ment agencies judge it essential to keep confidential and who is

giving information about persons associated with criminal activity or public disorder. Such an individual will typically have a criminal history, habits or associates and will be giving the information freely whether or not in the expectation of a reward, financial or otherwise (para. 1.14.1).

And a participating informer is defined (*ibid.*: para. 1.14.2) as: 'An informant who is, with the approval of a designated authorising officer, permitted to participate in crime which others already intend to commit.' The first definition places emphasis on the need to protect the informer's identity as well as noting that this type of informer will usually be someone who is or was an active criminal, and who has been given approval to commit a specific crime in specific circumstances in order that others are convicted. Within the world of drugs, the participating informer is particularly useful, as possession and supply are victimless crimes with no 'victim' to make a complaint.

At a time when policing claims to be increasingly intelligence led, the value of informers cannot be doubted. Yet informers operate in that murky world where accusation and counter-accusation are common-place, and where mistrust and deceit are the tools of the trade. John Grieve (1992) says, after years of experience as a police officer dealing with drug offenders and informers generally, he can only conclude that the drug scene is imbued with treachery. He believes there are more informers in the drug field, in aggregate and proportionate terms, than in any other area of crime. The problem for the police, according to Grieve, is how to stem the flow of information, not to acquire it, and how to use that information appropriately. Yet how do we deal with the informer who is prepared to deceive those who are his or her colleagues? And what will he or she do to those who are not his or her colleagues? Here I want to look closely at the special problem of informers in relation to the drugs field. I also look at corruption and informers, as corruption and drugs are closely linked.

Traditionally, the police have been reluctant to talk about informers. They fear that disclosing their methods and secrets will jeopardise operations. The obvious response is that outsiders do not want to know the details or have access to confidential material, but they are entitled to know that the methods fit basic legal requirements, are cost effective and are appropriate to basic standards of justice. Moreover, the more the police try to hide their activities, the more will the rest of us be suspicious and think they are up to no good. Too often the police seem to take pride in their secrets, believing this adds to that aura of being special. Giving secrets away takes away some of the mystery. It also shows up failures.

There has until recently been no guidance on how to handle informers – experience was seen to be the best way to learn. This led to some spectacular successes but to some equally disastrous failures. Under the RIPA, new procedures have been introduced aimed at reducing the risks, and matched by a new sense of openness. Both are welcome and would have not occurred a decade ago.

The legal authority for informers

As noted above, until recently there was no formal framework for the regulation of informers, although legal decisions created precedents for their use and conduct. The introduction of the Human Rights Act 1998 changed that with its demands (under Article 8 of the European Convention on Human Rights) that law enforcement be examined from the viewpoint of the citizen. Article 8, which asserts the 'right to private and family life', has led to a radical rethink of the situation. The UK government's response has been to produce a formal legal instrument to meet the demands of the Human Rights Act that allows informers to be retained. The RIPA was rushed through Parliament in time to beat the Human Rights Acts in October 2000 (Neyroud and Beckley, 2001). Informers by their very nature violate their subjects' 'reasonable expectations of privacy' (Article 8 of the European Convention on Human Rights), so that when through a deceptive relationship an informer covertly uses that relationship to obtain information or covertly discloses information obtained through that relationship this is an infringement of the subject's rights (Neyroud and Beckley, 2001: 166).

The RIPA provides the police with a legal framework that allows them to use informers. Informers in the RIPA are not defined on the basis of the evidence they provide but on what they do. They are called a 'covert human intelligence source' (CHIS), which places them alongside other covert operations such as undercover policing. The RIPA permits informers to operate under certain basic conditions. These are as follows:

1. *Subsidiarity.* The means of investigation should cause the minimum interference with the privacy and rights of the individual.
2. *Compulsion.* The outcome can only be achieved by the use of a specific registered source.
3. *Accountability.* The use of a registered source must be in accordance with the proper systems of accountability.
4. *Legality.* The investigatory method must not be unlawful.

5. *Proportionality*. The use of a registered source must be commensurate with the seriousness of the offence.

Points 1 and 2 are relatively straightforward. Subsidiarity means that minimum interference is required, which extends to collateral intrusion (i.e. that the privacy of other persons is also considered). Compulsion means an informer must be a registered source. The third point, accountability, has far-reaching consequences. It requires the introduction of an administrative system whereby the police must introduce checks and supervision of the informers and their handlers. The basic principles are supervision and control, which mean *inter alia* that an informer is not the property of one police officer but a resource deployed for the benefit of the law-enforcement agency to which the informer reports. Point 4 is straightforward, but point 5 on proportionality requires consideration to be given to any adverse impact on the community (including the confidence of the community) which may arise as a result of the use of an informer. In practice this means a risk assessment must be made at certain key stages of the investigation, including an assessment of the overall impact of the operation. When the risk is too great, the operation must be stopped.

For the first time in Britain, formal recognition is given to the use of informers; formal procedures are to be implemented for their use and conduct, and the RIPA requires informers and handlers to comply with existing legislation. This means informers are supervised and controlled more closely than hitherto and some of the risks are removed, whether to the police, the informer or the community. No system can completely eliminate risks, and dealing with informers is always going to require skill, care, integrity and, above all, being able to anticipate the dangers, but the RIPA tries to reduce those risks as far as possible. Informers are by definition a risky business.

Protecting the informer

Protecting the informer's identity has always been paramount and must remain so. The legal authority for this is found in *Swinney & Another* v. *Chief Constable of the Northumbria Police 1999* where it was held there was a duty of care owed by the police to take reasonable care to avoid unnecessary disclosure of information an informer had given to the police. The claim was in respect of information given by a witness about a murder enquiry but which found its way into the hands of one of the suspects, resulting in threats and harassment to the witness. It was also held in an earlier case (*Hill*) that 'The public interest will not accept that good citizens should be expected to entrust information to the police without also expecting that they are entrusting their safety to the police'. Failure to provide that protection will not only compromise the informer but also deter witnesses and others from coming forward. This duty of care exists at all stages of the informers contacts with the police. It is particularly important during the trial where there is extensive pressure to disclose the informer's identity.

The police can point to legal authority involving the granting of public interest immunity (PII), which allows them to seek from the court the right not to disclose the informer's identity nor their methods of work. These legal authorities for PII stem from three important cases: first, *Attorney General* v. *Briant 1846*; secondly, *Marks* v. *Beyfus 1890*; and, thirdly, *Hallett* v. *Others 1986*.

In the first (*Attorney General* v. *Briant 1846*) it was held that 'a witness cannot be asked such questions as will disclose the informer if he be a third person, ... and we think the principle of the rule applies to the case where a witness is asked if he himself is an Informer'. In the second (*Marks* v. *Beyfus 1890*) the judge went beyond the 1846 decision and reaffirmed that the Director of Public Prosecutions is entitled to refuse to disclose the names from whom he has received information and the nature of information received. He said:

> I do not say it is a rule which can never be departed from; if upon the trial of the defendant the Judge is of the opinion that the disclosure of the name of the informant is necessary to show the prisoner's innocence, the one public policy is in conflict with another public policy, and that which says an innocent man is not to be condemned when his innocence can be proved is the policy that must prevail.

This judgment reaffirmed the earlier rulings found above. More recently in *Hallett* v. *Others* (1986), the judge said disclosing the identity of an informer to the defence is not required unless it is necessary to avoid a miscarriage of justice. The appellants appealed against their conviction for importing and being in possession of cocaine from Germany as to the court's ruling that the identity of the informer should not be disclosed to the defence.

These rulings began to be challenged by the defence claiming that protecting the identity of informers produces injustices for their clients. They asserted that an accused has the right to know and cross-examine those making the accusations. In *R.* v. *Turnball 1976* and *R.* v. *Taylor 1994*, the judgments tipped the balance back towards the defence. In *Turnball* the court ruled the identity of the informer should be revealed if it was relevant to the defence case, and added that verbatim records of the PII applications should be made available to the Court of Appeal. In the second (*Taylor*), the judge ruled that a defendant in a criminal trial has a fundamental right to see and know the identity of his or her accusers, including witnesses for the prosecution, and this right should only be denied in rare and exceptional circumstances.

There the matter rests, at least for the present, except that in *R. v. Agar* the court held that if a defence was manifestly frivolous and doomed to failure, a trial judge might conclude it must be sacrificed to the general public interest. Occasionally the defence had become involved in what were called 'fishing expeditions' aimed at identifying whether or not an informer was involved. In *Agar* the defendant appealed against his conviction for possession with intent to supply after he was arrested in a trap set by the police and an informer. The judge refused to allow details of the trap to be put to the jury. However, the judge said that, if there was a tenable defence, the rule of public policy protecting the informer was outweighed by the stronger public interest in allowing a defendant to put forward a case.

The point at which the balance is struck is always going to be difficult for it must meet the needs of the prosecution witnesses and the fairness of the trial. The pendulum is likely to swing back and forth as one judgment follows the other, the first in favour of the prosecution only to be reversed in favour of the defence. The informer's safety has to be set against the rights of the defendant.

Included, too, is the safety of witnesses, who are not informers (at least in the sense defined here), and who need guarantees of safety – otherwise they will not come forward. Informers whose identity is compromised may require witness protection (Bean, 2001a). Every major trafficking operation involves an informer; for some, a witness protection scheme will be required. For how long and in what form (i.e. whether the family will need to be relocated with a new identity in another country or whether a short-term programme would be sufficient) depend on a number of matters, including the nature of the criminal organisation. It is said triads and yardies have long memories. Not all on witness protection are informers, and not all informers require witness protection – but witness protection is for those who need it and it encourages others to come forward to give information. Schemes must operate according to the highest standards of secrecy for, in the world of drugs and crime, violence is all too common and informers know they pay heavily for the information provided to the police, even if sometimes that leads to a reduction in their sentence.

Reducing the sentence

The value of informers is well recognised – by none other than the Lord Chief Justice:

> For many years it has been well recognised that the detection of crime was assisted by the use of information given to the police by members of the public. Those numbers might be either professional informers who gave information regularly in the expectation of financial or other reward, or public spirited citizens who wished to see the guilty punished for their offences. It was in the public interest that nothing should be done which was likely to encourage persons of either class from coming forward (*R. v. Rankine 1986*).

Not only that but, as Lord Justice Bingham said, there were rewards too, particularly when it comes to drug traffickers and dealers:

> It was particularly important that persons concerned with the importation of drugs into the UK should be encouraged by the sentencing policy of the Courts to give information to the police. An immediate confession of guilt, coupled with considerable assistance to police could therefore be marked by a substantial reduction in what would otherwise be a proper sentence (*R. v. Afzal*, reported in *The Times* 14 October 1989).

In this case, a sentence of 7½ years was reduced to 6 years. There was not, however, an expectation for a reduction in sentence just because the offender was an informer. Reductions had to be related to Index offences. In *Regina v. Preston and McAlery* (reported in *The Times* 14 December 1987), Mr Justice Farqarlarson in the Court of Appeal said that:

> What the courts should not take into account therefore as a result of this judgement is evidence of information given by an accused person which does not relate to the crime of which he now stands. The proper course to be taken was that where information is given by an accused person which does not relate to the crime of which he is charged then that is a matter which the authorities can properly take into account, but it is not a matter for the Court to consider in mitigation of the sentence passed.

Information to the court is given in what is called a 'text'. The text sets out any assistance given by an informer and details about how the informer was recruited. Here, *R.* v. *Taylor* is relevant where the defence claimed it had the right to know the nature of the text and, of course, the name of the informer. In an important judgment (*R.* v. *Piggott 1994*), the court held that it was no longer a matter of discretion by the police as to whether an informant text was issued. The defendant has the right to have all relevant information put before the court in mitigation.

In so far as a reduction in the sentence was possible, claims by the defendant had to be supported by the police. In *R.* v. *X 1999* it was held that a defendant's unsupported assertions were not likely to make any difference to the sentence. The courts had to rely on the completeness and accuracy of the report, and the greatest of care had to be taken in the preparation and presentation of such a text.

Informers: who are they, and how to control them?

There are many classifications of informers' motives (see Billingsley, 2001b), but there is probably as wide a range of motives as there are informers. Motives are likely to include revenge, pressure from the police, an active enjoyment of the role, the associated power that comes from being an informer and fear of a heavy sentence. Those involved in drug dealing are likely to seek ways to eliminate competition and, of course, what better way to do so than through informing? Financial inducements (mainly small at about £30 for information leading to a conviction and paid only after a successful arrest) are clearly not sufficient, although of course some receive much more where the information leads to the arrest of major traffickers and dealers. Street-level dealers will be concerned with more local, mundane problems, in which case something else must drive them along and this is usually the protection and extension of their drug markets. This is what makes them dangerous.

Dunnighan (1992) provides one of the few pieces of information on the type of people who become informers. In a survey of detectives and their informers in one police force area, he found the typical informer to be male, under the age of 30, unemployed and with previous convictions (also, incidentally, the typical criminal). Dunnighan (*ibid.*) also noted that about 30% of all informers will be drug users who will also inform on a wide variety of crimes other than drug use. A more detailed study by Roger Billingsley (2001b) largely confirms these findings. He found that most informers were male, young and with criminal convictions, and over half were unemployed. Women informers constituted about 20% of his population of informers; there are no national figures on the gender ratio (Nemitz, 2001b: 99).

Controlling these informers is now a much more ordered affair. Informers are allowed to operate only if they are registered and act according to defined procedures. Handlers must be trained and all contacts with the informers recorded; where payments are made to the informer, another handler must be present. Procedures are tight, largely as a result of some catastrophic blunders when informers were out of control.

Of the different types of informer described earlier in this chapter, it is the participating informer who creates the most problems, whether it be for the handler, the controller or the court – the more so in the drugs field as participating informers must know a great deal about the crimes of which they inform. The problem for the police is that the participating informer is also the most useful for he or she 'goes beyond mere observation and report' (Grieve, 1992). Or, put differently, the informer needs to be 'dirty' to be useful, which, in the drugs field, means continuing to act as a trafficker or dealer where the more the informer is involved in drug dealing, the more valuable will be the information.

The problem is to decide the appropriate level at which participation should be permitted. In *R. v. Birtles 1969* it was ruled that the police are entitled to make use of information concerning an offence already 'laid on' (i.e. to be committed in any event) with a view to mitigating the consequences of the proposed offence (e.g. to protect the proposed victim). It may be perfectly proper for the police to encourage the informer to take part in the offence, but the police must never use an informer to encourage another to commit an offence he or she would not otherwise commit.

Victimless crime is difficult to detect by conventional methods. Informers are therefore central to police operations and, of course, these informers will know more about dealing if they are part of that network. This means they must continue to deal, sometimes in ways that might be 'laid on' and sometimes not. The central dilemma is how to obtain information, control the informer and yet allow the participating informer the necessary leeway to continue.

In the murky world of informers, how difficult is it to know where the truth starts and ends? Some dealers claim they have a 'licence to deal' from the police, and those who do not claim they know others who have a licence. These so-called 'licences' are said to be given to informers who, in return for information, enjoy a favoured relationship with the police. The police, somewhat naturally, deny they issue 'licences' but 'licences' are mentioned so often as to suspect they do, at least in some form or another.

Moreover, some dealers will say informers are able to learn about police methods and operations, thereby having an unfair advantage. In fact, some say they are placed there by higher-level dealers for that purpose. Other dealers say they take advantage of the informer's licence and use their houses to sell their own drugs, believing the informers had been granted some form of immunity. Where such claims exist and are true, the police have lost control; the informers are able to dictate their terms and the police are left to accept what is given to them. Once control has been lost it is difficult to regain it and, with a loss of control, there is also a loss of respect.

The introduction of new procedures and an emphasis on 'tasking' (i.e. requiring the informer to provide information about what the police want to know and not what the informer is prepared to give) have helped to change the ethos. Tasking produces greater control; it requires the informer to act under instructions and not to operate as a free-floating agent able to produce information the informer thinks fit to give. Those informers not producing the tasked information are deregistered, which increases their vulnerability and makes them less able to receive protected status.

Informers and drug dealing

All drug markets have informers – the police would not be able to operate without them, and are clearly grateful that informers are numerous and generous with their information. Yet how effective is the informer system, and are informers in the drug world likely to have a different impact on the overall level of drug offending from those informing in other types of criminality? Might it be that the use of informers makes the drug problem worse, when it would not, say, make armed robbery worse? (Billingsley, 2001).

As a general rule we can assume that, whenever dealers provide systematic information on other dealers operating at the same level or above, those informers are extending their own dealer networks. Their aim is to extend their networks to the point where they, as dealers, are increasingly difficult to prosecute, for they will then operate at an organisational level, rarely being in possession of the drugs. Understandably, the informer system makes some people uneasy. For example, Goldstein (1960, cited in Billingsley *et al.*, 2001b) gives three reasons to be wary of informers. First, he says police hesitancy to implicate informers encourages others to commit crime. Secondly he believes informers are encouraged by the police to continue to commit crime, this being especially damaging to those in the early stages of their criminal careers. Thirdly, he sees the practice of using informers as leading to widespread disrespect for the criminal law. Others doubt their effectiveness. They believe informers rarely penetrate to the high levels of trafficking organisations, this only being achieved by undercover police officers. They also believe informers increase the level of narcotic crime by making accusations against low-level dealers in order to eliminate them. This they see as particularly damaging to young offenders and others equally naïve about drug dealing because it brings them into the court system with all the deleterious impact court appearances have (*ibid.*, cited in Bean, 2001b: 30).

These arguments must be taken seriously. Goldstein (among others) believes informers rarely reach the upper levels, for organised crime can be stopped only through extensive police work using undercover agents. Other critics point to the number of crimes committed by participating informers and note they inform for their own benefit rather than for that of the police. They believe that leaving horizontal informers in the system leads to trouble, which is likely to increase levels of crime rather than reduce it (*ibid.*).

In response to Goldstein and others, we may say that whilst informers may not always be able to penetrate to the highest parts of the organisation, the undercover operator often needs the assistance of the informer as a means to gain entry. In fact, working alongside undercover operators might turn out to be the best combination, where the one assists the other. At street level it may be true that informers make things worse, but the solution is not to cease using them but to impose more stringent controls. At upper levels things may be different, but each case presents the opportunity of leading to deeper levels of penetration in the criminal organisation. The aim is to move beyond horizontal prosecution – the so-called 'sidewalk-level dealers' – to vertical prosecution that reaches higher-level dealers and meaningful levels of crime.

We must wait for research to help answer some of these questions but, in the mean time, we should welcome the changes introduced to establish greater measures of control over informers and the efforts made to offset some of the earlier criticisms. At the moment, however, we must expect the numbers of informers to increase, especially in the drugs field, and we should be aware that however distasteful we may find the actions of informers, the police and the courts recognise them as a necessary evil.

The special case of juveniles

We may find it distasteful for juveniles (i.e. those under 18 years of age) to become informers but many choose to do so and some choose to inform on their friends and family, including their parents. Juvenile informers come in various forms. For example, a juvenile may give information on a school friend who has enticed away her boyfriend. This is likely to be a one-off piece of information and relatively innocuous in the overall scheme of things. Alternatively, it may be the case a parent is a burglar or a relatively important local drug dealer, in which instance the information will be of greater interest to the police. Motives will vary; it may be spite, as in the case of the young girl who has lost her boyfriend, or it may be to earn money to purchase drugs, in the case of the young person informing on his or her family. Or it may be prompted by a wish to be rid of a parent or guardian who may be persistently violent to the family. Alternatively, as Teresa Nemitz (2001b) shows, informers, especially women informers, might give information as a way of protecting themselves and their family against domestic violence; children will do likewise.

The police will be reluctant to ignore this information, especially if it comes from a source they think is reliable. Moreover, if they are to make an impact on the high rates of drug use amongst young people, they must inevitably seek information from those familiar with that world – and that means informers of the same age. The question is not about whether juveniles should be accepted as informers (although some police forces do not accept them) – the question is how to regulate their use in ways which make it more ethically acceptable.

Under the RIPA, a statutory instrument (2000, no. 2793) was laid before Parliament on 16 October 2000 and came into force on 6 November 2000. Briefly, this instrument regulates the use of juvenile informers under the age of 18 and provides special regulatory powers for those under the age of 16. In line with the language of the Act, informers are referred to as a 'source' or CHIS. For informers under the age of 18, the instrument says that a risk assessment must be made at the time the source is authorised, and the risk assessment must be by a police officer of superintendent rank. Under para. 5 (ii), that risk assessment must demonstrate that the 'nature and magnitude of any risk of psychological distress to the source arising in the course of, or as a result of, carrying out the conduct described in the authorisation have been identified and evaluated'. The risks must be justified and properly explained to the source.

For the juvenile under the age of 16, no authorisation for the conduct and use of the source may be granted if (1) the source is under the age of

16; and (2) the relationship to which the conduct or use would relate is between the source and his or her parent or any person who has parental responsibility for him or her (para. 3). Informers under the age of 16 may be authorised (i.e. registered) but an appropriate adult is required to attend any meetings with the superintendent, and an appropriate adult means a parent or guardian, any other person currently responsible for the juvenile's welfare or any other responsible person aged 18 or over.

These regulations do not stop the police from taking note of the juvenile's information against family members. What they say is that the juvenile will not be authorised (i.e. registered). In practice, however, this means they cannot proceed. For example, assume they take notice of the child and arrest the father for burglary. If the defence asks about the basis of the information that led to the arrest, the police will have to disclose their source. The defence will then say, rightly the investigation was unlawful. That of itself is bad enough but without registration the juvenile is not given the formal protection of a duty of care (as provided by *Swinney & Another* v. *Chief Constable of the Northumbria Police* (1999)), although it would be reasonable to suppose that all juveniles would receive a duty of care from the police under any circumstances. A likely outcome, then, is the juvenile will supply the information as before but the police will not act on it. It would be unreasonable to expect them to ignore it so they may seek other ways to circumvent these regulations. Paradoxically, in order to protect the juvenile, these regulations may have the opposite effect. As noted above, sometimes that information is given to secure the juvenile's own (or other family member's) protection.

The regulations for juveniles generally (i.e. whether under 16 or not) are about providing information against those outside the family. They require a senior police officer to be present and an appropriate adult. The definition of an appropriate adult is that taken from the Police and Criminal Evidence Act (PACE). This is hardly satisfactory, including as it does 'any responsible person over the age of 18 years'. One would think some reference should be given to the suitability of the person to act as an appropriate adult: suitable in the sense of knowing what to do or say, how to respect confidentiality for all concerned, including the police and understanding the juvenile's situation. It would seem to require a rather special sort of person trained in the art of knowing how to react to a delicate situation yet not damaging the information to be given. The lack of training of appropriate adults generally makes it likely that those used will be local authority social workers or probation officers who may be sympathetic to the child but who come from organisations rarely sympathetic to the police. If juvenile informers are to be protected yet permitted to provide information, which may after all lead to the conviction of serious offenders, suitable appropriate adults are required who are trained and who are capable of acting in ways best suited to the task in hand. Otherwise it seems again as if Britain is producing the correct procedures then emasculating them by failing to provide the levels of support necessary for them to function.

There remains another pressing ethical question that centres on payments to be made to juvenile informers. The problem is the police may reward the juvenile quite handsomely in some cases when there is every reason to believe the juvenile will use the money to buy drugs, or spend it on gambling. Some police forces have tried to get round this problem by staggering the payments (i.e. paying only small amounts at any one time); others pay for the information with food vouchers or by some other means to assist the family. This is not always acceptable to the juvenile who, say, may be a heavy drug user, homeless and have a liking for cocaine. There is little the police can do if they want the information. They would be helped if the regulations set out the conditions under which monies can be paid and if they were required to clarify this with the juvenile concerned. Presumably, the regulations would say something like this: vouchers will normally be paid and only in exceptional circumstances will money be given and then only with the approval of a senior officer of assistant chief constable rank. That may not solve all the problems but it might ease some of them.

The use of juvenile informants carries particular risks, whether to their safety or psychological development, and the police have rightly been provided with detailed rules and procedures for dealing with them. Authorising officers are required to give close attention to questions of proportionality that is, to determine whether the use of a juvenile informer can be justified. This use must be on the basis that it is commensurate with the seriousness of the offence. The younger the informer the more pressing is the decision about proportionality. In every case, the controlling police officer must be satisfied the juvenile understands what is happening and has had the risks clearly explained. If the juvenile's identity is compromised, he or she faces additional obstacles: juveniles cannot usually move to another area and they cannot protect themselves against violent drug dealers. Carole Ballardie and Paul Iganski (2001: 113) show that most police officers in their study solved the problem of juveniles by not registering them – hardly a solution in the circumstances. The move to tasking using dedicated informer units will help reduce that practice, though it may still appear, albeit fitfully.

We may not like using juveniles as informers, might find it morally repugnant, but juveniles will keep coming forward with information clearly it is wrong if financial inducements or gifts are offered as inducements to give information, and so the best we can do is provide clear guidelines about how they should be handled and controlled. After all, the peak age of crime is 15 years, and the peak age group 14–17 years. If the police are expected to make inroads into levels of juvenile crime, they must expect to use informers to help them.

Corruption

Drugs are easy to transport and easy to hide, and small quantities produce massive profits. It is this message that Roy Clark (2001) graphically describes in his study of police corruption. He says corruption can be found in all organisations, including those within the criminal justice system, especially where drugs and informers are involved. He thinks the police have recognised this more than most and have unfairly been seen as the most corrupt because they have publicly displayed their anti-corruption activities. The police have also recognised where the dangers are, and Clark makes it clear that other agencies that refuse to accept that corruption exists are building up trouble for themselves by failing to turn over the stone to see what lies under it. Corruption can never be eliminated but it can be reduced. Clarke (*ibid*.: 38) again:

> The risk of allowing police officers to come into regular contact with criminals under controlled conditions is therefore justified. On almost every occasion the contacts and resulting police actions are conducted according to high ethical standards. There are however rare occasions when standards fall, supervision fails and people become vulnerable to temptation. Under such circumstances the dangers of informers and police officers becoming corrupt are high.

Clark gives other examples of corruption, whether in the Crown Prosecution Service or HM Customs & Excise, and they almost all involve drug dealing. The incentive to bribe officials and engage in corrupt practices is a common and important feature of the contemporary drug trade. The large amounts of money and, from the trafficker's point of view, the need to launder that money, as well as finding better means of distributing the drugs, have meant that bribery and corruption are endemic. The bank clerk who is paid by the trafficker to look the other way or to fail to report large cash deposits, or the police officer who does not patrol a section of the coastline on selected evenings, operate at the low end of the corruption pyramid. At the upper end are the professionals, the lawyers and accountants able to promote shell companies or to engage in sophisticated trading techniques. Even higher are the corrupt politicians – some at the very top, whose practices promote and extend corruption nationally.

Some of the corrupt practices in relation to the drugs trade in the Caribbean and South American region have been documented (Paternostro, 1995). For example, in 1994 the US Attorney General's office filed in excess of 15,000 criminal corruption investigations against Colombian officials, including 21 Colombian Members of Congress. Although Colombia and the USA signed a Mutual Legal Assistance Treaty in 1900, Colombia has failed to ratify the treaty and it has not entered into force (Presidential Determination 1995). It would be wrong to single out Colombia; other countries have been found to have similar levels of corruption.

Corruption is thought to be most extensive in the producing and distributing countries (e.g. in South East Asia, Pakistan, Burma, etc., the Caribbean and South America). Levels of vertical corruption are thought to be less common in non-producing countries, although the BCCI Bank proved to be a notable exception. Corruption can be defined in legal terms as 'behaviour which deviates from the formal duties of a public role or violates rules against the exercise of certain types of private regarding influence' (Nye, 1970: 566–67). It is the abuse of a position for personal gain. Accordingly, corruption damages public interest as it is dysfunctional to the workings of an organisation, whether involving the law, business or whatever.

Almost all definitions of corruption have been in functionalist terms, where corruption is viewed as dysfunctional to the workings of an organisation or national economy. Recently there have been challenges to this legal definition (Lo, 1993), where the view is that functionalist legal definitions are rarely broad enough to cover the whole spectrum of corrupt practices. Many actions lie in a grey area where corruption in the legal sense would not exist or where it is not disfunctional but may be neutral or, at best, valuable. The handling of informers is a case in point. Skolnick (1984) argues that the enforcement pattern of 'working up the ladder' creates room for wide dissension to be given to narcotics officers who try to protect their informers by holding back information from their superiors. As a result, says Skolnick (*ibid.*: 124), opportunities are always there for corrupt practices and are always a problem. Insider trading is another grey area where corruption is always going to be near the surface, and what is and what is not a corrupt practice is open to debate. Also, the professionals such as lawyers and accountants noted below as well as bank clerks are likely to be operating in similar situations to the insider traders. If the law requires all cash deposits of £5,000 to be notified and a depositor repeatedly places £4,999, should the bank clerk ignore this?

Using a conflict perspective, Lo (1993: 153), in a study of corruption in Hong Kong and China, says corruption can be seen as more variable than that defined in moral and legal terms. It is, he says, determined by the actions of powerful political groups who are able to influence public opinion: 'If a political group succeeds in persuading the masses that a specific policy is in their interest its corrupt practices would be exonerated' (*ibid.*: 153). He goes on (*ibid.*) to say that as 'the dominant class has the capacity to mobilise the mass media and government institutions it is always in an advantageous position to articulate its own interests'. As an example he cites the Tiananmen Square massacre where the Chinese Communist Party claimed that counter-revolutionary riots had been suppressed to maintain law and order to uphold the people's interest when in fact it was the people's voice and freedom that had been suppressed (*ibid.*). Whether this is an example of corruption or simply of naked manipulation of power is debatable.

Clearly there is a point to be made about the way in which corruption is or is not defined by the dominant group – and the activities of some Caribbean governments illustrate this. Even so, it is not clear where such an argument takes us. If the definition of corruption varies from society to society (depending much on the political and economic structures and historical changes, as Lo would have us believe), then corruption can only be examined as another form of cultural relativism. Yet modern capitalist societies require large measures of conformity on those wanting to trade on the international market. The bank teller who takes a bribe in London is as corrupt as the bank teller taking a bribe elsewhere – hence the value of a functionalist theory. It may not be the only theory but it is likely to be the one most appropriate to drug trafficking that is, after all, about financial exploitation.

It is important to understand the structures that promote corruption. Organisations that are not corrupt or have no vertical corruption will, none the less, be prone to corruption if supervision is lax or if managers are not aware of the possibilities of corruption occurring. The poorly supervised bank clerk will not report a large cash deposit, the poorly supervised police officer will not report a cargo landing on his or her part of the beach, or the poorly supervised lawyer or accountant will accept a new client without asking too many pertinent questions. But they will report if supervision is close. On the other hand, Peter Reuter (1991: 17) sees the incentive to bribe as being not related to supervision but to the intensity of law enforcement: 'The greater the probability of long prison terms and loss of other assets, the more aggressively a dealer will seek out officials who can mitigate those risks and the more money he will be willing to offer such mitigation'. His conclusion is that active law enforcement induces corruption: 'This is one of the potential costs of more intense enforcement in raised corruption potential, particularly among the front line enforcement agencies' (*ibid.*).

Corruption and policing

Roy Clark (2001) gives the typical profile of the corrupt police officer in these terms: he (it is very rarely a woman) will be a very active police officer, usually with a reputation for being successful, having 'done a number of good jobs' and continuing to work at that pace. He will have served as a police officer for about 12 years and will have reached a reasonably high or middle rank. He will be divorced, probably paying a heavy maintenance allowance, or will have other similar monthly expenses. He will be working in one of the specialist detective units and will meet criminals who have ready access to large amounts of money.

It is difficult to believe that many police officers started their careers with the aim of becoming corrupt. More likely, they began with all the usual idealism of someone starting out in public service. What, then, goes wrong? How does an otherwise honest, hard-working police officer become corrupt? Almost certainly by gently sliding into corrupt practices beginning, first, with such matters as securing a lighter sentence in return for a relatively small payment. This is done by changing the records or finding other ways to avoid prosecution. Once involved it is easy to move to larger sums of money from more serious criminals and the point is soon reached where it is difficult (if not impossible) for him to regain his earlier reputation – and as a corrupt police officer he has lost control and becomes the employee of the offender population.

Clark (*ibid.*) describes the changes the corrupt police officer goes through from being honest and in control of the offender to being corrupt and in the offender's control. In the Metropolitan Police investigation he identified 'a new and more sinister problem' (*ibid.*: 41) with evidence that 'there was a complete reversal of the roles of the police officer and informer. The informer … became the recipient of police intelligence whilst the police officer became the informer.' He describes it (*ibid.*) thus:

> It became clear that this reversal process led to the criminals adopting many of the elements of police practices which relate to the recruitment and use of police officer informers. It was found that the criminals developed their own policy or set of standards which

closely mirrored the accepted law enforcement practices. These include the active recruitment of informers, protection from exposure, the use of pseudonyms, an acknowledgement that intelligence is to be shared, the tasking of informers, the provision of more than one handler, and reward in cash commensurate with the intelligence provided.

Paradoxically, it is the informer who provides the police with information about corrupt police officers. Clark says informers have been an important source of information, introducing several lines of enquiry and adding significantly to others. He says there is no such thing as honour among thieves; rivalry, jealousy and the settling of old scores create high levels of instability within criminal circles and ensure a constant stream of information to the police. He adds (*ibid.*: 48): 'Informers are also a vital component of any strategic response to corruption.'

For the trafficker and high-level dealer, corruption comes cheap. The police officer on the Caribbean island or the bank teller in a London bank when asked to look away at the opportune moment will not expect to receive a great deal of money. Clark describes an employee from the Crown Prosecution Service who was sentenced to 6 years' imprisonment for giving away the identities of 33 police informers. He had received just £1,000, although the court heard he expected to receive more (*ibid.*: 45). There is no point in the bank teller receiving £1 million for that would draw attention to his or her activities and so would be counterproductive. More likely, he or she will ask for enough to pay off existing debts, to buy a car and to go on holiday. And he or she will be hooked for life with no possibility of escape. In that sense corruption is a one-way street, dysfunctional to the organisation and dysfunctional to the corrupted – but highly functional and cost-effective to the corrupter.

It is reasonable to ask to what extent we should fear an extension of corrupt practices. Will corruption through the drug trade overwhelm our institutions, whether financial or otherwise? Peter Reuter (1991) is optimistic; he sees the fractionated structure of drug law enforcement as being its salvation. It means no force has exclusive criminal enforcement responsibilities (the police share much with Customs and Excise), and the often-cited lack of co-ordination between the agencies turns out to be but one aspect of the risks facing corrupt police: 'Taking money from dealers has become risky in an environment in which the individual paying the bribe has a reasonably high probability of being arrested by another agency' (*ibid.*: 18). Wing Lo (1993: 163) sees the solution in terms of changes in the dominant group so that all can contest the validity, target and purpose of the legal and moral censures of corruption.

The research evidence such as there is suggests that, in modern societies, drug dealers are unable to purchase the systemic and comprehensive protection that was available to many of their earlier bootlegging and gambling predecessors. Modern-drug dealing organisations in a country such as Britain are basically fragile and always subject to serious threats from law enforcement (Reuter *et al.*, 1990: 24). Of course, whilst they operate they do considerable damage, but they are always likely to be confined and always likely to be seeking new forms of corruption. The evidence to support Reuter *et al.*'s optimistic view in the face of the growth of organised crime needs to be evaluated. A comprehensive study of corruption – how it occurs and how it can be controlled – would seem to be necessary.

If, as is often claimed, about one third of all crimes are cleared up as a result of informers and, for drug crimes, the percentage is thought to be higher, informers play a key role in any police strategy. If the trafficking cases are disaggregated and counted separately, the percentage is likely to be much higher still. There is no suggestion the use of informers will decline but every indication it will increase and, almost certainly, change to meet the contemporary demands of law enforcement. Nowadays crime generally, and drug taking in particular, has a more international dimension, where the movement of drugs and the movement of criminals require a different approach than hitherto.

In October 1997 the UK government published *Rights Brought Home; the Human Rights Bill* and said it intended to incorporate the EU Convention on Human Rights into UK law. The use of informers was affected by the EU convention, particularly Article 8, which provides for the right of privacy. An informer clearly violates that right. Introducing legislation in the form of the RIPA resolved some of these difficulties and provided an opportunity (through speedy amendments to other legislation) to control and supervise informers generally. The old days when police officers learnt how to handle informers as they went along and then claimed an expertise in such matters that was never put to the test have gone. In their place is a new set of rules, infinitely more bureaucratic and cumbersome but with many more safeguards for all concerned.

The link with corruption has been well established and the impact of corrupt police officers well understood. Drugs, corruption and informers seem to go together; not always found together but, when they are, they can produce the most destructive consequences. At present there is no realistic alternative to the use of informers but there is a point to be made about the way they are handled and controlled. Clark (2001) says that any form of unethical or criminal behaviour involving an informer can now be detected, and long prison sentences invariably follow for the corrupt officer. He adds (*ibid*.: 44) that if high standards are allowed to fall, the courts would lose confidence in the informer system and that the consequences of this loss in confidence to policing would be massive. Conversely, the benefits to organised crime would be vast.

Chapter 9

Women, drugs and crime

Rarely in this book has reference been made to gender or even an acknowledgement made that gender is an issue. Obviously, this is not the case – gender *is* important. For example, Table 1.3 (on p. 5) shows that, of the 34,875 people starting agency episodes in the 6 months ending 30 September 1999, 25,750 were men and 9,125 were women (or about 25% of them were female). The ages at which women begin drug use are similar to those of men, the peak age group being the early to mid-20s. The drugs taken are also similar – although some American studies show that women are particularly fond of cocaine. However, Edna Oppenheimer (1991: 38) notes that the ratio of women to men coming to treatment in Britain is about 1 in 3. If this reflects the numbers using drugs generally, then probably about 25% of drug takers are women.

As noted in Chapter 1, data from the British Crime Survey (BCS) show there is a gap between the male and female rates and that this gap appears to be widening. Whereas female rates remained steady at 19% in 1999, for males it increased by 5%. Women also tend to enter treatment earlier than men, and often more successfully. Yet are these differences sufficient to warrant special policies, treatment programmes, policing or whatever? Do women drug users differ in a qualitative sense from their male counterparts and, if they do, is a different approach or a different set of standards required? In trying to answer these questions we face the obvious handicaps that, paradoxically, also apply to men: there are few good research studies that provide the necessary data. If 1 in 3 or 1 in 4 of the drug-using population are women and the services provided are failing, something clearly needs to be done and adjustments made in whatever areas are appropriate. But which and how?

At one level, of course, there are no differences. As Oppenheimer (1991) points out, women who misuse drugs are subject to the same risks as men. They will experience the same forms of ill-health, will die from the same overdoses, will experience the same severe weight loss, will have the same hepatitis B illness, will suffer the same muscle wasting and will be subject to all the other diseases related to the same chaotic lifestyle and the poor and erratic nutrition as their male counterparts. Yet in other respects their medical problems are unique, the most obvious being those related to pregnancy and childbirth and the effects of drugs on the unborn child. Related to these are the social norms surrounding being a mother and the plight of children whose mothers are substance misusers.

The aim here is to look at some of the matters surrounding women and substance abuse in order to highlight certain selected features that have received attention in the literature and in Parliament. Increasingly there is a developing interest in women's issues, especially concerning the number of women drug users in prison and in the treatment facilities inside and outside the criminal justice system.

Women, health and social norms

Women who use drugs are likely to be of child-bearing age; this will create additional problems for them and the unborn child if and when they become pregnant. A number of drug users do become pregnant, but how many and how many give birth as opposed to seek a termination is not known. Sheigla Murphy and Marsha Rosenbaum (1999), in their study of pregnant women on drugs, show how, for a variety of reasons, these women did not practise birth control – one reason being that the combination of long-term drug use and erratic eating habits resulted in menstruation cessation. They did not believe they could conceive and, when they did, it was sometime before they recognised it; they often attributed morning sickness to drug withdrawal (*ibid*.: 52–53).

Generally speaking, once they have conceived there are two main sets of problems: there are those occurring during pregnancy and those affecting the child immediately after birth. Of the first, Oppenheimer (1991) says that while congenital abnormalities occur primarily during early pregnancy, some drugs can affect the growth of the foetus and its post-natal behaviour producing mental problems (especially where exposure to drugs occurs later in pregnancy). She says (*ibid*.: 39–40) that even after delivery maternally ingested drugs can gain entrance to the neonate through feeding on mother's milk.

Women drug users who are pregnant face additional complications to their already-chaotic daily lives. If their major source of income is through prostitution, pregnancy will reduce their earning power. If they are 'busted' they will try to hide their pregnancy from the police and courts, fearing they will be remanded in custody to receive medical treatment. They know their lifestyles give cause for concern, especially if they are intravenous drug users. In the USA that concern is additionally justified. Many US states have public health laws where pregnant drug users can be detained until they give birth – and presumably a decision is also made about whether the mother may keep the child. The law operates as a form of preventative detention or preventative containment. In California (as in many other states), drug use during pregnancy can be interpreted as child abuse, and hospital staff are required by law to initiate child-protection or law-enforcement referrals (Murphy and Rosenbaum, 1999: 107). The aim of preventative containment is to produce a 'drug-free baby', thereby reducing the complications including the health costs of a child born of a drug-using mother.

The second set of problems surrounds the mother's future contact with child-care agencies and health services. Contact with the criminal justice system is also a potential minefield. Murphy and Rosenbaum (*ibid.*: 105) say that women must choose to disclose or not disclose and, in doing so, must confront their two biggest fears: first, that their babies might be born seriously impaired and secondly that their babies might be taken away from them – 'In the long term was it better for the baby to tell or not to tell?' (*ibid.*: 133).

Sometimes the role conflict works to the woman's advantage. There are some women drug users who recognise there are conflicts between being a 'junkie' and a mother and resolve this in favour of being a mother. If this is the case they seek treatment and are likely to be successful, the more so if they want their children returned to them to reconstitute their family. Murphy and Rosenbaum (*ibid.*: 58) describe how some women who had assumed they were infertile saw their pregnancy as a cause for joy, a living proof their drug use had not impaired their reproductive capacities: 'These women viewed their pregnancies as opportunities to change their life styles, almost as if the pregnancy was a special gift to provide them with new hope and resolve.' Male counterparts rarely see parenthood as sufficiently important to choose in favour of being a father rather than a junkie. Accordingly, they have fewer demands to make them grow up. Perhaps that is why women seek treatment at an earlier stage than men (Anglin and Hser, 1987a). Yet whilst a few see pregnancy as an opportunity to change for the better, many do not. Whatever advantages pregnancy brings to a small number of women, for the vast majority it brings 'seemingly never ending guilt' (*ibid.*: 7). They recognise that bringing up children in that unstable, violent world is likely to produce the same unstable, violent world for them as adults. Murphy and Rosenbaum (1999) describe – in that all too familiar way – how these pregnant mothers had been systematically abused as children and were being systematically abused as adults. They see the same prospects for their children. Yet many of the women in the Murphy and Rosenbaum study decided against an abortion. Pregnancy and motherhood offered them another chance of mending their flawed identities and of returning to a conventional role:

> For those women who had already been mothers and lost custody of their older children the decision to have another baby was another chance at being a good mother. Their decisions not to abort were often influenced by their guilt and remorse over past abortions or having failed in the past (*ibid.*: 65).

The baby offered an opportunity to do it right this time. Whether they were any more successful remains to be seen.

Women who are drug users and have young children living with them know they are at risk of having those children taken into care. Welfare workers rightly protect children, especially young children, from the dangers moral and physical of a mother who is a drug user. If she has a partner, that relationship is likely to be unstable where the demand for the drug interferes with any relationship between the adults. Each adult will believe the other is exploiting him or her by not giving them their share of the drugs – especially so where they are heroin users or are taking other addictive drugs. Fear, suspicion, distrust and violence are common to these relationships. Young children brought up in that atmosphere are bound to be damaged, psychologically at least. If as often happens the woman addict resorts to prostitution, the risk of HIV infection adds to the dangers.

Once the children had been taken away as many are it becomes an uphill task to get them back. How does a woman who was once a drug addict show she is reformed, has appropriate accommodation, is able to bring up children in an adequate way and convince everybody she will not return to drugs? Doesn't everyone know that 'once a junkie, always a junkie'? Increasingly it will become harder and harder to reclaim the children. Recent American legislation requires children who have been in care for 18 months or more to be considered automatically for adoption. The days are long gone where a mother could expect a child to remain in care for a number of years and then be able to reclaim it when she was ready. If this type of legislation is introduced into Britain it will work as in the USA – that is, reduce the mother's window of opportunity giving her less time to show she is suitable.

Oppenheimer (1994: 86) shows how the social norms surrounding the sexes differ widely so that a woman who becomes an addict violates those norms surrounding the expectations of her sex and gender roles. Or as Murphy and Rosenbaum (1999: 134, 135) say, losing her child and being regarded as unfit to reclaim it means the woman is being labelled an unfit mother. This has horrendous consequences of personal and social condemnation and social isolation. Failure to perform mothering resposibilities is tantamount to failure as a woman.

Broom and Stevens (1991), in their study of women drug dealers, say sex and gender roles and the structural position of women in society have been neglected by male researchers. Putting it more forcibly, they say research has typically failed to consider how women's lives differ from those of men. They believe one reason why drug abuse is viewed with such condemnation in women is that intoxicated women fail to perform one of their major roles – which is to act as 'God's police' by keeping men in order:

> The social expectation that intoxication is permissible for men but not for women has a long history in Australia where ... sexual stereotypes have had it that respectable women must function as 'God's Police' imposing restraint, civilisation and decorum on men who would otherwise behave in barbaric and anti-social ways (*ibid.*: 26).

That being so, presumably like all who were once beyond reproach and who acted as 'God's police', their fall will be regarded as all the more blameworthy and reprehensible. They will get little sympathy from others (men included), who will be merciless about such failings. The point is that male drug users can more easily reclaim their status; women find it harder to do so, especially where the label was that of a junkie. However, there are ways to avoid the stigma. Girl gang-members, in the study by Hunt *et al.* (2000: 350), protected their feminine status yet were able to drink more freely because they did so by:

> partying with the girls. On such occasions they did not need to worry about their drinking behaviour tainting their reputations nor did they need to worry about men taking advantage of their inebriated state. The context free from the presence of men was the only situation in which the women found themselves acting in an

environment where the wider society's double standards on female drinking did not operate.

Whilst Broom and Stevens (1991) see the problem in terms of a flawed identity, others (such as Rosenbaum 1981) see the woman drug user as trapped in a world that offers little to them, except drugs, and few ways of escape. Their world has less to do with having a flawed identity and more with the reduced number of options available to the addict as she becomes more involved with the drug world. Rosenbaum (*ibid.*), in one of the classical studies of women and drugs describes the woman's position as the 'career of narrowing options'. She goes on to say (*ibid.*: 49):

> Heroin expands her life options in the initial stages and that is the essence of its social attraction. Yet with progressively further immersion into the heroin world the social psychological exigencies of heroin create an option 'funnel' for the woman addict. Through the funnel the addict's life options are radically reduced until she is fundamentally incarcerated in an invisible prison. Ultimately the woman addict is locked into the heroin world and locked out of the conventional world.

Rosenbaum implies that 'the career of narrowing options' applies more to women than to men. She suggests that, when women are locked out of the conventional world, they find it more difficult to return or suffer greater hardship through that isolation. They mix only with other drug users, mostly men but of the type who will exploit women as and whenever they see it is in their interests to do so, or other women in a similar condition (i.e. junkies). Whether this is always so or only for American heroin addicts is a moot point. Clearly there is a shortage of comparable data for Britain, not just for heroin addicts but for women who take other drugs such as cannabis, LSD or ecstasy. Is their status similarly flawed to the point where they are reduced to that same career of narrowing options? We do not know. There is in Britain a view that women drug users are rather more fortunate than men. They are less likely to be given severe sentences for offences than men but they are less criminal anyway, and their drug taking is explained as being promoted and sustained by men. What is needed are some sound ethnographic studies describing the women's position, showing how that may differ from their American counterparts and seeing, too, if it varies according to the drug of choice.

All of which easily leads to a note of pessimism surrounding the woman drug user, a pessimism that is often misplaced and unjustified. The positive side is that women drug users seem to have more pressure on them to make them 'grow up' than do men, and often that is what pushes them into treatment. They can and often do break out of that 'career of narrowing options' and have a success rate in treatment that is no worse than for men and often rather better (Oppenheimer, 1994). It is never going to be easy for women drug users. Many of the pregnant women in the Murphy and Rosenbaum study (1999) were recipients of violence, poor parenting and poverty: 'For these women the American dream – a nurturing family with two kids, two cars, and a house with a garden and a white picket fence – was indeed a distant dream' (*ibid.*: 17). They conclude their study (*ibid.*: 157) with the view that:

> The greatest threat to effective parenting and child survival is a system that perpetuates poverty, violence, hardship and desperation. Rather than indicting pregnant drug users for their addictions and compulsions we should do well to look at their impossible conditions in which these women and their children are forced to live their lives.

For younger women, those in the 15–21 age group, it would seem that greater possibilities exist of being able to return to more conventional roles, especially if the drug-using episode is brief with little harm (i.e. not becoming pregnant) and the drugs taken were more of the 'soft' rather than the 'hard' variety. Yet for some young girls it is already too late. In our current unreported study of young prostitutes in Nottingham who are drug users (Bean, in preparation), preliminary results indicate there are about 60 young girls acting as prostitutes, aged between 12 and 16, many already in care, almost all are drug users (being supplied by their 'pimps'), and some of the pimps are women. It is difficult to be other than pessimistic about their future; their identity is already permanently flawed and their hopes of achieving conventional roles remote. How does a young drug-using prostitute, perhaps no older than 15 years, in care and has been so for nearly all her life, being 'pimped' and dressing in ways that emphasise her youth in order to attract paedophiles, expect to get out of that type of world? Her future, in whatever form it comes, will almost certainly be bleak.

Women drug users, crime and prison

In a written parliamentary answer it was said that, in March 1996, there were 2,120 women prisoners in England and Wales. In March 2000 the figure had increased to 3,392 (*Hansard* 2 May 2000: col. 922). Why the increase? The answer was that it was almost all due to drug offenders. Lord Bach explained: 'That does not mean possession of drugs but the selling of drugs and sometimes the importation of drugs.' He then went on to state what feminist criminologists have railed against for years – that 'There can be some mitigation for women – they can for instance be under pressure from male partners' and added, less controversially, 'but these are serious offences which are a danger to other women and to other people in general' (*ibid.*: cols. 923–24).

On 31 January 1999 there were 825 women in prison for drug offences (data taken from a written answer to the House of Commons on 24 February 1999). It is interesting to compare the women drug offenders serving 12 months or more as a proportion of other sentenced women prisoners serving similar sentences. On 31 January 1999, there were 782 women drug offenders serving 12 months or more out of a total population of 825 women drug offenders (or 94%). This compares with, 1868 other women offenders who were serving 12 months or more out of a total population of 2,391 (or 78%) (*ibid.:* col. 308). In other words, women serving 12 months or more were more likely to be drug offenders than others – 94% compared with 78%.

Some of these women drug offenders serving 12 months or more are foreign nationals. Many are charged with unlawful importation of drugs (448 of these were serving 12 months or more). The point prevalence figures for that day in January 1999 were that 274 foreign nationals were serving sentences for drug-related offences in England and Wales. However, on 31 December 1999, some 11 months later, that figure had risen to 312, serving an average sentence of 6.7 years.

The foreign nationals serving long sentences for drug importation have been the cause of much interest and concern. In the early 1990s, these women came mostly from Nigeria but after drastic action by the Nigerian authorities the numbers dropped steadily and, by February, were down to about 20. Most are now from Jamaica. Ian Burrell (reporting in *The Independent* 21 February 2000) says women smugglers from Jamaica are being arrested so frequently at Heathrow and Gatwick airports that they account for 1 in 16 of the female prison population in England and Wales. He says there are now (at February 2000) 184 Jamaican women in jail serving 10 years or more, and that those from Jamaica are over-represented and are five times greater in number than any other nationality in women's prisons. Back in Jamaica the traffickers are 'targeting mothers with no criminal records. They are targeting hospitals in the Caribbean to recruit women who need money for medical treatment' (*ibid.*). The money is presumably for their families as well as for themselves.

These foreign nationals distort the figures for women offenders in

England and Wales as, of course, do drug offenders generally. They accentuate the already-rising rate of female prisoners and, with so many serving long sentences, they produce a lop-sided female prison population. What sort of problems these women create for their families and children back home we can only guess. Stories abound of their naïvety and gullibility. One was of a courier or 'mule' as they are called from Nigeria and, having been told heroin was legal in Britain, declared her cargo at Heathrow and was promptly arrested. This is probably apocryphal but perhaps not too far off the mark. If, as Burrell says, the trafffickers target those women wanting medical treatment, there will always be a ready-made pool of potential recruits who are in similar desperate straits and prepared to take the risk. We do not know how many successfully deliver their drugs and return crime free.

Interestingly enough, the problem seems not to be confined to Britain. Huling (1996) reports that a high percentage of women in prison in Latin America were detained or sentenced under drug-trafficking laws. In Cuenca, Ecuador, it was 62%, in Guayaquil, Ecuador, it was 40%, in Rio de Janeiro, Brazil, it was 28%, in Caracas, Venezuela, it was 51% and in Los Teques, Venezuela it was 43%. Presumably there would be similar figures for prisons in South East Asia.

For the other prisoners (i.e. the non-drug offenders in prisons in England and Wales), many have a drug history and some have a serious drug problem. On 3 July 2000 it was reported in *Hansard* that, in 1998–99 when almost 16,000 women were screened on reception into prison by health-care staff, 3,091 completed drug detox programmes and 413 completed alcohol detox programmes. Moreover, the minister (Paul Boateng), in a reply to a written question, reported a study undertaken in 1997 that indicated that in the year before entering prison, 36% of women on remand and 39% of sentenced women reported engaging in hazardous drinking, and 54% of women on remand and 41% of sentenced women reported some degree of drug dependence (*Hansard* 3 July 2000: cols. 70W–72W). This is a considerable proportion of imprisoned offenders who require treatment whilst in prison.

There is little information to allow comparisons to be made between men and women prisoners. A study by Brook *et al.* (1998) on 995 unconvicted prisoners randomly selected from all prisons in England and Wales (750 men and 245 women) shows that, before arrest, 145 (19.3%) men were dependent on street drugs compared with 72 (29.4%) women. There were 91 men (12.1%) and 16 women (6.5%) who were solely dependent on alcohol. Seventeen men (2.3%) reported injecting drugs during the current period of imprisonment compared with 4 women (1.6%). Out of the 995 subjects, 235 (24%) wanted treatment whilst in prison – 172 men and 63 women. Extrapolating this figure to the prison population generally, the authors concluded that 1,905 prisoners (male and female) wanted treatment for their substance abuse whilst in prison.

The treatment of women prisoners has long stimulated interest and controversy, whether of drug offenders or not. The accusation is that women prisoners are given too much treatment and usually of the wrong sort. For example, it has been a source of concern that women prisoners generally have been over-prescribed neuroleptics and other heavy tranquillisers such as Largactil. A debate in Parliament was on the motion that:

> this House is gravely concerned at evidence of the over prescribing of damaging and addictive medicinal drugs in womens prisons ... [that] neuroleptic drugs are routinely prescribed to young women prisoners who mutilate themselves, and that medicinal drugs are used as pacifiers which move prisoners from non addictive illegal drugs to highly addictive medicinal drug use (*Hansard* 22 October 1998: col. 1400).

This debate was initiated by Mr Flynn, a member who had previously taken up the cause of over-prescribing neuroleptics and tranquillisers for women prisoners. He did not get the result he required but did succeed in bringing this to public attention. In an earlier question he wanted to know how many prescriptions for Largactil or Melleril and other anti-psychotic drugs were issued. The reply was that:

> The prison service recognises that many women received into custody have complex medical histories and have very often already been prescribed the types of medications cited ... Efforts are being made to reduce the prescribing of major and minor tranquillisers and neuroleptic drugs except where their use is clinically essential (*Hansard, Written Answers* 14 July 1998: col. 98).

There it seems is where the matter rests – at least for the time being. It still leaves open the question: what is 'clinically essential'? How is that to be interpreted? To use terms like 'clinical judgements' walks around the problem, for they imply there is something definitive or scientific about these judgements when they could as easily represent the less than unbiased views of the physician. That prescribing and over-prescribing in women's prisons have been a long-established practice is not in doubt, and questions about that practice need to be asked. Mr Boateng again:

We believe that it is important to ensure that in prisons there is a regime that does all that it possibly can not only to keep drugs out – that is why we emphasise creating in some prisons completely drug free wings where it is possible to provide the necessary alternative to counteract offending – but to educate prisoners to come to terms with their drug misuse that led them to be there in the first place (*Hansard, Prisons and Drugs* 10 December 1998: col. 540).

This statement applies equally to men and women. It does not answer the question about prescribing in women's prisons nor, perhaps, was it intended to do. That efforts are being made to reduce prescribing is to be welcomed, although many would say not before time.

Women as users and dealers

Anglin and Hser (1987b) say women tend to report first drug use at a later age than men and are frequently initiated into use by their male partners, who are often their main suppliers in the course of their addiction. They go on to say that women report a briefer transition from first drug to addiction. Anecdotally, it seems women tend to be more rapacious in their drug use, at least in the initial stages, but then for the reasons given above are more likely to see the dangers. There is also a current belief that women who see themselves involved in a mission to save their menfolk from the evils of drugs invariably finish up addicted. They also become heavier users than their men.

Distinctions need to be made between middle-class drug users and others. Middle-class women cocaine users (the drug in question is almost always cocaine and the studies almost always American) say that women use drugs for recreational reasons to add to their lives or 'just for fun' (Sterk-Elifson, 1996). Cocaine is seen as the perfect lady-like drug (Greenleaf, 1989). There are no unsightly injection marks and no pressure to hang around bars to obtain it. 'Also its slimming, you're not in a stupor, you don't slur your words, and you can carry it around in your cosmetic case just like the lipstick.' Or, as one user said, 'I can feel this good and lose weight too' (*ibid*.: 12). The problem comes when the demand for the drug begins to get out of hand or when they begin to feel and recognise they are losing control. What then? Sterk-Elifson (1996) says women at this point begin to recognise they must give up the myth of using just for fun. They are then faced with a number of dilemmas: 'If their use is discovered the women might lose their jobs, their relationships, and if they are mothers the custody of their children. The women do not want to lose what they have; they want cocaine to add to their lives not destroy them' (*ibid.*: 72). The other problem is that once the drug use begins to get out of hand, women become less selective about their partners. Their decision is then based more around cocaine than the quality of any prospective relationship (*ibid.*: 70).

Outside this rather protected middle-class world, Morgan and Joe (1996) suggest that women users, with very few exceptions, are restricted to passive or victimised roles in a social world dominated by men. Their drug use is limited to their relationship with men and they rarely consider that their use was shaped by choices outside their gendered relationship. Some (a small number) become dealers, and a few are successful. In our study of drug dealing in Nottingham (Bean and Wilkinson, 1988), we found a small number of women dealers who successfully operated using their boyfriends or current partners to collect debts and enforce discipline. These women changed partners regularly and the street talk was that they informed on them to remove them, either because they were not up to the task or because they were likely to take over the business. Similarly in their study of women crack users in New York, Johnson *et al.* (2000) found that crack-using women in Harlem claimed (and were so observed) to be relatively equal to male counterparts in their performance of street-level distribution roles as sellers or low-level distributors.

Morgan and Joe (1996) identified what they called the 'citizen dealer' who was mainly middle class (or aspiring middle class) and who was living in the mainstream of social life, regardless of the drug being used or the level of dealing. They also identified the 'outlaws', whose lifestyles were such as to be significantly immersed in deviant activities and who were living marginal lives. The former were either high-level dealers – in this case usually selling amphetamine that provided them with a major source of income – or part-time dealers selling to a small selective group of friends while maintaining regular employment. They felt pride in their accomplishments as dealers. Being 'able to retain or return to a measure of stability and respectability they were found to be living in good neighbourhoods. They had money, often a husband and family and sometimes a regular job' (*ibid.*: 132). In contrast, the outlaw dealer fitted more closely the view of women as operating in a passive and victimised role in which men dominated their social world. The outlaws come in one of two forms: either as victims when they are heavy users often working as prostitutes whose dealing is to make a living to furnish their own supplies or as survivors. Whether as victim or survivor, the life chances were limited, all had previous convictions and all lived marginal lives (*ibid.*: 135–142).

Most studies see women dealers as more likely to be outlaws than citizens. They support the view that the position of women in the drug world is 'parallel [to] the division in the straight society' (Broom and Stevens, 1991: 27). Typically, Broom and Stevens describe women as prostitutes and couriers, whilst men occupied the high-prestige position as dealers. Johnson *et al.* (2000), in their ethnographic study of Brooklyn, reported gender and ethnic biases directed at women. They found that crack-using women were left with virtually no option other than sex work, primarily because they would not be hired as day labourers by crack-selling crews (*ibid.*: 35–36). Whilst women may resist male domination as best they can, none the less, Murphy and Arroyo (2000) argue that women are at a decided disadvantage when they try to enter and operate in the drugs markets. What they called 'ambient violence' or emotional violence (or simply physical abuse) was an all too common occurrence. They say that in the subculture of addiction, masculine values relegate women to secondary roles, making them dependent on the dominant males. Drug use, ambient violence, gender roles and inadequate retaliation capacities meant that most women did not sell for long periods of time (*ibid.*: 105).

The emphasis in the research suggests that women are in the minority when it comes to dealing: there is no suggestion they become dealers at the highest level nor that they are high-level traffickers. However, things might be changing. Dunlap and Johnson (1996) think there may be more women dealers coming forward so that, whereas women have traditionally been on the demand side of drug markets (i.e. working as prostitutes in order to purchase drugs), they may increasingly be moving into the supply side. If so, this would mark an important development.

Women in treatment

There is general agreement that drug-using women have different treatment needs from their male counterparts. How and in what form is difficult to say; too often it depends on the drugs taken, the lifestyle and their perceptions of themselves based on their life experiences. Certainly the reasons women enter treatment seem to be different from those of men – although, once in treatment, outcomes remain comparable. American research suggests that, for men, the routes into treatment are invariably through the criminal justice system whereas, for women, they are through counsellors or social workers. Grella and Joshi (1999) studied gender factors associated with having a history of drug treatment; this involved a study of 7,652 individuals admitted to the national Drug

Abuse Treatment Outcome Study (DATOS). They concluded (*ibid.*: 385–86) that:

> Prior drug treatment among men was associated with factors related to family opposition to drug use and support for treatment, whereas for women prior drug treatment was associated with anti-social personality disorder and self initiation into treatment. Moreover, treatment initiatives among men appear to be facilitated by social institutions such as employment, the criminal justice system and one's family. In contrast treatment re-entry among women was associated by referral by a social worker suggesting that family service agencies can facilitate women's entry.

In other words, men were pushed into treatment by threats but women entered after counselling. If so, this supports the general view that drug-dependent women have treatment needs different from men, and that these needs should be recognised and dealt with. Too often the accusation is that they are not. At its worst, women in treatment are seen as there to assist with the treatment of men ('Would someone take the part of this man's wife/girlfriend/mother in this next role play' type of situation). Slightly better but no more helpful is the assumption that women are to receive the same therapeutic inputs as men, which may be wholly irrelevant ('All he [the therapist] keeps saying is that patients should exercise and receive more controls. Its because I had too much control from my father/husband/boyfriend that I became a drug user in the first place' type of comment). Greenleaf (1989: 7) reports that women are more passive and depressed about their situation than male drug users in treatment: 'They're just not dealing with their problems and are not assertive about how they feel about things.'

Wellisch *et al.* (1993) note the shortage of data on women drug users, especially on those women in treatment. They believe two models of treatment have emerged: the first is an empowerment model where women are encouraged to perceive of themselves as actors rather than victims, able to direct their own lives. The second is more practical, aimed at providing women with coping skills that will permit them to make the desired changes to their lives. These may relate to their status as parents (single parents and otherwise) or to family planning, alongside assertiveness and vocational training. The aim is to recognise the failings of women drug users (defined as 'a combination of inadequate and maladaptive social-behavioural and cognitive skills' (cited in *ibid.*: 8)) and yet remedy these whilst, at the same time, treating the substance abuse. Wellisch *et al.* argue that all treatment programmes for women, including those for women in prison, should, irrespective of the main theoretical formulation, contain the following components:

1. Provide the means for women to maintain or re-establish contact with their children.
2. Provide vocational training and career opportunities in higher-paying fields for women.
3. Ensure women offenders receive adequate health care.

Wellisch *et al.* (*ibid.*: 23) say that many women do not understand the child-care system or how to present their case. Also, there may be shame and resentment from both mother and children, which makes it difficult to re-establish and maintain contact. Visiting their mothers in prison is never an edifying experience for children, but that will be the only way to continue the relationship so it has to be done and made the best of. However, in the last few years the climate has changed and the rights of the child are being seen as increasingly important. For whilst every effort must be made to assist the mother to provide a life for herself and her family, the onus is on her to make the necessary changes to her life. She must make the effort; she must get off drugs and stay off if she is to be allowed to have her children back. She must convince the authorities she is serious, and that her intentions are firm about accepting treatment and about staying drug free. There are limits to the amount of time children can be expected to wait for their mothers to make the decision. They, too, have a life to lead and have the right to be brought up in a drug-free environment with parents who place children above the importance of using drugs.

In the second the aim is to persuade the women drug users to think about training for higher-paid jobs and away from seeing themselves as capable of working only in the traditional low-paid industries generally reserved for women. Wellisch *et al.* (1993) say that most women are the sole providers for their children, rarely receiving help from the fathers. Worse than that, most at the time of arrest or at the end of any sentence were less equipped to earn a high wage than many men in a similar situation (*ibid.*: 23). Opportunities are available. Sometimes all that is needed is for women to have the confidence and encouragement to train and apply. Their motivation is not in question; the hurdle to be overcome is more about self-belief than anything else.

Finally, access to health care is, for obvious reasons, less of a problem in Britain than the USA, but the point needs to be made, none the less. Wellisch *et al.* (*ibid.*) say that women have special health problems, such as those relating to gynaecological care, alongside the need for mammary examinations. In addition, women dependent on drugs are likely to have sexually transmitted diseases, which may include being HIV positive and that will need special attention. They also say that, since a large number of female drug users have also been subject to sexual abuse, counselling and psychological support are also required (*ibid.*: 24).

These three components are regarded as essential in any treatment plan for women drug users. How far they are part of the programmes for treatment in Britain is not known – nor is it known the extent of support they could expect from significant others in their families or friends. There is a suggestion that little support is forthcoming; indeed, Grella and Joshi (1999) report that women should expect little support from their partners and family members. They say they will more likely receive opposition, which sometimes includes intimidation and threats. That being so, the task is greater and the level of pessimism mentioned earlier increasingly justified. Hence, Wellisch *et al.* (1993: 25) conclude that 'it is incumbent on policy makers to increase treatment availability and to the extent that current knowledge permits, optimise the effectiveness of treatment programmes'.

A note on juveniles

Children who are brought up in substance-misusing families face additional problems. (Some local addiction units are now treating the grandchildren of methadone-maintenance users.) These children are likely to spend periods in care and their physical health may also suffer. We have not taken upon ourselves to determine the outcome of children in these substance-abusing families. Notwithstanding that, problem drug use generally often begins with children under the age of 15 years, some of these will be problem drug users by the time they are 18. Presumably many will simply stop taking these substances and come to no harm, but some will not; hence the need for good longitudinal studies to find out how many continue to take drugs.

As far as the criminal justice system is concerned, astonishingly the youth court system in Britain appears not to have made provisions for juvenile drug users; for example, drug use is not mentioned in the large number of new provisions found in the Crime and Disorder Act 1997. We have parenting orders, orders that deal with unruly children, etc., but these are not tied into a debate about children as drug misusers. This omission is all the more noticeable when set against the conclusions reached in American drug courts – namely, that it was neither possible nor practicable to transplant drug courts on to the juvenile justice system without adjusting to the special demands of children. That is to say, the treatment of juveniles is qualitatively different from that of adults. Treatment must include treatment of the child's family for, without agreement and support from the parents and family members, treatment programmes are quickly undermined. Children in treatment have to be separated from their erstwhile peer group lest treatment is also undermined, albeit for different reasons. Most of all, children should not to be seen as young adults but as children. Children are children. Treatment for children requires a different approach and a different schema that are more labour intensive than with adults and a great deal more complicated. Yet the rewards are also greater: a child treated successfully will be cost-effective in terms of future criminality and be a significant success in terms of a reduction in the extent of drugs to be consumed.

In Britain, the *UK Anti-Drugs Coordinator's Annual Report 1999–2000* has a section on young people and another on treatment (Cabinet Office 2000). In the first, considerable attention is given, rightly, to prevention and drug education in schools, the latter to be linked to primary health-care professionals. These programmes take various forms, most are imaginative and many will improve the levels of drug education and prevention. There are programmes that include targeted drug prevention focusing on young people at risk. These are important given the data that came out of the schools' survey of drug prevalence carried out by the Office for National Statistics (cited in *ibid.*: 47). The survey was carried out among more than 9,000 pupils aged 11–15 in about 340 schools in England. Results show that 7% (about 1 in 14) had used drugs in the last month prior to the survey. In 1999, of pupils aged 11–15, there were 12% who had used drugs in the last year. Cannabis was by far the most likely drug to have been used; fewer than 0.5% of 11–15-year-olds had used opiates (heroin and methadone) in the last year, but 3% had used stimulants, including cocaine, crack, ecstasy, amphetamines and poppers. This gives some indication of the extent of the problem, but which children are those who will stop using drugs and which are those who will not are the key questions here.

Chapter 10

Suggestions for the way forward

Although there is a general sense of gloom surrounding the drug problem in Britain, that pessimism is misplaced. There is nothing inevitable about the current level of substance abuse; we do not have to live with high levels any more than we have to live with high crime rates. There are a number of things we can do but most require changes, and change is not always welcome. Resistance can come from the unlikeliest quarters. For example, American judges in drug courts often say they do not believe British judges and magistrates will adopt the necessary procedural changes required to introduce drug courts into the UK. They may turn out to be wrong; resistance to change may come from other quarters, such as those involved in treatment who, on the face of it, would be expected to support greater measures of treatment for offenders. Or that partnerships will be unwelcome because some criminal justice organisations are reluctant to set aside their ideological differences. Change means more than making adjustments to new ideas – it means accepting changes in status and influence.

The 1960s and beyond

Writing in 1974 on the links between drug taking and crime, I remember saying that the relationship was complex and the research evidence inconclusive – at worst poor and at best able only to identify a small number of the many strands that made up the debate. Few attempts were made to establish a causal connection between the two morbidities. Now, looking back over 30 years, it seems we have not moved very far except, perhaps, we now have different pictures of the drug users – and this might not be an advance. Then, drug takers were seen as victims of social and psychological pathologies; now they are more likely seen as predatory criminals. Not entirely, but the image of the drug taker as predator would more than likely be dominant. Changes can be seen in small things, such as the way drug takers are encouraged to receive treatment – not for therapeutic benefits but to stop them taking drugs. The emphasis is different: in the 1960s the converse was true.

Also in that earlier period, few specific questions could be formulated, so wide and vast appeared the subject and so limited was the UK experience. One question that has emerged and remains uppermost is the links with crime. The debate then, such as existed, was dominated by the rights and wrongs of the maintenance prescribing of heroin or cocaine. Did prescribing reduce or encourage criminality? The answer then as now is that it all depends. On what does it depend? Well, it depends on whether the drug user is 'basically criminal' – a term derived from America in the 1930s when Commissioner Anslinger said 'it was the criminal type who became the addict'.

In Britain in the 1930s, the crime figures show drug takers were not given much to criminal activity but this had changed by the 1960s when prescribing was at its height. Then, Ian James (the prison medical officer at Brixton Prison) found that at any one time about 200 addicts were in his prison. This represented about one quarter of all known male heroin addicts. He noted, too, that most addicts sold their prescribed drugs, later buying them back having used up their own supplies. He described most addicts as 'full time addicts whose daily routine was scoring and fixing, allowing no time for anything but casual work' (cited in Bean, 1974). They had no regular employment, presumably supplementing what they had by crime. Yet (and here was the essential point), others, about half, were also prescribed heroin and cocaine but were not criminal, whether before drug taking or later. It is this non-criminal group of drug users, especially those taking heroin or cocaine, who undermine any argument about the inevitability of the links with crime.

In the 1960s the general consensus was that about 40% of heroin addicts were 'basically criminal', defined as having criminal convictions prior to drug taking (Bean, 1971). Drug takers, it seemed, came from two distinct groups: one from lower social-class backgrounds (who were, antecedently, delinquent before drug taking) and the other from a higher social class who were not. The former saw drug taking as an extension of their deviant lifestyles whilst the latter saw drugs as an extension of a worldview influenced by such writers as Aldous Huxley where drugs provided new forms of spiritual salvation. These two groups remain. The difference then was that the middle-class group dominated; now it is those who are 'basically criminal'. There remains, however, a sizeable middle-class group who take drugs to enhance social relationships and to produce more intense psychological experiences. For these, cocaine remains the champagne drug (these are, in addition, the so-called 'recreational' users who take ecstasy and cannabis occasionally). Nowadays, such terms as 'basically criminal', or 'ideologically motivated' (the latter for the middle-class group) are not used; others are preferred, but they simply put a different label on the same product.

In the 1960s, no one spoke of traffickers or thought of dealers as importing drugs into Britain to sell for profit. The world of organised crime was alien to that period: organised crime took place somewhere else, in Italy or the USA. Dealers, such as there were, bought and sold drugs from their friends or other users in Piccadilly Circus and the like. These were not the shadowy figures from overseas but locals who sold their surpluses to create a new group of users who, in turn, found their own over-prescribing doctors and received their own inflated supplies. In the mid-1970s, when prescribing was reduced (i.e. after the introduction of treatment centres and licensed doctors), the first imports of 'Chinese heroin' appeared on the streets and, with them, the first traffickers and dealers in their modern form. In the 1980s the cocaine epidemic confirmed the identity of the trafficker and dealer and the role of the organised criminal as a potent force in the British drug scene. Back in the 1960s, the American position and policies were derided; now they are hardly distinguishable from the British.

In one respect the British system remains distinct, iconoclastic almost, in that prescribing continues, even for the opiates. Controlling the prescribing habits of the medical profession remains a less than easy task, and it is now undertaken by the Home Office Inspectorate with the assistance of the General Medical Council, but what constitutes over-prescribing and its corollary of serious professional misconduct will always be difficult. During the 1960s the largest 'pusher' of drugs was the National Health Service (NHS) through its over-prescribing doctors – small in number but gross over-prescribers, none the less. Alongside these were another group, much larger in number, who prescribed rather more than the average. The NHS is no longer seen as an over-prescriber but over-prescribing still exists. There may not be the gross over-prescribing of the 1960s but there remain a number of doctors who 'prescribe rather more than the average' – whether to typical drug users or to the less typical, such as those receiving repeat prescriptions for such drugs as Valium and other benzodiazepines, and in large amounts. As before, the surpluses can be sold producing the same type of 'spillage' as occurred in the 1960s when over-prescribed heroin users sold their surplus supplies.

Maintenance prescribing of opiates remains, although there is probably little over-presribing. (This in contrast to methadone. The case for prescribing methadone as an alternative to heroin has not, in my view, ever been adequately made – but that is a different question.) Currently, there are about 200 drug users in Britain receiving maintenance supplies of heroin. These are almost the forgotten users: no one mentions them and no one knows much about them, yet their numbers remain steady and they continue to receive their supplies. They raise the age-old question, so dominant in the 1960s, about the role of the prescribing physician, supplying addicts with the drug of their choice. What is the place of the maintenance prescribing of heroin in any system of control? Should it be permitted, encouraged or banished? If, as it appears, maintenance prescribing is, *inter alia*, a delinquency-prevention device, can this form of medical intervention be justified or should prescribing be permitted only in exceptional circumstances and, if so, what are they? Not much thought appears to be given to these matters, so keen are we nowadays to push drug taking into criminal justice and to see the drug user as a property offender funding a habit.

Again, as far as comparisons with the 1960s are concerned, we have no reliable national database and, if anything, the situation has deteriorated. In the 1960s there was the Home Office Index. This peculiarly British institution was scrapped in the late 1990s, leaving only the British Crime Survey – which is hardly a database. The Home Office Index was neither reliable nor valid but it was of some value, producing interesting socio-demographic material on selected addicts over a long period. It could have been improved had there been the political will to turn it into a large-scale national longitudinal database, but that was not forthcoming.

Its history is interesting. It began in the early 1920s in a haphazard way when a number of addicts notified the Home Office they were drug users and said they were receiving supplies of heroin and the like from their physicians. Other addicts followed, some asking to have their names recorded on a register. The myth of the so-called 'registered' addict was born and was sustained throughout the 1960s and beyond. Being on the register produced no favours or privileges but, presumably, the addicts thought it did or at the very least thought it protected them in some way. In fact, it merely gave the Home Office information about the extent of use and the numbers on prescription.

This Index illustrated the measure of trust that existed between the addict and the government in ways unrecognisable today. Losing that

Index and subsequent trust has not been wise, for where else in the world would this happen? That is, where would drug users inform a government department responsible for their control they had been involved in illegal activities, that they had recently used a drug illegally and wanted to change into a fully fledged protected and lawfully supplied drug addict? There were attempts to make registration a less haphazard process where, under the Notification of Addict Regulations, selected professional groups were required to inform the Home Office of the users they were treating or meeting in other areas of their professional work. This they seldom did and, mainly for this reason, the Index fell into disrepute. Attempts to revive it have not been successful. As a result, a potentially valuable research and planning instrument has been lost and will not easily be revived.

Finally, and continuing with comparisons with the 1960s, the quality of research (then as now) was poor. It offered little help to policy-makers and governments – the difference being that, in the 1960s, there was little understanding of the research agenda and more of an excuse for short-comings. Government policy then, as now, was based on a set of *a priori* assumptions driven by political rather than pragmatic, empirical demands. In the 1960s when drug use was rare and spoken of by a small number of interested physicians only and by a few government officials such as H.B. (Bing) Spear, such research as existed was basic and of an exploratory, descriptive nature. There was no research tradition and little to go on, nationally or internationally. This has changed; there is more of a research tradition now but whether this has intruded on government policy is another question.

Earlier research was dominated by a psychiatric worldview – a fairly common phenomenon in the early stages of a new social problem. Later, as academic interest widened, other social scientists began to take an interest but even then the range was narrow. That problem remains; for example, there are too few economists interested in drug research and too few lawyers but rather too many of what Bing Spear disdainfully called 'policy analysts'. We badly need research on the impact of prices on drug use, on the way confiscation orders operate, on the cost-effectiveness of treatment programmes and policing, and on some of the jurisprudential questions raised by current legislation. We have a surfeit of small-scale epidemiological studies showing that drug use has increased and criminality has increased likewise, but little that sheds light on, say, the supply system or the treatment services. We have only one or two longitudinal studies able to provide data showing patterns and trends, and this is a serious failing.

We need two or three high-quality research centres with guaranteed funding undertaking a long-term research programme. Sadly, there is not the political will to push ahead with this type of programme. Instead we produce reports by committees where the enthusiastic amateur holds sway. The journalist and the celebrity are given more credence than the researcher. It is a recipe for going nowhere except to re-examine and debate the same old questions – usually it seems about whether cannabis should be legalised or its penalties be reduced. There are more pressing questions than this: about the quality of life on drug-ridden housing estates, or levels of violence by dealers (whether on dealers or by dealers), or on the impact of drug abuse on fragile communities. Yet as long as we continue with this type of blue ribbon committee where members are experts in other fields (in fact, in almost any other but substance abuse), we shall make few advances. The opportunities are there; we have a government strategy and public recognition that something must be done if the next generation is to be protected from the drug scourge. If we waste this opportunity now it may not come easily again.

Contributions from the drugs–crime debate

What can the drugs–crime debate offer to help promote a reduction in drug use? The answer is quite a lot. We may not know much but we know a great deal more than before, and we are beginning to know what we do not know. We are also increasingly aware that time is not on our side; the problem increases daily. In the USA drug use is declining but largely among students and the middle classes, not in the inner cities that produce the most intractable problems. There it remains, defying all obvious and apparent solutions, wreaking havoc as before.

A comment by James Inciardi and Duane McBride (1991: 75) sums up for me the essential elements of the current position. I want to pick up some of these points in the discussion in this chapter:

> In the final analysis drug abuse is a complicated and intractable problem that cannot be solved with quick fix approaches tended to by politically appointed boards. Deploying more patrol boats in the Caribbean or diverting additional high technology military hardware will not guarantee an end to or even a slowing of the war. Intercepting drugs at the border or cutting off illegal drugs at the source are praiseworthy goals but they are likely impossible ones. And pressurising source countries into compliance with US objectives is also an elusive task, even when there is willingness.

So what, then, is the answer? Inciardi and McBride (*ibid.*) again:

> Thus if total elimination of the supply of drugs is impossible then more attention should be focussed on the demand side of the equation. For after all without drug users there would be no drug problem. The weapons here are treatment and education, initiatives that seem to be both working and failing – working for some but failing for others.

Inciardi says we must concentrate on demand, for we can expect only limited success from interdiction policies or from other forms of law enforcement. John Grieve (1993), an experienced police officer concerned with drugs in London, said a good day for the police was a day when the problem gets no worse, and this echoes the views given above. He added, however, these days are few and far between (*ibid.*: 8). We should not lose the appetite for interdiction or enforcement but, at the same time, reducing the supply side of the equation cannot solve the problem. There will always be limits to what can be achieved by reducing supply, although of course we could still do better. For example, undermining the profits by a more efficient confiscation policy would help. But the demand side is the key; only by reducing demand will we achieve the best long-term results.

We can begin by saying what does *not* work. For example, sending police officers into schools to frighten children about the effects of drugs does not work, nor does the so-called 'Scared Straight' programme work where young people on the edge of criminality (drug abuse) meet convicted offenders (addicts) who have landed up in gaol. Nor, it appears, do programmes such as DARE (Drug Abuse Resistance Education) where children are taught to say 'no to drugs'. These programmes come in various forms. For example, the DARE programme in Nottingham is run by the police who teach the courses in primary schools – I would add at enormous cost, probably about £750,000 per annum – but there are other, much smaller ones, run by different agencies. To say these do not work is premature; rather we do not know if these programmes work as they have rarely been evaluated – except by DARE itself, which hardly gives confidence that the findings were unbiased. Some of the smaller programmes have been evaluated and, whilst early results are encouraging, the long-term effects are not yet forthcoming.

We also know what does not work in the criminal justice system; that is, we know that fining drug users, placing them on probation or sending them to prison has little effect. Long-term street addicts are unsuitable for fines or for probation as, indeed, are almost all drug users; they rarely pay fines and probation is unlikely to have a sufficient impact. Everything we know about treatment and its effects says probation cannot be the answer. As for prison, all too often it holds back drug abuse until release, although there are some imaginative and successful treatment programmes in prison nowadays. For most drug users, a prison sentence means their drug used is suspended rather than treated – and often not then as drugs are available in the prisons as well as in special hospitals such as Broadmoor, Rampton and Ashworth.

To those programmes that do not work we should add those that do but that are unacceptable because they infringe, violate or simply ignore civil liberties. The most common are those involving preventative treatment (sometimes called preventative containment), which are used to detain drug users *qua* drug users – that is, without there first being a conviction for an offence and without the safeguards provided by due process of the criminal law. Preventative treatment permits detention in a hospital for as long as necessary to cure the addiction. The justification is that drug abuse is also a public health measure. It involves treating a disease (albeit self-inflicted) that, if left untreated, will take disproportionate amounts of health resources to the detriment of the non-addicted population. Preventative treatment is widely used in the USA, especially where the drug user is pregnant and taking heroin or cocaine. It is suggested that, if left untreated, the patient will incur extensive health care costs – not just for herself but for her child. Better, therefore, to detain her early and provide treatment before it is too late (i.e. before giving birth).

Going down that route, in my view, leads to an unjustifiable loss of liberty and is certainly not acceptable on the basis of health-care costs. I am aware that certain notifiable diseases permit civil courts in Britain to detain a person until cured, but drug use would not in my judgement meet the necessary criteria for such detention. After all, why select drug abuse? Preventative treatment could as easily be used for those activities likely to incur disproportionate health costs – riding motorbikes, for example, or skiing or playing football? One suspects that drug abuse has been selected for preventative treatment more on the basis of mere dislike than anything else, but it provides a precedent that permits measures of control far above that which is acceptable. It does so in ways that not only circumvent the safeguards provided by the criminal law but that also come dangerously close to providing a new control system based on behaviour adjudged on financial terms. To misquote Brenda Hoggett (1984: 70), in effect this creates a special sort of crime called 'anti-social financial disorder'. If so, should we not admit to it?

What, then, *does* work? The route we should be going down was identified first by the Treatment Alternatives to Street Crime (TASC) programme, which linked treatment and the judicial process (Nolan, 1998: 81). TASC began in Delaware in August 1972 and those prisoners who volunteered for the programme were sent to a local treatment programme where their treatment was monitored and progress reported back to the court. TASC is essentially a diversion programme, aimed at taking offenders out of prison to treatment. At its peak there were 130 TASC sites in 39 states, making it the most respected organisation of its kind (*ibid*.: 82). It has now been overtaken in popularity and funding by drug courts.

The TASC programme organisers were very conscious of the philosophical differences between a traditional criminal justice perspective and a treatment one, recognising also the potential for conflict. They sought not to fuse the two operations but to act as a bridge between them. They saw the justice system's legal sanctions as reflecting community concerns for public safety and punishment and the treatment community as recommending therapeutic interventions to change behaviour and reduce the suffering associated with substance abuse and related problems (*ibid*.). Bridging the gap has not been easy or always successful but it has been worth while, and the services provided under TASC produce a model that is worth introducing into Britain. That bridge is ever more urgently required.

There was no better example of the need for a TASC-type programme than that which occurred during a research project conducted in Leicestershire in the mid-1990s. There, we found that offenders seeking treatment were almost always refused admission to the local statutory treatment agency if subject to a court order, or there was a direct requirement from the court to seek treatment. Those not under an order or who were prepared to enter treatment voluntarily were often given appointments 2 or 3 weeks in advance. It was not clear whether this was part of the treatment provider's policy to test motivation or to assess levels of determination, or whether it was because the agency had few vacancies; either way, by the time of the appointment the drug users invariably had appeared in court for other offences or were unable to attend having been earlier remanded in custody. There was no drug testing. Inciardi (in Inciardi and McBride, 1991: 75) sees the solution to the shortage of treatment as 'easily solved by a financial restructuring of the war on drugs'. Were it that simple. 'Financial restructuring' might be a long-term solution but the short-term problem involves bridging the ideological divide. That will be no easy task. There has been no grassroots movement in Britain aimed at bridging the gap. For example, there were no such preparations for the DTTO that (although it goes nowhere near the distance required by TASC), none the less, requires a measure of co-operation between treatment and criminal justice.

The TASC model could be used for all drug offenders who are referred for treatment, irrespective of the source of referral. For example, there are arrest referral schemes where the police send drug users to treatment programmes whether as a condition of bail or simply as a recommendation to receive help. Referral could also come from the courts, again as a request or as a condition of an order such as probation. In Britain, the results of these schemes are often less than satisfactory: either the drug users fail to attend or if they do they give up quite quickly.

Nor is there an overarching agency responsible for treatment programmes the likes of which TASC would provide. In effect that means users slip through the net or, as with the Leicestershire study, see the treatment facilities as irrelevant. Yet the impact would be pronounced were certain groups to be targeted. For example, there is a small group of heavy users who account for at least three quarters of the total volume of drugs used in Britain, especially cocaine and heroin. These people use a disproportionate amount and are persistent offenders, having served lengthy and frequent sentences. Their prognosis is poor and will remain so as long as their drug use continues. Reducing or removing their habit will have two important effects: it will reduce their criminality, which is persistent and serious, and it will reduce overall demand for the drug. John Grieve (1993) is correct when he says we need to undermine the acquisitive base on which drug purchases are derived. The vast sums of money that fuel inter-dealer status and violence in a paranoid treacherous environment are the product of thousands of burglaries by the same criminals who are arrested again and again (*ibid.*: 8). This type of offender needs a treatment programme that takes account of the chronic nature of the problem, the high relapse rate and the persistent, offending, accompanying drug use. They present an obvious case for a TASC-type programme. TASC could act as an umbrella for this and other treatment programmes, dealing with all phases of referral from the criminal justice system and directing the offender to the appropriate treatment programmes.

Modern thinking behind successful programmes is based on a three-pronged approach involving treatment, mandatory drug testing and supervision. All have to be linked, with the programme delivered in such a manner as to demonstrate to all – patients and treatment providers alike – that integration is complete. Each feature is important but of itself cannot produce satisfactory results. It is no good producing treatment facilities, producing a drug-testing programme or having supervision unless the treatment facilities are underscored by testing, and supervision can back up the programme, details of which must be agreed in advance especially about the quality of supervision. Inciardi talks of the value of treatment. If it is to be of value it must be linked to supervision and testing; it is of little use on its own.

In the USA the TASC programme was able to show that this three-pronged approach worked – and, incidentally, it formed the basis for the drug courts and their impact has been dramatic. Britain, by contrast, has the DTTO. As I said earlier, in my view this order will not work. Moreover, the government has failed to take advantage of a set of opportunities uniquely favourable to change and of a period of time when it would have been possible to instigate a thorough-going examination of criminal justice policies. No attempt was made at integration in the DTTO. The three main features were themselves poorly developed, reducing further the possibilities of success.

Take first – supervision. Here the DTTO was simply added on to the probation service workload. Yet the probation service as currently constituted is not, in my opinion, the appropriate service to undertake such a task; nor would it be were drug courts to be introduced. Too often probation officers retain their social-work value system and are antithetical to the demands of coercive treatment where, as the American research shows, the longer the offender remains in the programme the better the chances of success (Anglin and Hser, 1991). A 90-day treatment period would likely be the minimum required, supported by clear un-equivocal guidelines. Fudging issues, accepting excuses for short-comings and ignoring violations do not help offenders in treatment. Different rules might need to be applied to patients outside the criminal justice system but, for those within it, a greater measure of certainty is required.

Nor are the drug-testing facilities adequate. There are too many op-portunities to manipulate the system and to allow offenders to avoid or escape the consequences of their illicit use. Drug testing under the DTTO is an amateurish affair falling far short of what should be expected. The report on the DTTO describes drug testing thus:

> The frequency of urine testing varies markedly between pilot areas. Very frequent testing may not be good use of money and can be counterproductive in those who are reducing the amount of drugs they use. However testing does appear to be a valuable tool in reinforcing the motivation of those who are drug free … We think that testing needs to be integrated fully with treatment pro-grammes, with testing regimes tailored to the objectives set for individual offenders (Turnbull *et al.*, 2000: 85–86).

The drug court programme, which uses drug testing, requires more exact criteria; it starts from the premise that drug testing must be certain. Elements contributing to the reliability and validity of drug testing are, *inter alia*:

1. direct observation of urine sample;
2. specific detailed written procedures regarding all aspects of urine samples collection, sample analysis, and result reporting;
3. a documented chain of custody for each sample collected;
4. quality control and quality assurance procedures for ensuring the integrity of the process; and
5. procedures for verifying accuracy when drug test results are contested (US Deptment of Justice 1997: 21–22).

Under the DTTO, these minimum procedures are rarely met. The evaluation report describes staff attitudes to treatment in ways that cast doubts about the possibility of them seeing eye to eye with the sentencers, who were more enthusiastic about the tests and who regarded them as valid and, hence, the tests gave them confidence in their decisions to make a DTTO in the first place. The treatment staff, in contrast, said:

- Tests worked well in reinforcing good progress.

- Frequent testing was expensive and pointless for those who continued to use drugs.

- Tests were very destructive to the motivation of those who were reducing drug use considerably but were continuing to test positive.

- Tests were crude instruments which did not reflect different patterns of use (Turnbull *et al.*, 2000: 37).

Some of these comments illustrate a basic misunderstanding about the function of drug testing. The staff at the testing and treatment centres are correct when they say drug tests do not reflect different patterns of use, but they do show which drugs had been used – and that is a pattern of sorts. They are also correct to say drug tests work well in reinforcing progress. Yet, as far as being expensive and pointless for those who continued to use drugs, it would be an obvious rejoinder to say that tests provide the major source of data on these users and provide evidence as to the motivation to continue drug use. Also, when staff say tests were destructive of motivation, etc., presumably it does not occur to them to insist that offenders try harder; after all, no one ever suggested that getting off drugs would be easy. Successful programmes admit to no such compromises, that is why they are so successful and point to another reason why the DTTO will fail. If the procedures are not appropriate, enforcement will not be appropriate either, and the system will lose the respect of all concerned. It will become an unnecessary irritant no one takes seriously when it should be the linchpin of the programme providing verifiable results about the offender's progress and drug-taking practices.

Yet treatment facilities *are* adequate in Britain – in fact, better than almost anywhere else. The range is wide and the quality of treatment provided is often more than satisfactory. The defects are ideological rather than practical. For example, an attempt was made under the DTTO to produce a clear line of accountability about treatment where interagency practices differed and where conflicts and disputes could be resolved. The final evaluation report (*ibid.*: 82) noted that interagency working practices were 'perhaps the single most important factor to address in establishing programmes'. The report showed that rarely had the problems been resolved. It said (*ibid.*):

> It would be wrong to discount the difficulties encountered by the schemes [the three schemes in the pilot programme] as a function of personality clashes or deficits in skills. They are a consequence of work on a difficult joint enterprise involving organisations with big differences in working styles, traditions and values. We think they are likely to be widespread when DTTOs are rolled out nationally.

This comes as no surprise given that little or no attention was paid to this in the first place. What it shows is that developing a team approach within criminal justice is difficult, time-consuming but necessary; otherwise the programme ends up as interagency rivalry. Attempts to resolve some of the difficulties in the pilot programme involved the interchangeability of staff, where community psychiatric nurses, probation officers and drug workers all did the same work. This was not given much approval by the evaluators who said they were sceptical about aiming for interchangeability (*ibid.*: 83) and that 'requiring criminal justice competence from CPNs [community psychiatric nurses] and medical skills from probation officers is an inefficient use of the skills of both groups' (p. 57). The muddle we get ourselves into arises because no attempt is made to seek out information from others who had a tried and tested track record. Consideration of TASC would have helped.

In contrast, the American drug court programme offers that integrated approach. I have argued elsewhere that, initially, we should introduce a limited drug court programme into selected cities in England and Wales (Scotland is in the vanguard here with drug courts expected by late 2001. Eire already has one, and Canada is to have drug courts in all major cities in 2001). This should then be evaluated. The programme would be aimed at the more serious offenders and, if successful, be extended to other cities and other types of offender. What is needed is the political will that, I fear, might not be there unless and until the DTTO has run its course.

There might also be the possibility of extending drug courts to the juvenile justice field, for there is no reason why the youth courts should be excluded (Nemitz, 2001a). Initially in the USA, drug courts were introduced into the juvenile justice system on the basis of the model of the seamless web, that is, they could be transferred to the juvenile system as there was no need to offer a different approach to juveniles. Juveniles were seen as young adults. This view had to be revised to include the child's family in the treatment programme, alongside the school and other educational establishments, concentrating too on dissociating the child from his or her peer group. A new programme had to be devised to take account of these differences. The result was juvenile and family drug courts that seek to retain all the features of adult drug courts but adapted to the juvenile system.

Before leaving the subject of drug courts I want to clarify a point. I do not want to suggest that drug courts are without blemish and should be introduced at all costs. I have said elsewhere (Bean, 2001b) they are open to criticism, not necessarily because of the type of regime they offer but because of the way they resurrect many of the earlier features of re-habilitation discredited in the late 1970s and beyond. I have, however, argued that the advantage we have is that we can learn from what has gone before, whether in America or elsewhere, and adapt these features to local circumstances. The DTTO will be a failure, and we need to think out the next stage. Drug courts offer the possibility of moving to that stage, and do so with a track record from which to draw.

What impact could education have on the drugs–crime debate, and could it assist in any drug-reduction programme? Again, the answer is yes. Too little is made of the point that everyone purchasing illicit drugs explicitly buys into and supports the most violent and cruel set of criminal organisations yet known. Drug markets are violent places, and purchasing the products tacitly if not openly gives *de facto* support to that level of violence. Presumably few people would buy products from legitimate organisations where employees were treated with such violent disdain, so what is different about the illegitimate? The usual answer would be that the violence occurs only because the product sold *is* illegal and, by implication, legal markets would therefore be different. That is, the illegal ones would somehow be expected to whither away.

If so, then such a position should be challenged. It fails to understand the nature of trafficking; legalising drugs would simply permit traffickers to undercut the legal price and continue as before. They might shift their activities to other drugs when it suited them (cigarettes might be smuggled rather than cocaine), but that would depend on the prevailing economic conditions. Traffickers do not have a problem about supply; there is no shortage of the product they wish to sell. Their problems are of distribution, of discipline within their employee networks and of collecting money from sales. Their methods would not change were it likely that their product was legal. Suggesting that legality would produce a different ethos is to avoid looking at the reality. It is not possible to escape the moral opprobrium attached to purchasing drugs by suggesting things will somehow be different one day.

It is also worth emphasising that drugs have a destructive effect on the social fabric of many of our inner cities. These areas are not pleasant places in which to live for, as the residents of King's Cross made known, young children were exposed to discarded syringes and used condoms. Inner-city areas are often inhabited by those living on the margins of social life, separated culturally, socially and politically from the mainstream where all too often their adaptation to ghetto life is drug use (Inciardi and McBride, 1991: 75). Young teenagers able to earn £100 a night trading in drugs are likely to taunt others with their new-found wealth. This undermines the fabric of the community as well as having a more immediate destructive effect on their families. The end product of these actions is likely to be the downfall of the local dealers. This, too, needs to be emphasised, whether it be out-of-control drug use or violence from the other dealers, for one or the other will almost certainly occur. Either way impoverishment will be the end product, whether financially or otherwise, leading to further damages to the community. That local drug markets might add to the wealth of a few absentee high-ranking dealers merely adds to the sense of decay. It will take a long time to erase the damage.

The message needs to be conveyed that drug markets (at whatever level) undermine the democratic institutions of any society. The aim of the high-level dealers is not to empower but to extract the maximum profit from local transactions and to leave with the institutions under their control. Vulnerable institutions easily fall to the traffickers, as a number of small Caribbean countries have found to their cost – as, too, have a number of commercial activities when used by the traffickers.

Falling prey to the dealers can only lead to impoverishment in the same way it does to those who sell the drugs on the streets. If these type of messages are conveyed, this might assist with other demand-reduction programmes. To repeat the point: demand reduction is the key to reducing the use of drugs and must eventually make inroads into the problem if we are to be successful.

There are no easy solutions and, of course, a reduction in drug-related crime will not produce solutions to the crime problem. At best it will produce a significant reduction in the use of drugs and, consequently, a significant reduction in criminal behaviour, but there is no reason to suppose that ex-drug users will stop all criminality once free of drugs. This is an assumption made by drug courts and it seems unwarranted: treatment could quite easily turn some drug-using offenders into non-drug-using offenders. Aims, therefore, should be modest and realistic.

References

Advisory Council on the Misuse of Drugs (ACMD) (1994) *Drug Misusers and the Criminal Justice System. Part 2: Police, Drug Misusers and the Community.* London: HMSO.

Advisory Council on the Misuse of Drugs (ACMD) (1998) *Drug Misusers and the Environment.* London: HMSO.

Advisory Council on the Misuse of Drugs (ACMD) (2000) *Reducing Drug-related Deaths* (June). London: Home Office.

Aldridge, J., Parker, H. and Measham, F. (1999) *Drug Trying and Drug Use across Adolescence.* London: DPAS/Home Office.

Anderson, M. and de Boer, M. (eds.) (1992) *European Co-operation: Proceedings of a Seminar.* Edinburgh: University of Edinburgh.

Anglin, M.D. (1988) The efficacy of civil commitment in treating narcotic addiction. In_Leukefeld, C.G. and Tims, F.H. (eds.) *Compulsory Treatment of Drug Abuse; Research and Clinical Practice. NIDA Research Monograph 86.* Washington, DC: US Department of Health and Human Services.

Anglin, M.D. and Hser, Y.I. (1987a) Addicted women and crime. *Criminology* 25, 359–96.

Anglin, M.D. and Hser, Y.I. (1987b) Sex differences in addict careers. *American Journal of Drug and Alcohol Abuse* 13, 253–80.

Anglin, M.D. and Hser, Y.I. (1990) Treatment of drug abuse. In Tonry, M. and Wilson, J.Q. (eds.) *Drugs and Crime.* Chicago: University of Chicago Press.

Anglin, M.D. and Hser, Y.I. (1991) Criminal justice and the drug abusing offenders; policy issue of coerced treatment. *Behavioural Sciences and the Law* 9, 243–67.

Ashworth, A. (1995) *Principles of Criminal Law.* Oxford: Oxford University Press.

Association of Chief Police Officers (ACPO) (1985) Drug related crime (the Broome Report) (mimeo).

Balenko, S. (1999) Research on drug courts; a critical review. *National Drug Court Institute Review* 2(2), 1–58.

Ballardie, C. and Iganski, P. (2001) Juvenile informers. In Billingsley, R. *et al.* (eds.) *Informers: Policing, Policy, Practice.* Cullompton: Willan Publishing.

Bean, P.T. (1971) Social aspects of drug abuse. A study of a group of offenders in London magistrates courts. *Journal of Criminology, Criminal Law and Police Science* 62(1), 80–86.

Bean, P.T. (1974) *The Social Control of Drugs.* Martin Robertson.

Bean, P.T. (1991a) Policing the medical profession. The use of tribunals. In Whynes, D. and Bean, P.T. (eds.) *Policing and Prescribing.* Basingstoke: Macmillan.

Bean, P.T. (1991b) 'Ice' in Britain. *British Medical Journal* 303(20 July), 152.

Bean, P.T. (1994) Ecstasy: supply and use. Report to Business Against Drugs (mimeo).

Bean, P.T. (1995a) Report to the Home Office on the use of crack/cocaine in Nottingham. London: Royal Society of Health (mimeo).

Bean, P.T. (1995b) Policing drug offenders and the Broome report. In Dickerson, J.W. and Stimson, G.V. (eds.) *Drugs in the City.* London: The Royal Society of Health.

Bean, P.T. (1998) Dual diagnosis and beyond. *Alcohol Update* 37(October), 2–3.

Bean, P.T. (2001a) Violence and substance abuse. In Pinard, G.-F. and Pagani, L. (eds.) *Clinical Assessments of Dangerousness.* Cambridge: Cambridge University Press.

Bean, P.T. (2001b) Drug courts, the judge and rehabilitation (forthcoming).

Bean, P.T. (2001c) Informers and witness protection schemes. In Billingsley, R. *et al.* (eds.) *Informers: Policing, Policy, Practice.* Cullompton: Willan Publishing.

Bean, P.T. and Billingsley, R. (2001) Drugs, crime and informers. In Billingsley, R. *et al.* (eds.) *Informers: Policing, Policy, Practice.* Cullompton: Willan Publishing.

Bean, P.T. and Nemitz, T. (eds.) (2002) *Treatment: What Works?* London: Routledge.

Bean, P.T. and Wilkinson, C.K. (1988) Drug taking, crime and the illicit supply system. *British Journal of Addiction* 83(5), 533–39.

Beare, M.E. (1995) Money laundering: a preferred law enforcement target for the 1990s. In Albanese, J. (ed.) *Contemporary Issues in Organised Crime.* Monsey, NY: Criminal Justice Press.

Beare, M.E. and Schneider, S. (1990) *Tracing of Illicit Funds. Money Laundering in Canada* (report 1990-05). Solicitor General Canada.

Benn, R.S. and Peters, S.I. (1975) *Social Principles and the Democratic State.* London: George Allen & Unwin.

Bennett, T. (1998) *Drugs and Crime: The Results of Research, Drug Testing and Interviewing Arrestees. Home Office Research Study* 193. London: Home Office.

Bennett, T. and Sibbitt, R. (2000) *Drug Use among Arrestees. Home Office Research Findings* 119. London: Home Office.

Billingsley, R. (2001a) Informers. Unpublished PhD thesis, University of Loughborough.

Billingsley, R. (2001b) Informers' careers, motivations and change. In Billingsley, R. *et al.* (eds.) *Informers: Policing, Policy, Practice.* Cullompton: Willan Publishing.

Billingsley, R., Nemitz, T. and Bean, P.T. (eds.) (2001) *Informers: Policing, Policy, Practice.* Cullompton: Willan Publishing.

Bin-Salama, W. (1996) Confiscation orders. Unpublished PhD thesis, University of Loughborough.

Birch, R. (1991) International co-operation of the police. *Police Journal* 64(4), 289–98.

Birch, R. (1992) Policing Europe. Current issues. *Home Office PRSW Bulletin,* 4–6.

Birks, P. (1995) *Laundering and Tracing.* Oxford: Oxford University Press.

Boldt, R. (1998) Rehabilitation, justice and the drug court. *Washington University Law Quarterly* 76, 1205–306.

Boyce, D. (1987) Narco terrorism. *FBI Law Enforcement Bulletin* 56(11), 24–27.

Brain, K., Parker, H. and Bottomley, T. (1998) *Evolving Crack Cocaine Careers. Home Office Research Findings* 85. London: Home Office.

Brook, D., Taylor, C., Gunn, J. and Maden, A. (1998) Substance misusers remanded to prison; a treatment opportunity. *Addiction* 193(12), 1851–56.

Broom, D. and Stevens, A. (1991) Doubly deviant; women using alcohol and other drugs. *International Journal of Drug Policy* (2), 25–27.

Bruno, F. (1991) *Cocaine Today. Its Effects on the Individual and Society.* UN Inter-regional Crime and Justice Research Institute.

Burrows, J., Clarke, A., Davison, T., Tarling, R. and Webb, S. (2000) *The Nature and Effectiveness of Drugs Throughcare for Released Prisoners. Home Office Research Findings* 109. London: Home Office.

Cabinet Office (2000) *UK Anti-Drugs Coordinator's Annual Report 1999–2000.* London: HMSO.

Carver, J.A. (1991) Pre-trial drug testing: an essential step in bail reform. *BYU Journal of Public Law* 5(1), 371–407.

Carver, J.D., Boyer, K.R. and Hickey, R. (1995) Management information systems and drug courts: the District of Columbia approach. Paper prepared for the National Symposium on the Implementation and Operation of Drug Courts, District of Columbia Pre-trial Services Agency.

Caulkins, J. and Reuter, P. (1996) The meaning and utility of drug prices. *Addiction* 19(9), 1261–64.

Chaiken, J.M. and Chaiken, M.R. (1990) Drugs and predatory crime. In Tonry, M. and Wilson, J.Q. (eds.) *Drugs and Crime.* Chicago: University of Chicago Press.

Chaiken, J.M. and Johnson, B.D. (1988) *Characteristics of Different Types of Drug Involved Offenders.* National Institute of Justice.

Charles, N. (1998) *Public Perceptions of Drug Related Crime. Research Findings* 67. London: Research and Statistics Directorate, Home Office.

Clark, R. (2001) Informers and corruption. In Billingsley, R. *et al.* (eds.) *Informers: Policing, Policy, Practice.* Cullompton: Willan Publishing.

Cloward, R. and Ohlin, L. (1960) *Delinquency and Opportunity.* Free Press.

Coid, J., Carvell, A., Kittler, Z., Healey, A. and Henderson, J. (2000) *The Impact of Methadone Treatment on Drug Misuse and Crime. Home Office Research Findings* 120. London: Home Office.

Cooper, M.H. (1990) *The Business of Drugs. US Congressional Quarterly.* Washington, DC: US Government Printing Office.

Corkery, J.M. (1997) Statistics of Drug Addicts notified to the Home Office, UK, 1996. *Home Office Statistics Bulletin 22/1997.* London: Home Office Research and Statistics Department.

Corkery, J.M. (1999) The nature and extent of drug misuse in the UK: official statistics, surveys and studies. London: Home Office (mimeo).

de Leon, G. (1998) Legal pressure in therapeutic communities. In Leukefeld, C.G. and Tims, F.H. (eds.) *Compulsory Treatment of Drug Abuse; Research and Clinical Practice. NIDA Research Monograph* 86. Washington, DC: US Department of Health and Human Services.

Department of Health (1960) *Report of the Interdepartmental Committee* (first Brain report). London: HMSO.

Department of Health (1965) *Report of the Interdepartmental Committee* (second Brain report). London: HMSO.

Department of Health (1978) *Review of the Mental Health Act 1959* (Cmd 7320). London: HMSO.

Department of Health (1996) *Report of an Independent Review of Drug Treatment Services in England (Task Force Report).* London: HMSO.

Department of Health (1999a) *Drug Misuse and Dependence – Guidelines on Clinical Management.* London: HMSO.

Department of Health (1999b) *Review of the Mental Health Act 1983 (Report of the Expert Committee, December).* London: HMSO.

Ditton, J. and Hammersley, R. (1994) The typical cocaine user. *Druglink* 9, 11–12.

Dorn, N. (1993) Europe and drugs. *Criminal Justice Matters* 12, 19.

Dorn, N. and Murji, K. (1992) Low level drug enforcement. *International Journal of the Sociology of Law* 20, 159–71.

Dorn, N., Murji, K. and South, N. (1990) *Traffickers; Drug Markets and Law Enforcement.* London: Routledge.

Drug Enforcement Administration (DEA) (1982) *Narcotics Investigators' Manual.* Paladin.

Duke, K. (2000) Prison drugs policy since 1980. *Drugs Education: Prevention and Policy* 7(4), 393–408.

Dunlap, E. and Johnson, B.D. (1996) Family and human resources in the development of a female crack seller's career; case study of a hidden population. *Journal of Drug Issues* 26(1), 175–98.

Dunnighan, C. (1992) Reliable sources. *Police Review* 14 August, 1496–97.

Dziedzic, M.J. (1989) The international drugs trade and regional survival. *Survival* 31(6), 533–48.

Edgar, K. and O'Donnell, I. (1998) *Mandatory Drug Testing in Prison; an Evaluation. Home Office Research Findings* 75. London: Home Office.

European Community (1992) *Report Drawn up by the Committee of Inquiry into the*

Spread of Organised Crime Linked to Drug Trafficking in the Member States of the EC (EP Document A3-0358/91), 23 April.

European Community (1993) *Inventory of Legal Texts on Drugs*. Office for Official Publications of the European Community.

Fagan, J. (1990) Intoxication and aggression. In Tonry, M. and Wilson, J.Q. (eds.) *Drugs and Crime*. Chicago: University of Chicago Press.

Farabee, D., Prendergast, M. and Anglin, M.D. (1998) The effectiveness of coerced treatment for drug abusing offenders. *Federal Probation* 62(1), 3–10.

FATF (1990) *Report on Money Laundering*. Financial Action Task Force.

Florez, P. and Boyce, B. (1990) Colombian organised crime. *Police Studies* 13(2), 81–88.

Fortson, R. (1996) *The Law in the Misuse of Drugs and Drug Trafficking Offences* (3rd edition). London: Sweet & Maxwell.

Foster, J. (2000) Social exclusion, crime and drugs. *Drugs Education: Prevention and Policy* 7(4), 317–30.

Gallagher, R. (1990) *The Report of Mr Rodney Gallagher of Coopers and Lybrand on the Survey of Offshore Finance Sections in the Caribbean in Dependent Territories* (the Gallagher report). London: HMSO.

Gebelein, R.S. (2000) *The Rebirth of Rehabilitation. Promise and Perils of Drug Courts*. National Institute of Justice (May).

Ghodse, H. (1995*) Drugs and Addictive Behaviour. A Guide to Treatment* (2nd edition). Oxford: Blackwell.

Gillard, M. (1993) The pain in Spain; Europe's southern frontiers. *Police Review* 25 June, 28–29.

Gilmore, W. (1991) *Going after the Money. Money Laundering: The Confiscation of the Assets of Crime and International Co-operation. A System of Police Co-operation after 1992. Working Paper Series*. Edinburgh: University of Edinburgh.

Gilmore, W. (1992) *International Efforts on Money Laundering. Cambridge International Documents Series* Vol. 4. Cambridge: Grotius Publications.

Goldstein, P. (1985/1995) The drugs–violence nexus; a tripartite framework. *Journal of Drug Issues* 1985(Fall), 493–506. Also in Inciardi, J. and McElrath, K. (eds.) (1995) *The American Drug Scene*. Los Angeles: Roxbury.

Goldstein, P., Brownstein, H., Ryan, P.J. and Rellucci, P.A. (1991) Crack and homicide in New York City, 1988; a conceptually based analysis. *Contemporary Drug Problems* 16, 651–87.

Gossop, M., Marsden, J. and Stewart, D. (1997) The National Treatment Outcome Research Study in the UK; sixth month follow up and outcomes. *Psychology of Addictive Behaviour* (11), 324–37.

Gossop, M., Marsden, J. and Stewart, D. (1998) *The National Treatment Outcome Research Study (NTORS). Changes in Substance Use, Health and Criminal Behaviour One Year after Intake*. London: Department of Health.

Greenleaf, V.D. (1989) *Women and Crime*. Lowell House.

Grella, C.E. and Joshi, V.J. (1999) Gender differences in drug treatment careers among clients in the National Abuse Treatment Outreach Study. *American Journal of Drug and Alcohol Issues* 25(3), 385–406.

Grieve, J. (1992) The police contribution to drugs education; a role for the 1990s.

In Evans, R. and O'Connor, L. (eds.) *Developing Educational Strategies in Partnership*. London: David Fulton.

Grieve, J. (1993) Thinking the 'unthinkable'. *Criminal Justice Matters* 12, 8.

Hammersley, R., Forsyth, A., Morrison, V. and Davies, J.B. (1989) The relationship between crime and opioid use. *British Journal of Addiction* 84, 1029–43.

Haughton, G. (2001) Dublin Metropolitan District Drug Court. Address to the Scottish Seminar on Drug Courts (mimeo).

Healey, K. (1989) Bolivia and cocaine; a developing country's dilemma. *British Journal of Addiction* 83(1), 19–23.

Hearnden, I. and Harocopos, A. (2000) *Problem Drug Use and Probation in London. Home Office Research Findings* 112. London: Home Office.

HM Government (1995) *Tackling Drugs Together; a Strategy for England 1995–8*. London: HMSO.

HM Government (1998) *Tackling Drugs Together to Build a Better Britain; the Government's Ten Year Strategy for Tackling Drug Misuse*. London: HMSO.

Hoggett, B. (1984) *Mental Health Law*. London: Sweet & Maxwell.

Home Office (1986) The border war on drugs. London: Office of Technology Assessment (mimeo).

Home Office (1993) *A Practical Guide to Crime Prevention for Local Partnerships*. London: Home Office.

Home Office (1998a) *Drug Treatment and Testing Order; Background and Issues for Consultation*. London: Home Office.

Home Office (1998b) *Tackling Drugs in Prison; the Prison Service Strategy*. London: Home Office.

Home Office (1999) Codes of practice on informant use. London: Home Office (mimeo).

Home Office (2000) *Guidance for Practitioners Involved in Drug Treatment and Testing Order Pilots*. London: Home Office.

Hough, M. (1996) *Drug Misusers and the Criminal Justice System; a Review of the Literature. Drugs Prevention Initiative Paper* 15. London: Home Office.

House of Commons (Home Affairs Committee) (1990) *Practical Police Co-operation in the European Community*. London: HMSO.

House of Commons (2000) *Criminal Justice and Court Services Bill. Explanatory Notes (15 March 2000)*. London: HMSO.

Huling, T. (1996) Prisoners of war. Women drug couriers in the US. In Green, P. (ed.) *Drug Couriers*. London: Quartet Books.

Hunt, G., Joe-Laidler, K. and Mackenzie, K. (2000) 'Chillin, being dogged and getting buzzed'; alcohol in the lives of female gang members. *Drugs Education: Prevention and Policy* 7(4), 331–53.

ICPO Interpol (1989) Heroin trafficking in Africa; its impact on Europe (General Secretariat Drug Subdivision). *International Police Review* Sept/Oct(44.420), 25–28.

Inciardi, J. (1988) Compulsory treatment in New York. A brief narrative history of misjudgement, mismanagement and misrepresentation. *Journal of Drug Issues* (28), 547–60.

Inciardi, J. (1991) *Handbook of Drug Control in the US.* Westport, CT: Greenwood.

Inciardi, J.A. and Harrison, L.D. (eds.) (1998) *Heroin in the Age of Crack-Cocaine.* Thousand Oaks, CA, and London: Sage.

Inciardi, J., Lockwood, D.A. and Pottieger, A.E. (1993) *Women and Crack Cocaine.* Macmillan.

Inciardi, J. and McBride, D.C. (1991) The case against legalisation. In Inciardi, J. (ed.) *The Drug Legalisation Debate.* Thousand Oaks, CA, and London: Sage.

Inciardi, J., McBride, D.C. and Rivers, J.E. (1996) *Drug Control and the Courts. Drugs, Health and Social Policy Series* Vol. 3. Thousand Oaks, CA, and London: Sage.

Inciardi, J. and Pottieger, A.E. (1995) Kids, crack and crime. In Inciardi, J. and McElrath, K. (eds.) *The American Drug Scene.* Los Angeles: Roxbury.

Johnson, B., Dunlap, E. and Tourigny, S. (2000) Crack distribution and abuse in New York. In Natarajan, M. and Hough, M. (eds.) *Illegal Drug Markets; from Research to Prevention Policy.* Monsey, NY: Criminal Justice Press.

Johnson, B.D., Goldstein, P., Preble, E., Schmeidler, J., Lipton, D.S., Spunt, B. and Miller, T. (1985) *Taking Care of Business; the Economics of Crime by Heroin Users.* D.C. Heath.

Johnson, B.D., Williams, T., Dei, K.A. and Sanabria, H. (1990) Drug abuse in the inner city; impact on hard-drug users and the community. In Tonry, M. and Wilson, J.Q. (eds.) *Drugs and Crime.* Chicago: University of Chicago Press.

Kleiman, M.A. and Smith, K.D. (1990) State and local drug enforcement. In search of a strategy. In Tonry, M. and Wilson, J.Q. (eds.) *Drugs and Crime.* Chicago: University of Chicago Press.

Labour Party (1996) *Breaking the Vicious Circle* (October). London: Labour Party.

Langer, J.H. (1986) Recent developments in drug trafficking; the terrorist connection. *Police Chief* 52(4), 44–51.

Lee, R.W. (1989) *The White Labyrinth; Cocaine and Political Power.* Transaction Books.

Leukefeld, C.G. and Tims, F.H. (eds.) (1988) *Compulsory Treatment of Drug Abuse; Research and Clinical Practice. NIDA Research Monograph* 86. Washington, DC: US Department of Health and Human Services.

Levi, M. (1991) Pecunia non olet; cleansing the money launderers from the temple. *Crime, Law and Social Change* 16(3), 217–302.

Levi, M. and Osofsky, L. (1995) *Investigating Seizing and Confiscating the Proceeds of Crime.* London: Police Research Group, Home Office.

Lewis, P. (1980) *Psychiatric Probation Orders.* Cambridge: University of Cambridge, Institute of Criminology.

Lightfoot, J. (ed.) (1994) *Towards Safer Communities.* CDF/Crime Concern.

Lipton, D.S. (1995) *The Effectiveness of Treatment for Drug Abusers under Criminal Justice Supervision.* National Institute of Justice (November).

Lo, T.W. (1993) *Corruption and Politics in Hong Kong and China.* Milton Keynes: Open University Press.

Lo, T.W. and Bean, P.T. (1991) Heroin traffickers in Hong Kong. Report to the British Council (unpublished).

MacCoun, R. and Reuter, P. (1998) Drug control. In Tonry, M. (ed.) *The Handbook of Crime and Punishment.* Oxford: Oxford University Press.

MacDonald, D. and Mansfield, D. (2001) Drugs and Afghanistan. *Drugs Education: Prevention and Policy* 8(1), 1–16.

MacDonald, S.B. (1989) *Mountain High. White Avalanche; Cocaine and Power in Andean States and Panama.* Praeger.

MacKenzie, D.L. and Uchida, C.D. (eds.) (1994) *Drugs and Crime. Evaluating Public Policy Initiatives.* Thousand Oaks, CA, and London: Sage.

Martin, J.M. and Romano, A.T. (1992) *Multinational Crime; Terrorism, Espionage, Drugs and Arms Trafficking.* Thousand Oaks, CA, and London: Sage.

McBride, D.C. and Swartz, J.A. (1991) Drugs and violence in the age of crack cocaine. In Weisheit, R. (ed.) *Drugs, Crime and the Criminal Justice System.* Anderson Publishing.

Merton, R.K. (1957) *Social Theory and Social Structure.* Free Press.

Meyers, P.H. (1991) Pre-trial drug testing: is it vulnerable to due process challenges? *BYU Journal of Public Law* 5(2), 285–340.

Ministerial Drugs Task Force (1994) *Drugs in Scotland; Meeting the Challenge.* Scottish Home and Health Department. Edinburgh: HMSO.

Mitchell, A., Hinton, M. and Taylor, S. (1992) *Confiscation.* London: Sweet & Maxwell.

Morales, E. (1989a) *The White Gold Rush; Peru.* Tucson, AZ: University of Arizona Press.

Morales, E. (1989b) The Peruvian case; the political economy of cocaine production. *Latin American Perspectives* 17(4), 91–109.

Morgan, P. and Joe, K.A. (1996) The private and public lives of women in the illicit drug economy. *Journal of Drug Issues* 26(1), 125–42.

Mott, J. (1987) The relationship between alcohol and crime; a review of the literature. Paper presented at the British Society of Criminology conference.

Murji, K. (1998) *Policing Drugs.* Aldershot: Ashgate.

Murphy, S. and Arroyo, K. (2000) Women as judicious consumers of drug markets. In Natarajan, M. and Hough, M. (eds.) *Illegal Drug Markets; from Research to Prevention Policy.* Monsey, NY: Criminal Justice Press.

Murphy, S. and Rosenbaum, M. (1999) *Pregnant Women on Drugs.* New Brunswick, NJ: Rutgers University Press.

NACRO (1993) *Diverting Mentally Disturbed Offenders from Prosecution. Policy Paper* 2. London: NACRO.

Natarajan, M. and Hough, M. (eds.) (2000) *Illegal Drug Markets; from Research to Prevention Policy.* Monsey, NY: Criminal Justice Press.

National Association of Drug Court Professionals (NADCP) (1997) *Defining Drug Courts: The Key Components.* NADCP.

National Crime Squad (NCS) (2000) *Service Authority for NCS. Annual Report 1999–2000.* NCS.

National Criminal Intelligence Agency (2000) Destroying the glamour of organised crime. *Nexus* 9, 7–9.

National Criminal Intelligence Service (NCIS) (2000) *Annual Report 1999–2000.* NCIS.

Nee, C. and Sibbitt, R. (1993) *The Probation Response to Drug Abuse* (paper 78). London: Home Office Research and Planning Unit.

Nemitz, T. (2001a) Report to the Youth Justice Board on the development and use of juvenile drug courts (mimeo).

Nemitz, T. (2001b) Gender issues in informer handling. In Billingsley, R. *et al.* (eds.) *Informers: Policing, Policy, Practice.* Cullompton: Willan Publishing.

Neyroud, P. and Beckley, A. (2001) Regulating informers; the regulation of the Investigatory Powers Act, covert policing and human rights. In Billingsley, R. *et al.* (eds.) *Informers: Policing, Policy, Practice.* Cullompton: Willan Publishing.

Nolan, J. (1998) *The Therapeutic State.* New York: New York University Press.

Nye, J.S. (1970) Corruption and political development; a cost benefit analysis. In Heidenheimer, A.J. (ed.) *Political Corruption.* Transaction Books.

O'Hare, T. (1996) Court ordered *v.* voluntary clients; problem differences and readiness for change. *Social Work* 41(4), 417–22.

Oppenheimer, E.A. (1991) Alcohol and drug misuse among women; an overview. *British Journal of Psychiatry* 158(Suppl. 10), 36–44.

Oppenheimer, E.A. (1994) Women drug misuse; a case for special consideration. In Strang, J. and Gossop, M. (eds.) *Heroin Addiction and Drug Policy; the British System.* Oxford: Oxford University Press.

Parker, H. and Newcombe, R. (1987) Heroin use and acquisitive crime in an English community. *British Journal of Sociology* 38, 331–50.

Parlour, R. (ed.) (1994) *The International Handbook of Money Laundering and Practice.* London: Butterworths.

Paternostro, S. (1995) Mexico as a narco democracy. *World Policy Journal* 12(Spring), 41–47.

Peters, R.H. (1993) Drug treatment in jails and detention settings. In Inciardi, J. (ed.) *Drug Treatment and Criminal Justice.* Thousand Oaks, CA, and London: Sage.

Porter, L., Arif, A. and Curran, W.J. (1986) *The Law and the Treatment of Drug and Alcohol Dependent Persons; a Comparative Study of Existing Legislation.* WHO.

Preble, E. and Casey, J. (1969) Taking care of business; the heroin user's life on the street. *International Journal of the Addictions* 4(1), 1–24.

Presidential Determination (1995) *Confiscating Major Narcotics and Transit Countries* (no. 95-15, February). Washington, DC: US Government Printing Office.

Prison Reform Trust (1998) *Drug Use in Prison.* Prison Reform Trust.

Ramsay, M. and Partridge, S. (1999) *Drug Misuse Declared in 1998. Latest Results from the British Crime Survey. Home Office Research Study* 172. London: HMSO.

Ramsay, M., Partridge, S. and Byron, C. (1999) *Drug Misuse Declared in 1998. Key Results from the British Crime Survey. Home Office Research Findings* 93. London: HMSO.

Ramsay, M. and Percy, A. (1996) *Drug Misuse Declared. Results of the British Crime Survey. Home Office Research Study* 15. London: HMSO.

Reiss, A.J. and Roth, J.A. (eds.) (1993) *Understanding and Preventing Violence.* National Academy Press.

Reuter, P. (1988) *Sealing the Borders.* Rand.

Reuter, P. (1991) *On the Consequences of Toughness.* Rand.

Reuter, P. (2001) *The Limits of Supply Side Drug Control.* Rand.

Reuter, P. and Kleiman, M.A. (1986) Risks and prices. In Tonry, M. and Morris, N. (eds.) *Crime and Justice. An Annual Review of Research (Vol. 7).* Chicago: University of Chicago Press.

Reuter, P., MacCoun, R. and Murphy, P. (1990) *Money from Crime; a Study of the Economics of Drug Dealing in Washington, DC.* Rand.

Reuters News Agency (1993) Italy; Mafia look towards Europe without frontiers. *Criminal Justice Europe* 3(1), 15.

Robertson, R. (ed.) *Management of Drug Users in the Community. A Practical Handbook.* London: Arnold.

Rosenbaum, M. (1981) *Women on Heroin.* New Brunswick, NJ: Rutgers University Press.

Royal College of Psychiatrists (2000) *Drugs: Dilemmas and Choices.* London: Gaskell.

Ruggiero, V. and South, N. (1995) *Euro-Drugs, Drug Use, Markets and Trafficking in Europe.* London: UCL Press.

Rydell, C.P., Caulkins, J.P. and Everingham, S.S. (1996) Enforcement or treatment? Modelling the relative efficacy of alternatives for controlling cocaine. *Operations Research* 44(5), 687–95.

Seivewright, N. (2000) *Community Treatment of Drug Misuse; more than Methadone.* Cambridge: Cambridge University Press.

Sen, S. (1989) Narco terrorism. *Police Journal* 62, 297–302.

Skolnick, J. (1984) The limits of narcotics law enforcement. *Journal of Psychoactive Drugs* 16(2), 119–27.

Skousen, R.C. (1991) A special needs exception to the warrant and probable cause requirements for mandatory and uniform pre-arraignment drug testing in the wake of *Skinner* v. *Railway Labour Executives Association* and *National Treasury Employees Union* v. *von Raab.* BYU *Journal of Public Law* 5(1), 409–348.

South, N. (ed.) (1995) *Drugs, Crime and Criminal Justice.* Dartmouth.

Sterk-Elifson, C. (1996) Just for fun? Cocaine use among middle class women. *Journal of Drug Issues* 26(1), 63–76.

Stutman, R. (1989) Crack stories from the states. *Druglink* 4(5), 6–7.

Swartz, J. (1993) TASC – the next 20 years; extending, refining and assessing the model. In Inciardi, J. (ed.) *Drug Treatment and Criminal Justice.* Thousand Oaks, CA, and London: Sage.

Tonry, M. and Wilson, J.Q. (1990) *Drugs and Crime.* Chicago: University of Chicago Press.

Turnbull, P.J., McSweeney, T., Webster, R., Edmunds, M. and Hough, M. (2000) *Drug Treatment and Testing Orders; Final Evaluation Report. Research Study* 212. London: Home Office.

US Department of Health and Human Services (1998) *Continuity of Offender Treatment for Substance Use Disorder from Institutions to the Community.* Washington, DC: US Government Printing Office.

US Department of Justice (1997) *Defining Drug Courts; the Key Components.* Washington, DC: Drug Courts Program Office.

US General Accounting Office (1990) *Drug Control; how the Drug Consuming Nations are Organized for the War on Drugs.* Washington, DC: Committee of Government Affairs, US Senate.

US Treasury Department (Financial Crimes Enforcement Network) (1992) *An Assessment of Narcotics Related Money Laundering.* Washington, DC: US Government Printing Office.

Verdun-Jones, S. (1997) *Criminal Law in Canada* (2 edition). Harcourt Brace.

Visher, C. and McFadden, K. (1991) *A Comparison of Urinalyses Technologies for Drug Testing in Criminal Justices.* Washington, DC: US Department of Justice.

Wagstaff, A. (1989) Economic aspects of illicit drug markets and drug enforcement policies. *British Journal of Addiction* 84(10), 1173–82.

Wagstaff, A. and Maynard, A. (1988) *Economic Aspects of Illicit Drug Enforcement Policies in the UK. Home Office Research Study* 95. London: HMSO.

Wardlow, G. (1988) Linkages between the illegal drugs traffic and terrorism. *Conflict Quarterly* (Summer), 5–26.

Webster, R., Hough, M. and Clancy, A. (2001) An evaluation of the impact of Operation Crackdown (mimeo).

Weinman, B.A. and Lockwood, D. (1993) Inmate drug treatment programming in the Federal Bureau of Prisons. In Inciardi, J. (ed.) *Drug Treatment and Criminal Justice.* Thousand Oaks, CA, and London: Sage.

Wellisch, J., Anglin, M.D. and Prendergast, M.L. (1993) Treatment strategies for drug abusing women. In Inciardi, J. (ed.) *Drug Treatment and Criminal Justice.* Thousand Oaks, CA, and London: Sage.

Welsh Office (1998) *Forward Together; a Strategy to Combat Drug and Alcohol Misuse in Wales.* London: HMSO.

Wish, E.D. (1988) Identifying drug abusing criminals. In Leukefeld, C.G. and Tims, F.M. (eds.) *Compulsory Treatment of Drug Abuse: Research and Clinical Practice. NIDA Research Monograph* 86.

Wish, E.D. and Gropper, B.A. (1990) Drug treatment in the criminal justice system. In Tonry, M. and Wilson, J.Q. (eds.) *Drugs and Crime.* Chicago: University of Chicago Press.

Subject index

Name index